The next day we went out to assess the
damage. The storm had ruined the crops.
The tender shoots of winter corn had
been wiped off the fields as if by a
gigantic duster. Saplings were uprooted.
Old trees lay writhing, kissed by the
terrible east wind. Slender cypresses hung
limply with broken spines. The fine
avenue of palm trees planted to the
north of our kibbutz thirty years ago by
the founders when they first came to
these barren hills had lost their crests to
the storm. Even their dumb submission
had not been able to save them from its
fury. The corrugated iron roofs of the
sheds and barns had been carried far
away. Some old shacks had been
wrenched from their foundations.
Shutters, which all night long had
beaten out desperate pleas for help, had
been broken off by the wind. The night
had been filled with howls and shrieks
and groans; with the dawn had come
silence. We went out to assess the
damage, stumbling over broken objects...

from A HOLLOW STONE by Amos Oz

New Writing from Israel
1976

Stories, Poems, Essays

Selected and edited by
Jacob Sonntag

CORGI BOOKS
A DIVISION OF TRANSWORLD PUBLISHERS LTD

NEW WRITING FROM ISRAEL

A CORGI BOOK 0 552 10284 9

First publication in Great Britain in association with
The Jewish Quarterly

PRINTING HISTORY
Corgi edition published 1976

This book is set in 10 pt Intertype Baskerville

Corgi Books are published by
Transworld Publishers Ltd.,
Century House, 61–63 Uxbridge Road,
Ealing, London W5 5SA
Made and printed in Great Britain by
Cox & Wyman Ltd., London, Reading and Fakenham

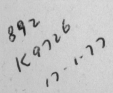

Contents

Editor's Note 7
Shimon Sandbank: Contemporary Israeli Literature 9
Aharon Appelfeld: Badenheim 1939 25
Daliah Ravikovitch: Two Poems 48
Yair Hurwitz: Two Poems 50
Shulamith Hareven: 'City of Many Days' 51
Zelda: Two Poems 63
Hayim Be'er: Two Poems 64
Ehud Ben Ezer: 'The flowers that you didn't give me' 66
Zelda: Poem 77
Moshe Tabenkin: The Parting 78
Nathan Yonatan: Another Poem on Absalom 79
Nathan Shaham: The Choice 80
Zerubavel Gilead: Three Poems 98
Israel Hameiri: Poem 99
Amos Oz: A Hollow Stone 100
Uzi Shavit: Poem 128
Elisha Porat: A Diagonal View 129
Yona Wallach: Two Poems 137
Nathan Zach: Poem 138
Abba Kovner: Because We Are Strangers 139
S. Yizhar: The Prisoner 140
Yehuda Amichai: Three Poems 157
Anton Shammas: Three Poems 158
Samih El-Kassim: Cinerama 159
Siham Da'oud: Three Poems 160
A. B. Yehoshua: Missile Base 612 161
Moshe Dor: Two Poems 196
Amir Gilboa: Three Poems 197
Meir Wieseltier: Poem 198
Shlomo Nitzan: A Stolen Hour 200

5

David Avidan: Antitear Gas — 206
Nathan Zach: Three Poems — 208
Aharon Megged: Levitin's Notebook — 210
Avner Treinin: The Day is Coming — 225
Yitzhak Orpaz: Little Woman — 228
Hanoch Levin: Pshishpash's Plight — 239
Abba Kovner: I Don't Know If Mount Zion — 253
Biographical Notes on the Authors — 255

LIST OF TRANSLATORS

Miriam Arad (Yehoshua); *David Avidan* (Avidan); *Mira Bar-Hillel* (Levin); *Chana Bloch* (Ravikovich); *Nicholas De Lange* (Oz); *Shula Doniach* (Nitzan); *Elaine Finestein* (Zach); *Richard Flantz* (Ben Ezer, Shaham, Orpaz); *Leonore Gordon* (Hurwitz, Wallach); *Hillel Halkin* (Hareven); *Chana Hoffman* (Zelda); *Arthur C. Jacobs* (Amichai, Dor, Hameiri, Shavit, Zach); *Sholom J. Kahn* (Zach); *Shirley Kaufman* (Gilboa, Kovner, Trainin, Wieseltier); *D. Krook-Gilead* (Gilead, Yonatan, Tabenkin); *Judy Levy* (Porat); *Stephen Mitchel* (Be'er); *Bettsy Rosenberg* (Appelfeld, Shammas); *V. C. Rykus* (Yizhar); *Jon Silkin* (Zach); *Edna G. Sharoni* (Zelda); *Sasson Somekh* (Da'oud, El-Kassim); *Samuel Whitehill* (Megged).

Editor's Note

Israel, the cradle of the three great world religions – Judaism, Christianity and Islam – is a modern state, sharing the kind of problems small countries in other parts of the world are faced with in this, our divided world, but having, in addition, problems of its own which are peculiar to its special character. One of these is having to adapt an ancient language – Hebrew – to the needs of the technological age.

Throughout their long history Jews have never ceased to use Hebrew as a language of prayer, study and dissertation; its revival as a living tongue, however, is of comparatively recent date – a mere hundred years or so. The return of Jews to their ancient homeland accelerated its growth, and with the establishment of the State of Israel in 1948, it struck firm roots in the upturned soil. Many of the modern Israeli writers began their careers as road builders and workers on the land; they also became the moulders of the reborn language, producing a colourful new literature. It was only natural that an earlier generation of Israeli writers should stress their national and social commitment while a younger generation, which emerged in the late fifties and early sixties, rejected this kind of commitment in the mistaken belief that it impairs the writer's freedom and individuality. In this they followed, and were influenced by, current trends in European and American literature.

Even so, at its best contemporary Israeli literature reflects the tensions in society and the soul-searchings and inner conflicts of the individual. As is the case with all minority literatures, modern Hebrew literature is accessible to the outside world in translations only. Thanks to the efforts of the Institute for Translation, especially designed to promote translations from the Hebrew, the work – and the art – of translations has greatly improved, both in quantity and quality, though in some cases it is still left to the enterprise of individual writers and publishers to reach a wider audience.

The present collection of stories and poems is intended to provide glimpses of the literary scene of Israel today. It

7

does not pretend to be representative of all current trends; this would be impossible in any case within this limited volume. The selection is based on available translations to the exclusion of those which have already appeared in book form.

The stories range from a most sensitive depiction of the uneasy calm 'before the flood' on the eve of the Second World War, with the shadow of the Nazi holocaust hanging over the peaceful guests in an Austrian summer resort – to the visit by a bewildered lecturer to a dugout of a missile site at the Suez Canal at the time around the Yom Kippur War in 1973. There are stories from Jerusalem, old and new; stories from the Kibbutz – the extraordinary creation of the Israeli pioneers in search of a new way of life – of an earlier and a later period. One remarkable story – 'The Prisoner' – tells of the conflict in the mind of an Israeli soldier torn between his own conscience and his military duty; it relates to an episode during the war of independence (1948/9). One story provides some insight into the world of ideas among the literati of Tel Aviv. Three of the stories may serve as examples of experimental writing on account of their innovations in style and subject matter.

I would like to thank the following persons for their helpful co-operation in making available to me the material from which the selection was made: Yael Lotan, editor of 'Ariel', a multi-lingual quarterly review, Jerusalem, where some of the stories and poems first appeared; Nili Cohen, of the Institute for Translation of Hebrew Literature, Tel Aviv; Lorna Soifer, of the Foreign Rights Department of the Association of Book Publishers in Israel, Tel Aviv; David Hardan, of the Publication Department of the Jewish Agency, Jerusalem; Moshe Dor, Counsellor for Cultural Affairs at the Embassy of Israel, London. I would also like to thank Mr. Patrick Newman, Managing Director of Transworld Publishers Limited, without whose encouragement I would not have undertaken the task which had to be accomplished within a very short time. Finally, I would like to thank the authors and translators for their agreement to be included in this collection which is published to coincide with the Israel Book Week 1976 at the National Book League in London.

Jacob Sonntag
September 1976.   Editor, The Jewish Quarterly

Shimon Sandbank

Contemporary Israeli Literature: The Withdrawal from Certainty

I

IN the midst of an elegant dinner-party, uneasy like many Israeli social occasions immediately after the 1973 war, something unpleasant happens to Izy Ornan:

... almost irrelevantly, perhaps because of the embarrassment, the expectation, the startled faces, the lobster left untouched on the bulky, altar-like table – a sound escaped his mouth, perhaps a tremor, a supplication, an undefined something which burst out from within.

A strange silence fell. Heads turned, searching. Then sudden sensitivity made them look away.

And then, still trembling, astonished at the meaningless sound that had escaped from him, locked up perhaps for a long time, he recognized it as the moment a person knows himself. He was speaking in a whisper, as if in self-defence:

'I don't know. I don't. I have been thinking, maybe. I have been afraid, yes. I had an uncle who used to tell a story about a certain Avreml. It doesn't matter. What he meant to say was that a man could wear himself out trying to decide whether he should get married or not. Doesn't matter. We've got something we carry with us wherever we go, and there's no escape, no escape. Sorry. I hope I'm wrong. I wish I were wrong. Only a question of time. Not even hope. For what, for nothing. No hope whatever. And whoever wants to can run away. If he can. Run away from himself. From ourselves. We can't even do that. And there's no hope. No. So, that's it? So there's no life? All over? And were it not for wars, there would be no death … sorry. It doesn't matter. O.K., so there isn't much, but surely there must be something. There's a bit of life. Who has the right to give it up? Even the tiniest bit. To say: I don't want children – that's easy. But to be a coward, yes. I claim my right to be a coward. And to have a home. And to love. And help each other. For what. Death eats us up every couple of years, but meanwhile … Perhaps there's greatness under the volcano. Perhaps.'

Izy Ornan is the poet-protagonist of *A House for One* (1975), the latest novel by the Israeli author Yitzhak Orpaz. His bachelorhood, his impassioned inarticulateness, his basic nausea with the world and himself – partly overcome in this epiphanic episode – are all reminiscent of J. H. Brenner, the grim chronicler of early-century Jewish life in Palestine.[1] But, though somewhat derivative, the sensibility and the style of Orpaz are perfectly contemporary. A return to Brenner's soul-searching, his renunciation of easy truths, and his withdrawal from the pretence that one can understand and articulate one's experience, would have been unlikely twenty years ago. It is only recently that attitudes in Israel have begun to make such a frame of mind possible. In the pathetic, meaningless sound which Orpaz's protagonist emits there is an admission that not only ideologies but words themselves have become inadequate.

2

It is perhaps late in the day for a modern literature to recognize the inadequacy of words. Didn't the literatures of Europe do so at the very beginning of a century now in its eighth decade? But the Hebrew language is a special case, in that, rather than to slough off all meaning, its real problem has been to slough off its inbuilt sacred meanings. For thousands of years it served as a written language only, steeped in religious tradition and permeated with biblical and talmudic associations. Its revival as a spoken language, with the rise of Zionism, required an adaptation to secular needs. This has been a painful process, perhaps not yet completed to this very day. The creative energy that has gone into this process has left little initiative for a 'modernistic' questioning of communication itself. To opt for silence, one must despair of language; to despair of language, perhaps one must first exhaust its possibilities. Hebrew literature, it seems, has not yet exhausted the possibilities of the Hebrew language.

There is a respectable body of Israeli literary critics – notably the late Baruch Kurzweill – who think that the paradox of a language or religious tradition serving secular goals has been the bane of modern Hebrew literature. Ever since the Haskalah, the Jewish Enlightenment movement, says Kurzweill, Hebrew literature has been forced to use the language of the absolute religious imperative only to contradict that imperative. To Kurzweill, who was an orthodox Jew, this complex situation offered no advantage. What could be regarded as a splendid opportunity for a rich ironical exploitation of the gap between sacred etymology and profane usage, was to him caricature and fakery: the use of the sublime to extol nihilism.

Others have stressed the 'new virginity', to use a phrase of Gershom Scholem's,[2] which Hebrew has acquired as a result of its development as a natural language. Modern Hebrew writers, says Scholem, 'are free to wrestle with the words in a completely new emotional setting and on a level of freedom previously unattainable'.

But this freedom, as Scholem notes, also involves a loss of form. 'When language,' he says, 'is no longer forged, first and foremost, by the study of texts and through conscious reflection, but rather by unconscious processes in which the power of tradition is a minor factor at best, that language becomes by nature chaotic.'[3] And, one may add, it can become doubly chaotic through the *conscious* endeavour of writers determined to liberate it from tradition. Hence, the apparent uneasiness with which Hebrew writers – even the most unorthodox – have been carrying out this 'liberation' of the language, constantly oscillating between the poles of ancient text and modern colloquialism, rejecting the smooth familiarity of old, comfortable collocations for the immediate, rough impact of modern speech, but yearning for the splendor gone. Dame Hebrew, the novelist Aharon Megged once said, has been a spoken language for a long time now, but she is still an aristocrat, still a lady. She has learned to carry out all household jobs, but she does them in her Sunday best, unlike that modest housewife, Yiddish. The same ambivalent feeling about the nature of Hebrew shows in a recent interview given by the novelist A. B. Yehoshua, in which he appears determined to drop his attempts at imitating colloquial speech. 'I think the answer – not just in my case – should be to return to a style as rich as possible. I've become allergic to lean Hebrew.' The same allergy to lean Hebrew was already there in an interview he gave ten years ago. But then he thought rich language was beyond his reach: 'I'm incapable of experiencing the entire associative burden of the language, the way Agnon can, for instance.' This new inclination to do what ten years ago he thought he couldn't, is, I think, highly significant.

3

The struggle to mould an idiom free from a tradition which has grown irrelevant, and yet as regular and elegant as the language of tradition, has left little room for the more radical experiments undertaken by literatures spared this dilemma. This may partly account for the non-modernist character of much Hebrew literature, and particularly of much Hebrew fiction. But language is not the whole story.

Beyond and above it, the entire mental climate connected with the state of Israel, with its foundation, its wars and other struggles, has made modernism a problem. For a central element in modernism is incompatible with this mentality – the element, I mean, of doubt and irony, which conflicts with the passion and conviction of national movements. Nor does 'dehumanization', in Ortega Y Gasset's sense, go together with them. There has been little room, in the Israeli climate of opinion, for a 'dehumanized' literature of pure aesthetic value.

It was only with the weakening of conviction that Hebrew literature could come closer to the mainstream of twentieth-century literature. In the following, I shall attempt an outline of three important phases in the development of Israeli literature: the 1948 War generation, the 'New Wave' of the 50s and 60s, and the literature of the present. These are by no means the only divisions possible, but they can serve to set off the process of maturation which is my main thesis. The division applies to both prose and poetry, but since it applies to each differently, I shall deal with them separately.

4

'It goes without saying,' said the late novelist Haim Hazaz at the Hebrew Writers' Association conference celebrating Israel's twentieth anniversary, 'that Israeli literature should be a responsible literature ... on concerned above all with the individual and the community, with the people and the country, the people and their neighbours, the people and the diaspora, and similar subjects requiring seriousness, courage, and honesty ... Above all: books shouldn't be mere books, writers shouldn't be anonymous, shouldn't be luke-warm, comfortable people ... they should be heroes of a national struggle, of a class-war, of culture; people of conviction and responsibility.'

This was as late as 1968, and definitely anachronistic. Falling back on attitudes no longer in fashion, Hazaz was voicing his discontent with fashion. The commitment to national and social causes which he was advocating, the backbone of Israeli literature about the time of the foundation of the state, had long been questioned. Interestingly, however, it had not really been done away with. It is a measure of the singular nature of literary life in Israel, that Hazaz's words, incredible as they would seem in any other part of the western world, could pass without much notice at an Israeli writers' conference in 1968.

Twenty years earlier, such ideas had been the norm. Any one of the many editorials and manifestoes published in literary supplements or journals around the 1948 war, can serve to illustrate the Socialist Realism approach of the time – an approach perhaps stricter than the literary practice itself, which often digressed, as a free literature must, from ideological commitments. 'Our generation,' wrote the novelist Moshe Shamir in an editorial for *Yalkut Ha-re'im* ('The Friends' Knapsack', a short-lived magazine published on the eve of the war, 'will be a generation writing realistic literature, searching and revealing. It will not necessarily be revolutionary in literary terms, but it shall, it must, follow the revolution of life.' Earnest symposia, published by the literary weekly *Massa*, were devoted to the idea of 'progressive art', and the question of whether art was supposed to serve society and ideology or to be progressive through its very greatness as art. To forestall the attacks of traditionalists like Kurzweill, who condemned the discontinuity between those 'progressive' youngsters and the Jewish tradition, moderate leftists, such as Aharon Megged, declared they loved 'not only what is far-away, the fighting Koreans, the liberated Chinese, the oppressed Blacks', but also new immigrants from the Jewish diaspora. Yigal Allon, now foreign minister, praised the literature that 'came out of the Palmach and served it' at a convention of Palmach (pre-State fighting units) veterans in 1953. The Palmach, said Allon, 'would have been unthinkable without our young writers and poets'. Its writing, he said, was a test of the quality of a Palmach unit no less than its training, weapons, or ammunition.

This confusion of art and life ('Our youth was not a mere "phase"; it was culture, it was spiritual life' – Aharon Megged) did not necessarily result in real observation of life. This, perhaps, is a paradox, inherent in all Socialist Realism: too preoccupied with revolutionizing life, it seldom looks at life itself.

Those writers seldom looked, for instance, at the living individual. One way, indeed, of distinguishing them from later Israeli writers is to contrast (as many writers on the subject have done) their 'collective' themes with their successors' concern with the individual. They defined themselves, says Robert Alter, 'through a repeated sifting of the various social, political, and ideological materials that were the particular circumstances of the Israeli self at a fixed point in time.'[4] Moshe Shamir's popular wartime heroes, Uri of *He Walked In The Fields* (1947) or Elik of *With His Own Hands* (1951), are more or less typical products of Youth Movement and Kibbutz, of the 'Religion of Labour' and collectivistic ideology.

At the same time, I am not entirely convinced that the concern with the broad issues of society and nation is peculiar to these writers. It is no less central, I suspect, to the literature of the fifties and sixties.[5] One could, indeed, argue that even Amos Oz's latest collection of stories *The Hill of Evil Counsel* (1976) has the birth of Israel, rather than any particular Israeli, for its real subject.

What *is* peculiar to the 1948 writers is their relative certainty about the values of their society. Though S. Yizhar, the most admired member of that group, had his misgivings about the treatment of Arabs, he did not question the very *raison d'être* of Zionism and Israel until *The Days Of Ziklag*, his most ambitious (and, for the time being, last) novel, which came out in 1958.

Self-satisfaction is hardly a writer's best friend, and it certainly does not sharpen his perception. Lack of nuance, abundant rhetoric, pomposity are some of the flaws which must be weighted against the attractive side of a literature passionately dedicated to a great vision. And, while 'following the revolution of life', it was not, to use Shamir's above-quoted understatement, 'revolutionary in literary terms'. Quite the contrary.

5

The literature of the late 1950's and the 1960's reacted against this confidence. This second phase of Israeli fiction has been labelled the 'New Wave'(the title of a study by the Israeli critic Gershon Shaked). In terms of our threefold division, it must be distinguished from a still newer wave of the 70s. To be precise: some of its members are 'new'; others are 'Newer'.

A. B. Yehoshua, perhaps the best of the first New Wave, has repeatedly said that his group's first concern was to get away from all indentifiable Israeli reality. 'We were determined to leave out what was local, which had so over-taxed the literature before us.' The result, in his case, was *The Death of The Old Man* (1962), a collection of allegorical fables, free of local flavour and diametrically opposed to the parochial naturalism of his elders. Though a wholesome corrective, this proved to be a dead-end, because its Kafkaism was external gesture rather than inner necessity. It was later repudiated by the author himself and followed by another collection of stories, *Facing the Forests* (1968)[6], more rounded and local in subject and colour.

The original impulse to blot out all Israeli colour and belong nowhere, is most revealing. It is related to the kind of embarrassment of seeing oneself in a mirror. It is the very opposite of the 1948 generation's firm identification with their own values, and it showed a weariness with those values.

It is surely significant, however, that this walk-out, the withdrawal to a no-man's land of existential *angst*, was so short-lived. In returning to the Israeli fold, Yehoshua opted to confront, not waive aside, the old values. In *Facing the Forests*, the title-story of the second collection, the Israeli student who becomes a tacit accomplice to an Arab in burning down the Jewish National Fund forest (that is, the forest planted by his parents' generation), is no longer a destructive Everyman. He is, rather, the destructive *Israeli*, questioning his parents' life-work to the point of gloating over its ruin. Significantly, the destruction of the Parents' Dream is here related to guilt-feelings towards the Arabs: a long-destroyed Arab village emerges out of the ashes of the burnt forest.

Thus, the younger generation's refusal to carry on the Great Work, was not exactly the 'Lo-ikhpatiyut' (devil-may-care attitude) for which their elders blamed them. Aharon Megged, whose many editorials in *Massa* can serve as a fascinating chronicle of Israeli literature in the fifties, angrily quotes a manifesto by the then new *Akhshav* ('Now') magazine:

Liberate Hebrew literature from its dependence on 'Jewish Life', on the 'Great Work'! Let the writer be moved by the dictates of contemporary life ...

This double repudiation, of Jewishness and of Socialism, shows, says Megged, a return to the notorious Jewish habit of self-denigration. It is, he says elsewhere, 'an evasion of the need to face the problem of the day; a flight to the individual, to meaninglessness.'

But it was not, of course. I cannot think, in fact, of a less 'meaningless', less nihilistic body of mid-twentieth-century literature. And I cannot think of a more hilarious piece of criticism than Kurzweill's attack on the 'nihilistic' Oz: 'If Satan had literary gifts, he would write like Amos Oz' (!). Even 'avant-garde' magazines like *Akhshav* (founded 1957) and *Yokhani* (1961–1967), or their precursor *Likrat* ('Towards', 1953–1954, with all their tirades against the literary establishment, gave one's human duties their full due. Their critics, notably the highly influential poet Nathan Zach, advocated fidelity to one's own inner life, a deliberate avoidance of what was public, a return to those neglected writers of the past who, unlike the popular names, had been 'unable to quelch their generation's thirst for grand certainties'. Surely, this had nothing to do with 'nihilism'.

It was, rather, the confrontation of one set of values by

another. The 'grand certainties' of the past were being questioned. At the same time, they were still strongly felt to be imperative, a necessary moral justification for unending political, military and economic strife. Thus, there was plenty of occasion for pitting the disillusioned individual against them. Yehoshua's student, gloating over the ashes of the Jewish National Fund forest, is only a particularly radical specimen in a long gallery of rebels populating the novels of Megged, Yizhar, Hanoch Bartov, David Shahar, Binyamin Tammuz and others in the 50s and 60s. But rebellion needs an object against which to pit itself, and the object was still very much there in those novels.

However, it now took on a more evasive form. Society and state became less explicit, more of a metaphor. Yehoshua's early allegorical Kafkaism, though later mellowed down, points to a change of style which was taking place. The 'grand certainties' though still very much there as objects of doubt, were now grappled with symbolically rather than directly. Guilt-feelings about the Arabs, for instance, were no longer discussed as a moral problem (as in Yizhar's wartime novellas) but implied in a symbolic plot, as in *Facing the Forests*. The same holds for the Holocaust; first it was a direct, literal experience, as in Uri Orlev's *Soldiers of Lead* (1956), later it was treated more metaphorically in two novels by poets: Haim Gouri's *The Chocolate Deal* and Yehudah Amicahai's *Not of This Time, Not of This Place* (both 1964).[7]

The dominant mode of the New Wave is thus symbolic. Outwardly, this mode is a reaction against the explicitness of earlier Israeli prose. More intrinsically, it is a result, I think, of a split in sensibility between the preoccupation with the individual self and the inability to dissolve the commitment to supra-individual issues. As a result, it uses individual life to suggest broader, social and national issues, or, alternatively, makes 'personal neurosis wear the guise of, fix on, national conflict' (Yehoshua). In either case, the result is symbolic.

The most obvious case in point is that of the novelist Amos Oz. The demonic power that permeates in his stories is inner violence, which women possess, men suffer, and animals symbolize. But this private violence, as often noted, is closely interwoven with Israel's threatened military position. In his recent story *The Hill of Evil Counsel*, the drives which

17

make Ruth Kipnis, a respectable housewife, elope with a British admiral (at the time of the British Mandate), and the Russian ladies from next door rape her child, are closely related to the totalitarian-messianic politics of the Kipnis' subtenant, a member of a dissenting terrorist organization on the eve of the 1948 war. And it is on both planes – of sex and of politics – that Dr. Hans Kipnis' enlightened vision of nice family-life and a nice state, with Martin Buber for president, is then shattered.

6

The first appearance of *The Hill of Evil Counsel* in the magazine *Keshet* in 1975, was followed by a highly perceptive review by the novelist Amalia Cahana-Carmon. Her observations show some of the tendencies of what I earlier referred to as the 'newer' wave, or the third phase in my scheme. The fact that she is older than Yehoshua or Oz shows that this has nothing to do with an age-group. Nor are members of the 'new' wave excluded from this 'newer' style.

All things in Oz's world, she says, 'are found and proved to be insubstantial, for a simple reason: they are of no interest in themselves. There is neither concern, nor love, nor tenderness, nor respect for them in themselves. Even all association with them, their use as mere props, is cautious, timid, reticent. Sooner or later they are bound to be sacrificed, deliberately, like pawns on a chess-board. Oz's eye is always on guard, always in search of something which exists beyond things, which alone is in focus. Something hostile, lurking, evil.' The same holds for Oz's characters, she says. They are set in a time and a place, but they don't belong there. They don't exist for their own sake, but only to be threatened by a murderous transcendent being, absolutely determined to wipe them off the face of the earth.

The reviewer's subsequent psychological speculations (Oz, she says, painfully discovers himself in that murderous being) are less illuminating than the literary desideratum implied in what she says: the return to a 'concern for things', to the sights and sounds of the world, which Oz misses because of an obsession with what is beyond them, or a constantly inward-turned eye, which is the same.

This is not to be understood as a call to return to the

1948 kind of realism. The respect for things in themselves, which the reviewer cannot find in Oz, is equally absent there. Yizhar, it is true, can beautifully convey the sheer physical magnificence of a horse on the run; or the sound of a well on a quiet night. In the last analysis, however, both the 1940s, the 1950s, and the 1960s, both 'realists' and 'symbolists', both the old and the new waves, read their own vision, or myth, – or anti-vision, or anti-myth, – into reality. They imposed a scheme on it, be it a highly virtuous scheme not unlike Socialist Realism, or a less virtuous one, skeptical towards the accepted norms.

Only recently has reality itself begun to come into its own in Israeli fiction. Cahana-Carmon's own collection of stories, *Under One Roof* (1971), and her one novel *And Moon in the Valley of Ajalon* (1971), are subtle, nervous accounts of the strange shapes and colours of a vibrating world, ever reflecting the changing moods of her adolescents and middle-aged women in love. Her marvellously flexible syntax and her peculiar blend of ancient diction and up-to-date inflections of tone, hardly retainable in translation, serve to underline her very personal sensibility. Yitzhak Orpaz, in *A House for One*, has outgrown the excessive symbolism of his earlier novels, though his deliberate renunciation of an over-all thematic pattern at times results in amorphousness. Yehoshua, too, has recently written one or two stories free, not only from his early Kafkaism, but also from the later combination of local flavour and symbolic meaning. These stories, though involving army life and other collective experiences which tend to drag both writer and reader in the direction of ideology, are down-to-earth accounts of psychological states, not at all meant to be sacrificed – 'like pawns on a chess-board' – to any 'transcendent being', murderous or otherwise. One could further mention, as examples of prose free from myth and symbol, some less recent phenomena in Israeli prose: Y. Knaz's gripping tales of Gothic pathology in rural life; Aharon Appelfeld's quiet, resigned account of lives truncated by the psychological after-effects of the Holocaust; or playwright Hanoch Levin's shabby men and women, ever engaged in a pathetic, sado-masochistic battle of the sexes.

In a recent interview, Yehoshua connects the recent change in his own writing with a general change in Israeli mentality since the 1973 war. The Israelis, he says, have lost much of their self-confidence. There is therefore no point in repeating what he did in *Facing the Forests* – pitting an alienated protagonist against a self-confident environment. Instead, his alienated protagonist can now return to the fold which has itself become alienated from its former certainties. His characters, in other words, can now move to the centre of Israeli life.

Like all generalizations, this is only partly true. There is certainly much opportunity left for individual alienation in a country constantly thrown into conflict with itself by the force of circumstances. What is clear, in any case, is that the last war has put in question, not only the original moral certainties, but also the subsequent anti-certainties, and has paved the way for a more receptive, more open frame of mind. All certainties gone, Israeli literature must do without the comfortable contents and forms which those certainties made safe.

7

Hebrew poetry has lately suffered three major losses: the poets Avraham Shlonsky, Nathan Alterman, and Lea Goldberg all died within the last seven years, leaving behind, as the only great survivor, Uri Zvi Greenberg, a highly individualistic expressionist, who is also one of our most militant nationalists. Hebrew prose, too, has recently lost two of its great names: Nobel-prize winner S. Y. Agnon, and Haim Hazaz. But while Agnon, with his unique blend of charming sageness and modernistic consciousness of crisis, still acts as a central influence on Hebrew prose, the three late poets have long served as targets for rejection. And the greater their spell on young Israeli poets, the more violent has the rejection been. One could claim, indeed, that their rejection has made contemporary Hebrew poetry possible.

The most articulate and insistent spokesman of the rejection was the poet Nathan Zach, who, in a series of essays in the fifties and sixties, did for Hebrew poetry what T. S. Eliot did thirty or forty years earlier for English poetry. He blamed Alterman for the same mellifluous, mechanically regularized, inauthentic, generalized, 'poetic' verbosity which Eliot had found in Tennyson or the Georgians. Like the New Critics, he advocated concreteness and adherence to time, place, and experience. Like F. R. Leavis, he spoke in the name of moral seriousness, commitment to feeling, empathy with others. 'Alterman versifies,' he said, 'as a substitute for what he should feel.'

Like Eliot, again, Zach revised, along with the critic (Sh.) Grodzensky, the canon of Hebrew poetry. As in Donne or Marvell, the virtues now admired were those of ironic distance, lack of pompousness, colloquialism. These qualities proved to belong, not to the great names like Bialik, the pre-State 'Poet Laureate', or Shlonsky, who rebelled against Bialik's authority and introduced a new, non-biblical style, but to lesser names: Ya'akov Steinberg, David Vogel, or Yehudah Karni.

The fact that the poets now favoured, unlike Alterman, or Bialik before him, had shied away from what was public, unable (to repeat Zach's words) 'to quench their generation's thirst for grand certainties', showed the development of Israeli poetry to run parallel to the above-outlined development of Israeli prose. In terms of sheer output, poetry has been much richer than prose, perhaps because it does not require the leisure and perspective which prose requires. And its sheer volume explains, in part, the greater number of individual achievements. As in prose, modernism in poetry has been made possible by the withdrawal from ideological certainties. Shlonsky and Alterman[8] were as deeply steeped in Socialist Zionism as were the prose-writers of the 1948 generation (who often were their great admirers), and the reaction against those prose-writers, was inseparable from a decline in ideology.

Shlonsky and Alterman, however, were brilliant craftsmen, and Alterman, in addition, was a much more complex poet that what I said may seem to imply. Not unlike Brecht, but with greater integrity, he was torn between a highly refined private sensibility and a deep commitment to public ideas. Zach's dismissal of his work, like Eliot's one-time dismissal of Milton, is subjective historiography and cannot possibly detract from his importance.

The fact remains, however, that the mid-fifties, headed by Zach, Yehudah Amichai and David Avidan, introduced a new style of poetry, marked by much which was antithetic to Alterman and his followers. If Haim Gouri, the representative poet of the 1948 War and a disciple of Alterman, later regretted, in an often-quoted poem, that his generation 'had no time', Zach and his friends now insisted on having time for themselves, on being less (and more) than mouthpieces for an era. This reductive tendency also involved a reduction in tone, which became understated, studiedly inelegant, ironized through obvious rhyme or parodied liturgical allusion. English and American poetry, which had become the only body of foreign poetry accessible to many young poets, replacing their elders' intimacy with Pushkin or Schiller, was also conducive to this new style.

This generalized account of the change calls, however, for at least two qualifications.

First, the switch from overstatement to understatement was central, but not universal. Yehudah Amichai's natural gift for profuse imagery is often closer – in colour, not in irregular syntax – to Dylan Thomas than, say, to Auden. And Daliah Ravikovitch's exotic geography of the unconscious shows little ironic restraint. They do, however, participate in the general retreat from the great issues, and in Miss Ravikovitch there is hardly a reference to collective experiences.

Second, the change described is not meant to draw an absolute line between the young and the old, for the simple reason that the old have often proved to be more capable of renewal than the young. Amir Gilboa, Abba Kovner, or Ozer Rabin, all 1948 poets in terms of their age, let alone Avot Yeshurun who is now in his seventies, have turned out to be more susceptible to change than some younger people I mentioned, who have either been chewing their cud or stopped writing altogether.

8

In a sense, Israeli poetry, too, now shows signs of entering a third and 'newer' phase. I don't think one could simply apply to it what we have said about prose, i.e. the switch from a thought-scheme imposed on reality to a free observation of reality. But recent changes in poetry seem related to those in prose in a more oblique sense.

In a recent interview, Me'ir Wieseltier, a much-discussed younger poet and a central figure in the influential quarterly *Siman-Kri'a* distinguished his own poetry from that of his predecessors also were 'uncommitted' and Romantic. They took the self to be an 'autonomous being'. His own self, on the other hand, is 'open, exposed in all directions, susceptible to constant influences and influxes'.

One uncommitted Romantic is, I suppose, Nathan Zach. His dismissal – which began ten years ago in the very same *Akhshav* magazine which had published and celebrated him – is the sort of poetic justice which no influential poet can escape. It is his turn now to be accused of being divorced from reality. Interestingly, however, fidelity to self was Zach's reality, which he found lacking in Alterman; openness to the world is Wieseltier's reality, which he seems to find lacking in Zach. In this, Wieseltier's objection to Zach is surprisingly close to Mrs. Cahana-Carmon's objection to Oz. Both poet and novelist want literature to expose itself – in very different ways, of course, – to the direct impact of 'things'. In Wieseltier, this tendency shows in a stark language, whose hard edges are cutting rather than suggestive.

To Zach and his followers, authenticity meant a colloquial, 'non-poetic' style. This is still often accepted, either by Zach's many imitators, or by independent talents such as Dan Pagis, who has moved away from a Rilkean Romanticism to a dry, highly personal idiom. At the same time, a breakthrough is felt – in the poets Ya'ir Hurvitz, Mordechai Geldman, or Yona Wallach – to a more luxuriant language. I doubt if one can relate this point to the previous one and say that the new openness to a many-coloured world calls for a more colourful language. This would be neat, but inaccurate, particularly since the poets just mentioned happen to be perfect introverts steeped in their utterly private worlds. But it is, I think, no accident that this change in style coincides with Yehoshua's earlier quoted words about the need to return to a style 'as rich as possible'. Both poet and novelist seem to feel that the limitation on expression owing to an over use of the colloquial layers of Hebrew and an avoidance of its higher, literary layers, is too heavy a price to pay for the direct impact gained.

We have come full circle and are back at what literature is really made of, i.e. words. It now seems confirmed by the brief outline I have drawn, that contemporary Israeli literature is marked, not by a distrust of words, but, on the contrary, by an ongoing discovery of the potentialities of language. Its paradoxical advantage, when compared to the literatures of Europe, is the many things it has not yet done with language. It has neither a Joyce nor a Rilke, and it can look forward to many adventurous explorations of the undiscovered terrains of language. In the meantime, its achievement appears in its present unembarrassed return to the treasures it had to relinquish in order to define itself as a contemporary, secular literature. Having reached relative freedom by denying its heritage, it can now come back to traditional forms and give them a pulse of life independent of tradition. The result, one hopes, should be extremely interesting.

NOTES:

1. His *Breakdown and Bereavement*, translated by Hillel Halkin, was published by the Jewish Publication Society, 1971.
2. 'Reflections on S. Y. Agnon', *Commentary* (December 1967), p. 60.
3. ibid., p. 59.
4. 'New Israeli Fiction', *Commentary* (June 1969).
5. This is Harold Fish's thesis in his review 'Unique and Universal' (*Commentary*, 1972).
6. English version: *Three Days and a Child*, translated by Miriam Arad, Doubleday.
7. Gouri's novel, translated by Seymour Simckes, was published by Rinehart & Winston, 1968; Amichai's novel, translated by Shlomo Katz, was published by Harper & Row, 1968.
8. Lea Goldberg had been a non-ideological poet all along.

Professor Shimon Sandbank is head of the Department of Comparative Literature at the Hebrew University in Jerusalem.

Aharon Appelfeld

Badenheim 1939

SPRING returned to Badenheim. Bells rang in the nearby country church. The shadows of the forest drew back into the forest. The sun scattered the remaining darkness, and its light spilled out along the main street, from square to square. It was a moment of transition. Soon the holidaymakers would invade the town. Two inspectors passed from street to street, checking the flow of sewage in the drains. Over the years, the town had seen many tenants come and go but its modest beauty was still intact.

Trudy, the pharmacist's ailing wife, stood at the window. She looked about her with the feeble gaze of a chronic invalid. The beneficent sunlight touched her pallid face and she smiled. A difficult winter, a strange winter, had ended. Storms had played havoc with the housetops. Rumours spread. Trudy's sleep was disturbed by hallucinations. She spoke incessantly of her married daughter, while Martin assured her that everything was all right. That was how the winter passed. Now she stood at the window, resurrected.

The low, well-kept houses looked tranquil once again. Islands of white in a green sea. This is the season when you hear nothing but the rustle of things growing and then, by chance, you catch sight of an old man holding a pair of pruning shears, with the look of a hungry raven.

'Has the post come?' asked Trudy.

'It's Monday today. The post won't arrive until afternoon.'

The carriage of Dr. Pappenheim the impresario charged out of the forest and came to a halt on the main street. Dr. Pappenheim alighted and waved in greeting. No one responded. The street was steeped in silence.

'Who's here?' asked Trudy.

'Dr. Pappenheim has just arrived.'

Dr. Pappenheim brings with him the moist breath of the big city, an air of celebration and anxiety. He'll be spending his time at the post office – sending off cables and express letters.

Apart from Dr. Pappenheim's appearance in town, nothing has happened. The mild spring sunshine shone out as it does every year. People met at the café in the afternoon, and devoured pink ice-cream.

'Has the post come yet?' she asked again.

'Yes. There's nothing for us.'

'Nothing.' Her voice sounded ill.

Trudy got back into bed feverish. Martin removed his jacket and sat down next to her: 'Don't worry. We had a letter just last week. Everything is all right.' Her hallucinations persisted: 'Why does he beat her?'

'No one beats her. Leopold is a very nice man, and he loves her. Why do you think such things?'

Trudy shut up as though she had been scolded. Martin was tired. He put his head on the pillow and fell asleep.

The first of the vacationers arrived on the following day. The pastry shop window was decorated with flowers. In the hotel garden Professor Fusshalt and his young wife were to be seen, also Dr. Schutz and Frau Zauberblit – but to Trudy they looked more like convalescents in a sanatorium than people on vacation.

'Don't you know Professor Fusshalt?' asked Martin

'They look very pale to me.'

'They're from the city,' said Martin, trying to mollify her.

Now Martin knew that his wife was very ill. Medicines would be of no use. In her eyes the world was transparent, diseased and poisoned, her married daughter held captive and beaten. Martin tried in vain to convince her. She had stopped listening. That night, Martin sat down to write a letter to Helena, his daughter. Spring in Badenheim is delightful, beautiful. The first vacationers are already here. But your mother misses you so.

Trudy's disease was gradually seeping into him. He, too, began to distinguish signs of pallor on people's faces. Everything at home had changed since Helena's marriage. For a year they had tried to dissuade her, but it was no use. She was in love, head over heels, as they say. A hasty marriage took place.

Dark green spring was now ascending from the gardens. Sally and Gerti, the local tarts, strolled along the boulevard dressed for the season. The townspeople had tried at one time to throw them out – a prolonged struggle that came to nought. The place had got used to them, as it had grown used to the eccentricities of Dr. Pappenheim, and to the alien summer people who transplanted themselves here like an unhealthy root. The owner of the pastry shop would not let the 'ladies' set foot on his premises, thus depriving them of the most delicious cream cakes in the entire world. Boyish Dr. Schutz, who liked Sally, once took some cakes out to the street. When the owner of the shop found out about it later, he made a scandal but that led nowhere either.

'And how are the young ladies?' asked Dr. Pappenheim merrily.

Over the years they had lost their big city haughtiness – they had bought themselves a modest house, and dressed like the local women. There had been a period of riotous parties but the years and the town's prostitutes had pushed them aside. But for their savings, theirs would have been a sad predicament. They had nothing left but the memories which they mulled over like widows on long winter nights.

'How was it this year?'

'Everything is fine,' said Pappenheim cheerfully.

'Wasn't it a strange winter, though?'

They were fond of Pappenheim, and over the years they had become interested in his strange artistes. Here, in alien terrain, they grasped eagerly at anything whatsoever.

'Oh don't worry, don't worry – the festival is packed this year – lots of surprises.'

'Who will it be this time?'

'A child-prodigy, a *yanuka*. I discovered him this winter in Vienna.'

'*Yanuka*,' said Sally maternally.

Next day, the vacationers were all over Badenheim. The hotel bustled. Spring-sunlight and excited people filled the town, and, in the hotel garden, porters hauled the brightly coloured luggage. But Dr. Pappenheim seemed to shrink in size. The festival schedule was ruined again. He ran through the streets. For years these artistes have been driving him mad, and now they wanted to wreck him altogether.

After leaving their luggage at the hotel, the people moved on towards the forest. Professor Fusshalt and his young wife were there. A tall man escorted Frau Zauberblit ceremoniously. 'Why don't we turn left?' said Frau Zauberblit, and the company did indeed turn to the left. Dr. Schutz lagged behind as though enchanted.

'Why do they walk so slowly?' asked Trudy.

'They're on vacation, after all,' said Martin, patiently.

'Who is that man walking with Frau Zauberblit? Isn't that her brother?'

'No, my dear. Her brother is dead. He has been dead for years.'

That night the band arrived. Dr. Pappenheim rejoiced as if a miracle had happened. The porters unloaded horns and drums. The musicians stood at the gate like trained birds on a stick. Dr. Pappenheim offered sweets and chocolates. The driver hurried the porters on, and the musicians ate in silence. 'Why were you late?' asked Pappenheim, not without relief. 'The car was late,' they answered.

Dressed in a frock coat, the conductor stood aside, as if all this were no concern of his. He'd had a struggle with Pappenheim the year before. Pappenheim was on the verge of dismissing him, but the senior musicians sided with their conductor, and nothing came of it. The conductor had demanded a contract for the usual three-year period. The quarrel ended in a compromise.

In the past, Pappenheim had lodged them on the ground floor of the hotel, in dark, narrow rooms. There was an emphatic clause in the new contract providing for proper lodging. Now they were all anxious to see the rooms. Pappenheim walked over to the conductor and whispered in his ear: 'The rooms are ready – top floor – large well-ventilated rooms.' 'Sheets?' asked the conductor. 'Sheets as well.' Pappenheim kept his promise. They were lovely rooms. Seeing them, the musicians were inspired to change into their blue uniforms. Pappenheim stood quietly by and did not interfere. In one of the rooms a quarrel broke out – over a bed. The conductor chided them: 'Rooms like these deserve quiet. Now get everything together before you go down.'

At ten o'clock, all was ready. The musicians stood in groups of three, instruments in hand. Pappenheim was furious. He would gladly have paid them compensation and sent them packing, but he could not afford to. More than anything else, they reminded him of his failures. Thirty years gone by. Always late and unrehearsed. Their instruments produced nothing but noise. And every year, new demands.

The evening began. People swarmed over the band like hornets. The musicians blew and hammered as though trying to drive them away. Dr. Pappenheim sat in the back drinking steadily.

Next day, the place was calm and quiet. Martin got up early, swept the entrance, wiped the dust off the shelves, and made out a detailed purchase order. It had been a hard night. Trudy had not stopped raving. She refused to take medicine, and finally Martin had tricked her into swallowing a sleeping mixture.

At approximately ten o'clock, an inspector from the Sanitation Department entered the pharmacy, and said that he wanted to look the place over. He asked strange questions. Ownership title. Had it come through inheritance? When and from whom was it purchased? Property value. Surprised, Martin explained that the place had been whitewashed and thoroughly disinfected. The inspector took out a folding yardstick, and measured. Then, neither thanking him nor apologizing, he went directly out into the street.

The visit made Martin angry. He believed in the authorities, and therefore he blamed himself. The back entrance was probably not in good enough repair. This short visit spoiled his morning. There was something in the wind. He went outside and stood on the lawn. A morning like any other. The milkman made his rounds bucolically, the musicians sprawled in the hotel garden sunning themselves, and Pappenheim left them alone. The conductor sat by himself shuffling a deck of cards. In the afternoon, Frau Zauberblit entered the pharmacy and announced that there is no place like Badenheim for a vacation. She was wearing a dotted poplin frock, but to Martin it seemed that her late brother was about to walk through the door.

'Isn't that strange?' he asked, not knowing what he was asking.

'Anything can happen,' she said as though she had understood the question.

Martin was angry. It was all because of Trudy.

The musicians stayed in the garden all afternoon. They looked pathetic out of uniform. For years they had been used to fighting with Pappenheim, now they fought among themselves. The conductor did not interfere. He set down his deck, and watched them. A gaunt musician took a pay receipt out of his vest pocket, and waved it at his colleagues.

They showed him his mistake. From Martin's garden this looked like a shadow play, perhaps because the light was fading. One by one long shadows unrolled across the green lawn.

At twilight, the conductor hinted that it might be advisable to go up and change into uniform. They took their time, like old soldiers worn out by long service. The conductor chatted with Pappenheim. For some reason, Pappenheim found it necessary to give a long-winded explanation of the festival programme. 'I hear Mandelbaum is on the programme too. Why, that's a spectacular achievement – how did you manage it?' 'Hard work,' said Pappenheim, and turned to go into the dining room. The guests were already eating hungrily. The waitress watched the kitchen door sharply. Her orders were late. But the cynical old waiters praised the food with an air of self-importance. Trudy's condition was no better. Martin's endless talk was futile. Everything seemed transparent and diseased to her. Helena was a prisoner on Leopold's estate, and when he comes home from the barracks at night, he beats her.

'But don't you see?' she asked.

'No, I don't see.'

'It's only my hallucinations.'

Martin was angry. Trudy frequently mentioned her parents, the little house on the banks of the Vistula. The parents died and all contact with the brothers was lost. Martin said that she was still immersed in that world, in the mountains, with the Jews. And this was, to a certain extent, the truth. She was tortured by a hidden fear, not her own, and Martin felt that her delusions were gradually penetrating into him, and that everything was on the verge of collapse.

Next day it was made known that the jurisdiction of the Department of Sanitation had been extended, and henceforth the Department would be entitled to carry out independent investigations. The modest announcement was posted on the town bulletin board. Without further ado, the clerks of the Department set about investigating all places designated on their map. The detailed investigations were carried out by means of questionnaires sent in from the district head office. One of the muscians, who bore his Polish name with pride, remarked that the clerks reminded him of marionettes. His name was Leon Semitzki. Fifty years ago he had emigrated from Poland with his parents. He had a fondness for his Polish memories, and when in good spirits he would talk about his country. Dr. Pappenheim liked his stories and he would sit with the musicians and listen.

The clouds vanished, and the spring sun shone warmly. A vague anxiety spread over the faces of the old musicians. They sat together and said nothing. Semitzki broke the silence all of a sudden: 'I'm homesick for Poland.' 'Why?' Pappenheim wanted to know. 'I don't know,' said Semitzki. 'I was only seven years old when I left, but it seems like only a year ago.'

'They're very poor there,' someone whispered.

'Poor, but not afraid of death.'

That night, nothing happened in Badenheim. Dr. Pappenheim was melancholic. He could not get Semitzki off his mind. He too recalled those rare visits to Vienna of his grandmother from the Carpathians. She was a big woman, and brought with her the odour of millet, the smell of the forest. Pappenheim's father hated his mother-in-law. Rumours flourished. Some said that the Department was on the track of a sanitary hazard, others thought that this time it might be the Tax Department masquerading as the Sanitation Department. The musicians exchanged views. The town itself was calm, co-operative, complying with all the Department's requests. Even the proud owner of the pastry shop agreed to give information. There was nothing noticeably different, but the old musicians surveyed the town, imparting a strange unease.

At the end of April, the two reciters showed up. Dr. Pappenheim wore his blue suit in their honour. They were tall and gaunt with an intensely spiritual look. Their passion was Rilke. Dr. Pappenheim, who had discovered them in Vienna seven years before, at once discerned a morbid melody in their voices which enchanted him. Thereafter, he simply could not do without them. At first their recitals drew no response, but in recent years people had discovered their elusive melody – and found it intoxicating, Frau Zauberblit sighed with relief: They're here.

The reciters were twin brothers who, over the years, had become indistinguishable. But their manner of reading was not the same – as if sickness spoke with two voices; one tender and appeasing, the remains of a voice, the other clear and sharp. Frau Zauberblit declared that without the double voice, life would be meaningless. Their recitals were balm to her, and she would murmur Rilke to herself in the empty nights of spring, as though sipping pure nectar.

The musicians, who worked at dance halls in the winter and resorts in the summer, could not understand what people found in those morbid voices. In vain did Pappenheim try to explain the magic. Only Semitski said that their voices excited his diseased calls. The conductor hated them – he called them the clowns of the modern age.

And meanwhile spring is at work. Dr. Schutz pines after the schoolgirl like an adolescent. Frau Zauberblit is engrossed in conversation with Semitski, and Professor Fusshalt's young wife changes into her bathing costume, and goes out to sunbathe on the lawn.

The twins are forever rehearsing. They can't do without the practice. 'And I was naïve enough to think that it was all spontaneous,' said Frau Zauberblit.

'Practising, practising,' said Semitski. 'If I had practised when I was young I never would have ended up in this second rate outfit. I wasn't born here. I was born in Poland. And my parents didn't give me a musical education.' After midnight, Dr. Pappenheim received a cable, worded as follows: *Mandelbaum taken ill. Will not arrive on time.* Dr. Pappenheim got up shaking and said: 'This is a catastrophe.' 'Mandelbaum,' said Frau Zauberblit. 'The entire arts festival is at stake,' said Pappenheim. Semitzki tried to soothe them, but Pappenheim said, 'This is the last straw.' He sank into his grief like a stone. Frau Zauberblit brought out a bottle of Pappenheim's favourite French wine, but he wouldn't touch it, and all night long he moaned: 'Mandelbaum, Mandelbaum.'

And the investigations showed reality for what it was. From this point on, no one could say that the Department of Sanitation was ineffective. A feeling of strangeness, suspicion and mistrust was in the air; still, the residents went about their usual business. The vacationers had their pastimes, and the local residents had their worries. Dr. Pappenheim was inconsolable over his great loss – Mandelbaum. Life was worthless since that cable had arrived. Professor Fusshalt's young wife declared that something had changed in Badenheim. The Professor did not leave the room – his definitive book was about to go to the publisher, and he was busy with the proofs. His young wife, whom he spoiled like a kitten, understood nothing about his books. Her interests were confined to cosmetics and dresses. At the hotel they called her Mitzi.

In the middle of May, a modest announcement appeared on the bulletin board, stating that all Jewish citizens must register with the Sanitation Department before the month was out.

'That's me,' said Semitzki. He seemed to be delighted.

'And me,' said Pappenheim. 'You wouldn't want to deprive me of my Jewishness, would you?'

'I would,' said Semitzki, 'But your nose is proof enough that you are no Austrian.'

The conductor, who had learned over the years to blame everything on Pappenheim, said: 'I have to get caught up in this bureaucratic mess all because of him. The clerks have gone mad, and I'm the one who suffers.'

People started avoiding Pappenheim like the plague. He seemed not to notice, and rushed back and forth between the post office and the hotel.

Trudy's condition worsened the last two weeks. She talked on and on about death. No longer out of fear – but rather as if she were coming to know it, preparing to inhabit it. The strong medications that she swallowed drew her from one sleep to the next, and Martin saw her wandering off into the other regions of her life.

People confessed to each other, as if they were talking about a chronic disease which there was no longer any reason to hide. And their reactions varied – pride and shame. Frau Zauberblit avoided talking and asking questions. She pointedly ignored them. Finally she asked Semitzki: 'Have you registered?'

'Not yet,' said Semitzki. 'I'll do it on a more festive occasion. You don't mean to say that I have the honour of addressing an Austrian citizen of Jewish origin?'

'You have indeed, sir.'

'In that case, we'll be having a family party in the near future.'

'Could you have thought otherwise?'

The sun stopped shining. The headwaiter himself served the white cherries for the cake. The lilac bushes climbed the veranda railing, and bees sucked greedily at the light blue flowers. Frau Zauberblit tied a silk scarf around her straw bonnet. 'Brought in from Waldenheim this morning – they ripened early.' 'That's simply marvellous,' said Frau Zauberblit. She adored these local voices.

'What are you thinking about?' asked Semitzki.

'I was remembering my grandfather's house – the rabbi from Kirchenhaus. He was a man of God. I spent my term vacations there. He used to walk along the river in the evenings. He liked growing things.' Semitzki did not stop drinking: 'Don't worry, children. Soon we'll be on our way. Just think – back to Poland.'

Dr. Schutz runs about in a stupor. The schoolgirl is driving him mad: 'Dr. Schutz, why not join intelligent company for an intelligent conversation?' said Frau Zauberblit. In academic circles, he was considered quite the prodigy – if a bit naughty.

'Have you registered?' said Semitzki.

'What?' he asked in surprise.

'Oh, you have to register, haven't you heard? According to the regulations of the Sanitation Department – which is, of course, a Government Department, a fine Department, a Department whose jurisdiction has been extended these last two months. And this most worthy Department earnestly desires that you, Dr. Schutz, should register.'

'This is no laughing matter, my dear,' said Frau Zauberblit.

'In that case,' he said, confused. He was the pampered darling of Badenheim. Everyone loved him. Dr. Pappenheim lamented his wasted musical talent. The prodigal son of his rich old mother, who never failed to bail him out at the end of the season.

A vague terror lurked in the eyes of the musicians. 'Don't worry,' said Dr Pappenheim, rallying his courage, though he was feeling melancholy. 'But aren't we guests? Must we sign as well?' asked one of the musicians.

'It is my opinion,' said Pappenheim dramatically, 'that the Sanitation Department wishes to boast of its distinguished guests, and will, therefore, enter them in the Golden Book. Now that is nice of them – don't you think?'

'Maybe it's because of the *Ostjuden*,' said one of the musicians.

Semitzki rose to his feet: 'What's the matter? You don't like me? I'm an Eastern Jew through and through – so you don't like me, eh?'

Badenheim's intoxicating spring was causing havoc again.
Dr. Schutz was penniless, and he posted two express letters
to his mother. The schoolgirl, it seems, was costing him a
fortune. Frau Zauberblit and Semitzki sit together all day
long. He might have been the only man left in the world. Dr.
Pappenheim is depressed – the intoxicating spring never fails
to make him sad. Frau Zauberblit already rebuked him: 'I'll
defray the losses. Hand me the bill. If Mandelbaum continues to give you the run around, I'll get the Krauss
chamber ensemble.' The twins wander through town looking
cryptic. People at the hotel talk about them in whispers, as if
they were sick. They eat nothing, and only drink coffee. The
headwaiter said: 'If only I could serve Rilke's death sonnets
maybe they would eat. That's probably all the food they can
digest.'
After breakfast, Frau Zauberblit, Semitzki and Pappenheim decided unanimously to register at the Sanitation
Department. The clerk did not so much as raise an eyebrow at
Frau Zauberblit's declarations. Frau Zauberblit praised the
Department for its order and beauty. No wonder it had been
promoted. Semitzki announced that his parents had come
from Poland fifty years ago, and that he was still homesick.
The clerk wrote all this down without a trace of expression.
That night Semitzki did not wear his blue uniform. The
band played. Everyone saw at a glance that Frau Zauberblit
had a sweetheart – she glowed like someone in love. The
young wife of Professor Fusshalt is going mad. Professor
Fusshalt is preoccupied with the book, and he doesn't leave
his desk. She's fed up with the people in Badenheim. What is
there to do here? Those readings again. They depress her.
One of the musicians, a cynic, tries to console her: 'Don't be
angry. In Poland, everything is beautiful, everything is
interesting.'
On the following day Trudy's screams were heard in the
street. From the hotel veranda, people watched the terrible
struggle in progress. No one went down to help. Poor Martin
fell on his knees in desperation, and begged: 'Trudy, Trudy,
be calm. There is no forest here – there are no wolves.'
An alien night descended on Badenheim. The cafés were
empty, people walked the streets in silence, as though being
led along. The town seemed in the grip of some other va-

cation, from another place. Dr. Schutz led the tall schoolgirl
about as though he were going to tie her up. Sally and Gerti
strolled arm in arm like school girls. The moist light of
spring nights slithered on the pavement. The musicians sat
on the veranda, observing the passing flow with sharp looks.

Dr. Pappenheim sat in the corner alone, reckoning sadly:
The trio has deserted me again. Nobody will forgive me.
And rightly so. Had I known, I would have planned it
differently.

The deadline for registration was approaching. Three in-
vestigators from the district office arrived at the Sanitation
Department. The conductor carried an interesting document in his vest pocket – his parents' baptismal certificates.
Dr. Pappenheim was taken aback, and he said: 'I would not
have believed it.' Strange, the conductor wasn't pleased.

'You're welcome to join the Jewish order, if you like. It's a
fine old order,' said Pappenheim.

'I don't believe in religion.'

'You can be a Jew without religion, if you like.'

'Who said so – the Sanitation Department?'

It poured that afternoon. They gathered in the lobby, and
were served hot wine as on autumn days. Dr. Pappenheim
was deep in a chess game with Semitzki. Towards evening,
Frau Zauberblit's daughter arrived. From her father, General Von Schmidt, she had inherited an erect carriage,
blonde hair, pink cheeks, and a deep voice. She was a student
at a lyceum for girls, far away from her mother.

General Von Schmidt is still remembered here. They
came to Badenheim the first year of their marriage, but Von
Schmidt had hated it there, and called it Pappenheim, after
the impresario. As far as he was concerned, it was no fit place
for healthy people – no horses, no tennis, no hunting – no
beer! They stopped coming after that and were gradually
forgotten. They had a daughter. Years went by, and Von
Schmidt, who had started his career as a lieutenant, rose
through the ranks. Soon after, they were divorced. After the
divorce, Frau Zauberblit, tall, slender, and suffering, appeared in Badenheim. That was the end of the matter.

The daughter stated at once that she had brought a document, a statement surrendering the so-called 'rights of the
mother'. Frau Zauberblit studied the document and asked:
'Is this what *you* wish?' 'What my father wishes, and what I

wish,' she said like someone who had learnt a part. Frau Zauberblit sighed. It was a hard and abrupt farewell. 'Excuse me, I'm in a hurry,' she said on her way out. The daughter's appearance shook the hotel. Frau Zauberblit sat mutely in the corner. A strange new pride seemed to show on her face.

Throughout the hotel, a secret was uniting the people. The conductor felt ill at ease for some reason, and sat down with the musicians. The twins were to perform that night. The proprietor of the hotel was arranging the small auditorium. They haven't been seen on the veranda for two days now. Cloistered. 'What do they do up there?' someone asked, and the headwaiter confirmed the fact that they had eaten nothing for two days. The people were standing by the windows, with the fading light on their faces. Pappenheim whispered, 'They're rehearsing, aren't they wonderful?'

The silence of a house of prayer filled the small auditorium that evening. The audience was early, and Pappenheim darted back and forth between the doors as if that would make the twins come down before it was time. They came down precisely at eight o'clock, and took their place by the table. Pappenheim retreated towards the door, like a guard.

For two hours, they talked about death. They spoke in a calm, modulated voice, as if they had returned from Hell and were no longer afraid. At the end of the recital, they stood up. The people bowed their heads and did not applaud. Pappenheim moved forward and took off his hat. He seemed about to fall on his knees.

Apple strudel was served in the afternoon. Frau Zauberblit had on her straw bonnet. Semitzki wore short trousers, and Pappenheim stood at the door like an unemployed actor. It seemed as if the old days were back.

At midnight, the *yanuka* arrived. The watchman refused to let him pass, because he was not on the lists. And Dr. Pappenheim, who was amused, said: 'But can't you see that he's Jewish?' When she heard, Frau Zauberblit said: 'Everything is going according to plan. Isn't that wonderful?'

'You'll love him too,' Pappenheim whispered.

'The impresario is a man of his word. By the way – in what language will the young artiste sing?'

'Why – Yiddish of course – he'll sing in Yiddish.'

When Pappenheim presented him, they saw before them neither a child nor a man. He blushed, his suit was too long.

'What's your name?' asked Frau Zauberblit drawing near. 'His name is Nahum Slotzker – and speak slowly,' Pappenheim interrupted, 'he doesn't understand German.' Now they saw wrinkles around the eyes, but the face was the face of a child. The adults were confusing him.

'Where are you from – Lodz?' asked Semitzki in Polish.

The boy smiled and said: 'From Kalashin.'

It was a strange evening. Frau Zauberblit was like an amorous young girl. Semitzki paced the corridor like a retired gym instructor. The conductor shuffled cards and joked with the cook. The cook gave him freshly baked poppyseed cakes. She was of mixed parentage. Orphaned at an early age, she had been for several years the mistress of Graf Schutzheim, until his death.

'Do you think they'll let me come too?' she asked slyly.

'There's no question about it. Who will cook for us in the land of cold?'

'But I'm not wholly Jewish.'

'Well I'm not wholly anything.'

'But your parents were both Jews, weren't they?'

'Yes, my dear, Jews by birth, but they converted to Christianity.'

Next day, the patroness of the twins arrived in town. Frau Milbaum was tall and elegant, and she had an aura of majesty. Dr. Pappenheim was extremely glad to see her. He was always glad to see people returning to Badenheim.

The secret surrounds them little by little, a dread born of other intimations. They tread lightly, and speak in whispers. The waiters serve strawberries and cream. The frenzied shadow of summer is spread out on the broad veranda. The twins sit beside Frau Milbaum, flushed and silent. They look like children in a roomful of adults. Pappenheim has planned a full programme, and there is a strange sense of anticipation in the air. The old people die between one interrogation and the next. The town swims in alcoholic fumes. Last night at the café, Herr Furst fell down and died. For years he had passed through the streets in his magnificent clothes. Next door at the lottery house, another man died by the roulette table. Sometimes it seems not to be the alcohol but a freshness not from the nearby forests.

And the interrogations proceed quietly at the Sanitation Department. This is the centre, and all the strands radiate from it. The Department is now omniscient. They have maps, periodicals, a library – a person can sit and browse if he wishes. The conductor registered at the Department and came back smiling. They had shown him a closetful of contracts, licences, and credentials. Strange – his father was the author of an arithmetic book in Hebrew. 'They know everything, and they're happy to show a man his past,' said the conductor.

A barrier was erected at the town gate. No entrance, no exit. But it was not a total blockade. The milkmen delivered milk in the morning and the fruit truck unloaded its crates at the hotel. Both cafés were open, and the band played every evening. Yet it seemed that another time, from another place, had broken through and was quietly entrenching itself.

The banquet given for the *yanuka*, the child prodigy, began late. The guests filed through the corridor, lamplight on their faces. There were soft woolly shadows on the carpet. The waiters served ice-cream in coffee. The tables were being laid in the hall. A few musicians played to themselves in the corner. Tongues of darkness climbed the long narrow windows.

Frau Milbaum sat on her throne, and green lights flashed from her green eyes. People avoided her look. 'Where are my twins?' she asked in an undertone. No one answered. They seemed caught in a net. The twins were talking to Sally. Sally, in a long, flowered dress, was making faces like a concert singer. The twins, who seldom conversed with women, were embarrassed, and started to laugh.

Sally told them about the first festivals. Gerti appeared and said, 'You're here.' 'Please meet two real gentlemen,' said Sally. The twins offered their long white hands. The *yanuka* sat mutely in the corner. Dr. Pappenheim explained in broken Yiddish that the banquet was about to begin. Everyone was anxious to hear him sing.

The guests drank heavily. Frau Milbaum sat enthroned, and now there was venom in her green eyes. So here, too, her life was becoming involved. She thought that there was a plot against her. That morning she had registered at the Sanitation Department. The clerk did not take her titles into account, the ones bequeathed her by her first husband; and he did not so much as mention her second husband, a nobleman of the royal family. There was nothing on the form but her father's name.

Semitzki was chattering away gaily in faulty Polish. He turned good-naturedly to Frau Milbaum, and said: 'Come and join our jolly circle. You'll find it amusing, I believe.' Her look was metallic. 'I am obliged,' she said.

'A fine society – Jewish nobility,' Semitzki was relentless.–

'I understand,' she said without looking.

'We would be delighted to have the lady's company,' Semitzki continued to pique her.

'Don't worry, the Duchess will get used to us,' whispered Zimbelmann the musician.

'She registered, didn't she? What's all this distance about?' added someone from the corner.

Frau Milbaum scanned them with her green eyes. 'Riffraff,' she finally spat out the word.

'She calls us riffraff,' said Zimbelmann, 'riffraff she calls us.'

The waiters served cheese wedges and Bordeaux wine. Dr. Pappenheim sat with the *yanuka*. 'There's nothing to fear. These are all very nice people. You'll stand on the stage, and sing, he said, trying to encourage the boy.

'I'm afraid.'

'Don't be afraid. They're very nice people.'

The conductor emptied one glass after another. His face was turning red. 'We're going to your native land, Semitzki. We must learn to drink.'

'They drink real alcohol there – not beer soup.'

'What will they do with a goy like me?'

'Don't worry, they'll only circumcise you,' said Zimbelmann, but felt he had gone too far. 'Don't worry. The Jews aren't barbarians for all that.'

Dr. Langmann approached the duchess and said: 'I'm getting out of here tomorrow.'

'But aren't you registered at the Sanitation Department?'

'I still consider myself a free citizen of Austria. They have to send the Polish Jews to Poland. That's the country for them. I'm here by mistake. One is entitled to a mistake, now and then, isn't one? You're also here by mistake. Are we to forfeit our freedom on account of a mistake?'

Now she scrutinized Sally and Gerti as they led the twins into a corner. 'Whores,' she glowered at them. The twins were greatly amused and as gay as two boys stumbling upon a wild party.

After midnight, they set the boy on the stage. He trem-

40

bled. Pappenheim stood over him like a father. The boy sang about the dark forest, the haunt of the wolf. It was a kind of lullaby. Seated around the stage, the musicians stared dumbly. The world was collapsing before their very eyes. Someone said, 'How wonderful!' Semitzki sobbed drunkenly. Frau Zauberblit approached him and asked: 'What happened?'

At that moment, Sally felt an oppressive fear. 'Dr. Pappenheim, may we go as well? Is there room for us?'

'What a question,' he scowled at her, 'There is room in our kingdom for every Jew and for everyone who wants to be a Jew. It is a mighty kingdom.'

'I'm afraid.'

'No need to fear, my dear, we'll all be going soon.'

Gerti stood aside as though she had no right to ask questions.

The town was empty. The light no longer flowed. It seemed to have frozen, listening intently. An alien orange shadow nibbled stealthily at the geranium leaves. Bitter damp seeped into the thatch of the creeping vines. Pappenheim worries about the musicians. He treats them to chocolate, cream cake. Such kindness makes them submissive. No more quarrels. Now the light filters through the thick drapery and illuminates the wide veranda. Dr. Schutz's love is not so easy as in days gone by. The orange shadow lingers upon him and his beloved. The high-school girl burrows ever more deeply into his summer coat, as though afraid of a sudden parting.

The post office is shut down. A cold light falls on the smooth marble stairs. The gate with its Gothic relief conjures up a memorial in ruins. The night before, Pappenheim stood outside the post office and laughed, 'Everything is closed.'

As Pappenheim stood laughing on the stairs of the post office, a terrible struggle was in progress at the pharmacy. Two men from out of town grabbed the poison chest. Martin fought them, snatched the jars from their hands, and shouted after them, 'I will not permit this.' These two skeletal men had arrived a few days before. Their faces were cold with desperation.

Mandelbaum and his trio arrived like thieves in the night. Pappenheim took them downstairs, and brought tea.

'What happened?'

'We got a transfer,' said Mandelbaum.

'Did you ask for it?'

'Of course we asked for it. A young man, a junior officer, has already sent on the documents. We told him that we had to get to the festival. He laughed, and he gave us a transfer. What do you say? We're in for it.'

'That's wonderful,' said Pappenheim. 'Oh, I can't believe it. You need to rest.'

'No, dear friend. That's not why we're here. We didn't have a chance to prepare anything. We have to rehearse.'

The tin sun was fixed on the cold horizon. 'How far is it from here to Vienna?' asked someone adrift in his own limp thoughts. 'I'd say – two hundred kilometres, no more.' These words hung in the air like tired ravens. The old favourite, apple strudel, was baking down in the kitchen. The sweet smell wafted on to the veranda.

'Why don't we ask for a visa?' said a musician who had travelled in his youth.

'Say you had a visa – where would you go?' The man was struck dumb by the question. The conductor put his card down and said: 'As for me, I'm willing to go anywhere.'

Martin took the winter clothes out of storage, and the house smelled of naphthaline. The dream of Poland calmed Trudy. Martin sits down and assures her, 'In Poland, everything will be right. That's where we came from, and that's where we're bound. Those who were there have got to go back.' There's music in his voice – Trudy listens and doesn't ask questions.

A group of angry people stood by the dead phone cursing the bureaucracy that, suddenly and without warning, had cut them off from their loved ones. Order, they grumbled, order. An energetic few wrote long letters of complaint. They described all the hardships that came from being disconnected. They claimed compensation from their travel agents, from all the authorities responsible for their being here. Of course, this was all futile. All telephone lines were disconnected, the post office was shut down. Domestic servants fled as if from a fire. The town began to live in a state of siege.

'What will they do to us in Poland?' asked one of the musicians.

'What do you mean? You'll be a musician as you've

always been,' answered a friend who dozed nearby.

'Then why all this moving around?'

'The force of circumstance,' was the reply.

'Kill me, I don't understand. My common sense doesn't grasp it.'

'In that case, kill your common sense and you'll start to understand.'

Silence enveloped the houses. The withered vines grew wild. The acacia flourished. It was autumn and spring in a strange coupling. At night there is no air to breathe. Semitzki is on the bottle. He drinks like a peasant, mixes Polish and Yiddish. Of all his languages, the language of his childhood seems to be the only one left.

'Why are you drinking so much, dear?' asks Frau Zauberblit tenderly.

'When a man goes home he ought to be happy.'

'It's cold there, really cold.'

'Yes, but it's a pure, healthy cold, a cold with hope.'

The registrations were over. The clerks at the Sanitation Department sit around, drinking tea. They've done their duty. Now they await orders.

But surprises never cease in the streets. Several days ago, a resident of Badenheim, who had been a major in the Great War, stood near the post office, and demanded to know why it was closed. Pappenheim, who had not given up his habit of a daily visit to the closed post office, answered, perhaps incautiously, that the town was cut off.

'I don't understand,' said the major, 'Is there a plague?'

'A Jewish plague.'

'Are you trying to make fun of me?'

'No, I'm not. Try leaving.' Turning his head with the narrow, metallic gaze that was used to scanning maps and fields, the major now focussed on the short figure of Dr. Pappenheim, and seemed about to reprimand him and send him away.

'Haven't you registered at the Sanitation Department?' Pappenheim continued to harass him.

For two days, he fought the Department. He cursed the Jews and he cursed the bureaucracy. He terrorized the deserted streets of town. Finally, he shot himself in the head. Dr. Langmann, who never left the window, said to himself: You must admit, the Jews are an ugly people. I find them useless.

Just then, the conductor put down his cards and asked: 'Do you remember anything from home?'

'Which home?' asked Blumenthal the musician, a simple man whose life was a prolonged yawn. The conductor used to taunt him in the early days, but it was no use, he was wrapped up in his doze.

'From your Jewish home.'

'Nothing.'

'My parents converted, damn it.'

'Then forget everything and go back to Vienna.'

'My friend, I am in good standing at the Sanitation Department.'

'What do they want of us?'

'It's hard to say,' said the conductor as though faced with a difficult musical score. 'If there's truth in those rumours that we're going to Poland, then we'd better start learning. I don't know a thing.'

'At our age, we're a little rusty in the head, wouldn't you say?'

'There's no choice. We'll have to learn Polish.'

'Is that how you imagine it.'

Grey days stretched across the town. Meals were no longer being served at the hotel. People queued by the serving hatch for dinner, barley soup and dry bread. The musicians opened their bags. A whiff of dead leaves and of drafty roads blew down the long corridors.

Suddenly, the old rabbi appeared in the street. Many years ago they'd brought him to Badenheim from the east. He had served as rabbi of the local synagogue, which was in fact an old-age home, until the last members had died, leaving the place empty. The rabbi had been stricken with paralysis. It was generally believed that he had passed away with the others.

The proprietor lowered his eyes and did not answer.
'Won't you come in, sir?' – more like a doorman than the proprietor of a hotel. Two musicians lifted the wheel-chair. The rabbi shaded his eyes, and a blue vein throbbed on his white forehead.

'Jews?' asked the rabbi.

'Jews,' said the proprietor.

'And who is your rabbi?'

'You are. You are our rabbi.'

44

The rabbi's face expressed some astonishment. His feeble memory tried to discover if they were playing a joke.

'Perhaps you will allow us to serve you a drink?'

The rabbi frowned: 'Kosher?'

The proprietor lowered his eyes and did not answer.

'Everyone here is Jewish?' the rabbi recovered. There was a sudden gleam of cunning in his eyes.

'Everyone, I believe.'

'And what do you do?'

'Nothing,' said the proprietor of the hotel, and smiled.

Semitzki rushed to his aid, 'We're planning to go back to Poland.'

'What?' said the rabbi, straining to hear.

'To go back to Poland,' repeated Semitzki.

The riddle was partially solved the next day. A kindly Christian woman had nursed him all these years, then a few days earlier she suddenly abandoned the house. After days of trying to manipulate the wheel chair, the rabbi had finally succeeded.

The rabbi poses questions, and the people answer him. Many years of isolation had made him forget the language, and he speaks Yiddish sprinkled with the Holy Tongue. Some musicians appear in the doorway carrying luggage. 'Who are they?' asks the rabbi.

'Musicians.'

'Are they going to play?'

'No, they want to go home, but the roads are barricaded.'

'Let them spend the Sabbath with us.'

'What did he say?' asked the astonished musicians.

The autumnal light, the tin light governs the town these days. The proprietor stands in the kitchen like one of the servants and ladles out soup. Supplies are not delivered. Provisions are running low. The dining room is like a soup-kitchen. Long shadows crawl on the tables at night. There is a faltering look in the eyes of the musicians. A few days ago they were still grumbling. Now, their hopes are dashed. They comprehend: there is no going back. Pappenheim's optimism has also dissolved, the owner of the pastry shops shakes a fist at the hotel, or, more accurately, at Pappenheim, whom he threatens to murder.

'What does the rabbi say?' asked Frau Zauberblit.

'He's sleeping,' whispered the proprietor.

The musicians took no pity on the hotel and stuffed their

bags with crockery and silverware. Semitzki took them to task: 'What for? No one uses fancy dishes in Poland.' 'What harm are we doing?' said one of them like an amateur thief. 'If we come back, we'll return it.'

The fleshy vines steal inside now, and spread over the veranda. This is their last burst of growth before winter. The forsaken chairs stand oafishly in place. A thick shadow nests inside the geranium pot. The flowers redden like rotten beets.

'What ever happened to the major?' asked someone.

'He killed himself.'

By the shuttered windows of the pastry shop stands Bertha Stummglanz. They brought her here last night. Her parents died some years before, and the house was transferred to the local council.

'Do you remember me?' asked Sally.

'I think I do, I think we were schoolmates.'

'No, dear. My name is Sally and this is Gerti.'

'Oh, I've made a mistake then, haven't I?' said Bertha apologetically.

'My name is Sally and this is Gerti.'

Bertha could not remember. Her memory was evidently deserting her. Her eyes wandered aimlessly.

'Why is everything closed?'

'The town is being transferred. Dr. Pappenheim says that everything is going to Poland, including us.'

'Dr. Pappenheim?'

'The impresario, don't you remember him?'

Strangers are brought in from the gate. Dr. Pappenheim stands at the entrance of the hotel like a doorman.

'Why did you come here?' someone asked.

'They were born here, so they had to come back.'

'It's a fine place,' Dr. Pappenheim interjects. 'Mandelbaum is with us, the twins are with us.'

'The twins? Who are the twins?'

'Where are you from, Jews?' asked the rabbi. An ancient grief glazed his eyes.

'This is our rabbi,' says Pappenheim proudly, 'A real one of the old school.'

The rabbi's questions never stop. The proprietor wears a skullcap, and serves him cold water.

No end to surprises. Last night, Helena came home. Her husband the lieutenant threw her off the estate. She had the face of her ailing mother. Incredulous, Trudy stroked her hands like a blind woman. Martin was drunk with joy. 'Now we can go. Together we can go anywhere.'

Every day brings more newcomers, decendants of former Badenheimers. The town's curse had pursued them all these years, and now they were caught. Dr. Pappenheim received a letter from the Sanitation Department, instructing him to put his articles at its disposal. Pappenheim rejoiced – a grand tour await us!

Autumn turns to dust. The wind growls in the empty streets. Mandelbaum tortures the trio, polishes the music. The twins are cloistered again. An air of gravity pervades the hotel. Pappenheim walks on tiptoe, saying, 'Hush, hush, you're disturbing the sound.' The musicians quietly nibble their bread. 'Practice won't do us any good. It's too late now for what you didn't accomplish when you were young.' Pappenheim comforts them: 'In the new place, there'll be time, you'll be able to practise. Where there's a will there's a way.' He himself plans to take up research.

Dr. Pappenheim makes continuing efforts to talk to the owner of the pastry shop. 'Why be angry with us? What have we done? We haven't committed a crime, after all. Tell us what our crime is. In Poland, you can open up a bigger shop. A person has to broaden his horizons.' Wasted words. The owner of the shop stands at the window, raving: 'If it weren't for this hotel, if it weren't for the corruption, they wouldn't have closed the town. It's all because of Pappenheim. He ought to be arrested.' He only stops at night.

Mandelbaum looks happier. The trio is inspiring him. He is getting new tones from his violin.

'When do we set off?' he asks Pappenheim, the way he used to ask his agent.

'Soon,' says Pappenheim like the bearer of a secret.

'We're improving, we're improving.'

It poured on Saturday night. The rabbi prayed loudly. People hugged the walls like shadows. The proprietor brought wine and candles, and the rabbi performed the Havdala service.

Immediately after the Havdala, the musicians went off to pack. The bags were big and swollen. Dr. Pappenheim was surprised at the commotion, and said, 'I'm going like this – empty-handed. If they want me, they'll take me like this – empty-handed.'

The next day was bright and cold. Mandelbaum rose early
and stood with the trio on the smooth steps of the hotel. The
rehearsals had left their mark. His distinguished brow had
turned white. Semitzki escorted Frau Zauberblit with a cumbersome elegance. Professor Fusshalt stood in his bathrobe as
if he'd been shaken out of a fitful sleep: 'The proofs, what
will happen to the proofs?' Zimbelmann the musician
wrapped the rabbi in two velvet blankets and put him in his
wheel-chair. The proprietor said: 'What must we bring?'
'Nothing, don't worry,' said Pappenheim. By the old orna-
mented gate, the clerk called the roll. The people answered
their names as at a morning parade. A long journey stretched
before them. At the familiar railway station there stood a
hissing engine with many empty carriages. No one pushed.
No one cried.

Translated by Betsy Rosenberg

Two Poems   *by* Daliah Ravikovitch

REQUIEM

The cantor was reading Psalms.
The trees whispered
like a flock of black priests.

We were not much taller than the gravestones
and we knew there would be
no resurrection in our day.

The ladder reached up from there
to the ranks of the holy and pure
who shine like sapphire
(most of them lay at our feet).

Our lives were like a grasshopper's
on the border of sun and shade.

But when the drowned girl passed through
all the chambers of the sea
we knew

it is the sea
that gives life to the rivers

FROM DAY TO NIGHT

Every day I wake up again
as if for the last time.
I don't know what's waiting for me,
perhaps that's a sign
that nothing's waiting for me.

This spring
is like the spring before.
I know what the month of Iyyar means,
but it means nothing to me.
I can't tell the moment
that divides day from night,
just that night is colder
though both are equally silent.

At dawn I hear the sound of birds
and my affection for them
eases me to sleep.
The one I care for isn't here,
perhaps he is nowhere.

I go from day to day
from day to night
like a feather
the bird doesn't feel
as it falls.

Translated by Chana Bloch

Two Poems   *by* Yair Hurwitz

WHISPERING IN ME

The dead man clutched me.
I went after him.
He revealed himself, night, that dead man.

Once he was a kingdom.
Years passed.
The crown that honored him is cracked.
Light filters through me broken.
I know those difficult days.

A man is walking in the street.
He sees me laugh – that man.
And how will I tell him
that a dead man clutches me and magic spells
whisper in me, hard.

AND STILL I LOVE ...

And still I love. And still I sit hidden.
And still I don't know. And still I don't know what.

What, as if amazed. I saw a face in sudden amazement.
And still I love. And still I'm captive.
And still I don't know. And still I'm not there and I

saw wonders in the vision of a face. Wondrous corruption.
And still I love and still I'm caught in wondrous embroidery.
And still I love wonder that holds that much corruption
like suffering and still I love and my mother
burst out of my dream, my mother out of my house

and still I love and my hands still seem to be sprouting
and the wind caresses inside me in her sweetness and still
      there's love
and still the kingdom.

Translated by Leonore Gordon

Shulamith Hareven

'City of Many Days'

SARA's father had never met morality in person and so could be forgiven his neglect of it. Even in the Jerusalem of those days, which was a passionate city of passionate quarters, Don Isaac Amarillo was considered an exceptionally passionate man who was unable to resist the general sweetness of things, such as the pure breeze that whistled down the oboes of the alleyways when a heat wave suddenly broke, driving before it sun-bronzed women, all colours of children, the smell of jasmine crying out in Arab courtyards from an overdose of evening, a dusty shepherd returning from the city's fields with a lamb on his shoulders, a fragrance of arak, thyme and repose. At such times his defences were down! Tears of utter helplessness flooded his good-natured, near-sighted eyes; he grew weaker than a baby; and he was capable of taking every cent that he had, his own soul had anyone requested it, tying it in one of his not always immaculate handkerchiefs, and giving it away. One might compare him then to a big, kind Gulliver with a horde of children perched on his hat brim, tweaking his ears to make him run and stamping their feet on his forehead for the fun of it. And when summertime came, bringing the wild red rut of watermelons piled high in the market by the Jaffa Gate, along the path that led down to the Hebron road from the Old City wall, he was at the mercy of the first woman who came along.

Perhaps it was just such a time, at the break of a heat-wave, when life began to flow again through the narrow streets as though blown out of a bellows, that saw him drying the face of Hannah, a young socialist pioneer from Russia who had come to live in Jerusalem, in the new part of Beth Israel. As her tears proved too much for him, he came back again and again, until she bore him a son whom she named Tanhum. Don Isaac Amarillo promptly acknowledged his paternity. Indeed, he might have acknowledged it if he hadn't been the father too, for how was a man like him to abandon an unclaimed baby, and a little boy at that? A white tropical hat on his head, he stood proud and penitent in the doorway of Hannah's room holding a bouquet of flowers. For a while he felt obliged to live with her in Beth Israel, so as to stand by her when she was taunted by the neighbours over the shameful consequences of his own too fond heart. But the neighbours too were young socialists: they went about unkempt, wore tattered Russian blouses, worked at their printing press until all hours of the night, and couldn't have cared less about the origins and ancestry of Hannah's squalling child.

Three months after Hannah gave birth to Tanhum, Don Isaac was summoned home, where his wife, Gracia, had given birth too, to a second daughter, named Ofra. Once again he stood proud and penitent in a doorway with a bouquet in one hand. This time it was his own wife's tears that proved too much for him. He moved back home.

Eventually Hannah took Tanhum and went to live in a village near the coast, where she taught school for a living – whereupon Don Isaac's escapades might have come to an end, had not a strange young woman turned up in Jerusalem several years later. A small, slender thing surrounded by bundles and suitcases, she arrived in a gigantic hat that resembled a wagon wheel, and a white muslin dress, chattering away in loud French. Rumour had it she was the daughter of a French count and countess. Since Don Isaac was one of the heads of the Jewish community, she appeared before him in his office one morning with a roll of pictures under one arm, looking like a starched hornet. The story she told was a strange one. The pictures, she said, had been painted by her late mother, and her one desire was for Don Isaac to help her *arranger une exposition*, that is, a public showing, in Jerusalem. Dipping her lips in a little coffee, she explained, seated opposite him, that she was the daughter of a French count and countess who had travelled to Lebanon and lived there for a while until, compelled one day to return to France on family business, they left her behind with their Arab servant and his wife. The two of them tragically perished at sea and she became an orphan.

Don Isaac was so overcome with compassion that his tongue clucked unconsciously in his mouth. The more it clucked, the less he was able to stop it, for the tale went from bad to worse. The servant and his wife brought the girl up, but they were vulgar, common people with whom it was impossible for her to live any longer. Not only that, it was just her misfortune that, as she matured – and her benefactor, Don Isaac, could see for himself that she wasn't exactly unattractive – her servant-guardian began making advances to her until she didn't have a moment's peace. She packed up a few of her belongings, just a smattering of what she owned, took her mother's paintings, which were her most precious possessions, and fled.

Don Isaac wiped his eyes. He would be only too happy, he declared, to come to her aid as best he could, even *arranger une exposition* of her mother's paintings in Jerusalem, though in fact no one in the neighbourhood knew what *une exposition* was, or how it might be arranged. In this and all other possible ways he could think of, he would help her raise the money to trace her legal kin in France. He was so carried away by his desire to be of assistance that he hardly bothered to listen to the rest of her story, which included such things as stock companies in Panama, diamonds her guardian had made off with, and various other financial details that could make a man's head spin round.

The exposition never was held. On one occasion the countess wasn't feeling well; on another she feared that there weren't enough paintings for a proper show; on still another she cancelled because not enough guests were invited, or because they weren't the right sort of people. Finally, when a hall had been rented and Don Isaac had taken care of everything down to the smallest detail, guaranteeing the presence of just the right number of just the right sort of guests, she sent him a messenger the morning of the opening with a note to inform him that the paintings had been stolen that night. And that was that.

Don Isaac Amarillo was a man of some means, and he spared no effort to see that she was properly looked after, with lawyers for her stocks, pawnbrokers for her jewellery, doctors for the mysterious attacks of illness that periodically befell her, and maids to iron her dresses. Eventually he became her slave. She sent him messages over every little thing, until he found himself devoting half his time to her and her affairs, and ultimately the whole of it. Before five

53

months were out Don Isaac disappeared from Jerusalem one fine summer day along with the Countess Claudine – who, it was rumoured, was not really a countess at all, and was perhaps half-an-allegorical-figment of Don Isaac's imagination to begin with.

Sara was seven at the time. 'An evil beast hath devoured Zaki,' her grandfather declared, as Jacob had of Joseph in the Bible. The members of the family didn't officially go into mourning; but they did mourn Zaki none the less, that is, Don Isaac, their pride and their joy, of whom it was difficult to say whether he had cast them out of his life or himself out of theirs. One way or another, he had suddenly ceased to be a husband, son-in-law, father and son, and had become as good as dead.

Sara was sick with a fever that week, covered all over with the chicken pox, which itched and itched, and she simply couldn't believe that her father could desert her at such a time. He had always been so nice to his daughters whenever they chanced to intrude on that invisible ballet of which his days were composed. Why, just the other evening, standing by her bedside after returning from his day's affairs, he'd gently wiped her moist brow and promised that if she didn't scratch the blisters and scar her face for life, he'd invite the Turkish army band to serenade her beneath her window on Saturday night. He'd promised in so many words – and now he was gone for good. In Jerusalem he was never seen again. It was said that he was in Panama. Or perhaps, like Elijah in his chariot, he was carried off in a storm to Brazil. Sara's mother kept a stiff upper lip and never mentioned his name. In all likelihood she had hated him down all the years, with a dark and ponderous hatred, for his stupid, compassionate heart. Indeed, now that he was gone it was remarked on in Jersualem that somehow one's contacts with Don Isaac Amarillo had always ended in disappointment. This feeling was well put by a local porch-sitter named Nissim Mizrahi, known slyly to the neighbours as Mirácolo Orientale because of his dandyish ways. 'It's as though,' said Mirácolo, a thin slip of a man who drove a wagon for the burial society, 'Zaki was always promising to take you to heaven in a speeding coach, and you trusted him so much that you didn't even look where you were going, and then suddenly, wham-bang, he reins in the horses and out of the wagon you fall!'

And yet he had been a good man.

In purely practical terms, nothing changed very much. The role of Sara's grandfather, Elder Amarillo, became even more clearly defined as that of paterfamilias. The family continued to live in one house with him and Sara's grandmother, a mean old woman who spent all her days bed-ridden in her alcove, from where she issued orders to the household. Grandfather Amarillo was a strong and taciturn man, strict and pious in his habits; he never patted the cheeks of the children and always met his obligations. He considered it his duty to look after Tanhum, whose grandsire he'd been made by his idiot son – nor was Sara unaware of the fact that he frequently sent money to a certain village near the coast, much to her mother's displeasure.

One day Sara met Tanhum. Hannah came with him to Jerusalem. A dry, bespectacled woman, she shut herself up with grandfather in his office, with its big, black, intricately carved safe. It was shortly after the Turks had left the country, and Hannah had come on hard times. Gracia retired at once to her room, whose curtains were drawn and well-tied, and lay there groaning with a headache, a handkerchief soaked in eau de cologne on her forehead, muttering *tranquil, tranquil* to herself in French as though it were a magic charm. Bukas, the cook, made a tomato omelette for Tanhum, who sat silently in the kitchen and refused to eat.

Sara saw him when she entered the kitchen: he was only a little shorter than herself, thin and intense, with electric, bristly hair. She sat without a word by his side and cut up everything on his plate into little bites, though he was at least nine years old and could have done it himself; yet he took the food from her hands and ate. 'Eat, Tanhum, eat,' she urged him on quietly, a lump forming in her throat. He didn't even shy away when she stroked his wiry hair. His arm was black-blue all over, because, Bukas said, that *pisgada* of a pioneer was always pinching it. The two of them sat on the window sill, swinging their legs; though they didn't talk, they were already fast friends. Afterwards Sara wasn't sure whether they really hadn't exchanged a word that day. She would have given anything to remember, for within the year they found out that Tanhum was dead of diphtheria. If Don Isaac Amarillo had any other son left, he could only be growing up in Panama, watered daily by his father's contrition. And if he didn't, he had only his two daughters.

Grandfather Amarillo prayed hard all week long; Bukas wiped her eyes in the corners of the house; and even Sara's mother was heard to remark, '*Pobro chico*, to think that such a good-looking boy could come from such an ugly old thing!' The day of her unbearable migraine, it appeared, she had sneaked a good look at the two of them through a crack between the curtains.

Hannah moved soon after to a kibbutz, several of whose members she knew from her old neighbourhood in Jerusalem. In time she married a pioneer from Germany, a fanatical socialist who was bald and loved sports. Grandfather Amarillo stopped sending her remittance, and even gifts for the holidays. The family lost touch with her.

The holidays were the worst times of all. On the first night of each, her mother's quarrels with her grandfather invariably came to a boil, frothing up like one of Bukas' pots that were always seething and simmering crossly like the cook herself. Gracia wanted a divorce in order to be able to remarry. Grandfather Amarillo wouldn't hear of it. 'Some day,' he would say, 'Zaki will come back. What will they say of you then? Shall we make a harlot out of you?' 'Then find him for me so that he can divorce me himself,' Gracia would scream in a desperate, drawn-out, up-and-down wail. 'You have no pity!' She knew perfectly well that Don Isaac was not to be found. There wasn't an agency through which Elder Amarillo hadn't tried to trace him; he had even turned to the British Government, whose tentacles were all over the world. Privately he was of the opinion that Zaki was no longer alive. 'The boy is crazy,' he admitted, 'that's true. And he's weak, that's true too. But it's still inconceivable that he would abandon his wife, and family, just like that. If he could write, he would write. Chances are that he's dead.'

Sometimes Grandfather Amarillo was brought lists by Captain Tony Crowther of His Majesty's army. In them were the names of all sorts of men whose bodies had been found, murdered perhaps in some violent brawl in one of the port cities of the world: under smoky, flickering lights, amid the smells of cheap alcohol, fish, seaweed and salt, astride rotting, slippery planks, in docks and piers licked by the ocean tides, in the shadows of mouldy warehouses greasy with petrol and tar, they had gone to their deaths. There were lists of the dead in railway accidents too, descriptions of men missing, of curious fatalities in India and Abyssinia, Turkey and British Guiana, of circumcised corpses of whom nothing else was known. Good Lord, how many weird, anonymous footloose Jews there are in Your world!

None of the descriptions fitted. The names on the lists were strange, even comical, each a joke in itself. Sara and Ofra would sit in a corner and repeat them one by one, roaring with laughter. Their lives seemed made up to them of the names and fragments of names of the anonymous dead. Men put on and took off names like clothing, changed them, threw them away like used rags, had them come to life again in some office in Jerusalem like a balloon blown gloriously up for a minute, for the sake of some document, clarification, only to be punctured again and discarded like bits of old scrap. None of them was Don Isaac, neither the official Isaac ben Rabbi Moses Amarillo of the record books, nor the Zaki whom everyone knew. One day Captain Crowther brought a faded, yellowed photograph of a man in a white hat, dressed in a white tropical suit and white shoes. Sporting a thin mustache, he stood leaning on a column in the patio of some villa against a background of palms. It was hard to say whether the villa was real or a painted backdrop in some photographer's studio. Elder Amarillo, his daughter-in-law, his children and grandchildren inspected this snapshot for three or four days through a magnifying glass until they returned it to the captain with a mixture of heartbreak and relief: no, it wasn't he. The Englishman, who happened to be in dress uniform with a diagonal belt on his chest and a swagger-stick under one arm, sipped his arak on ice, the cloudy complexion of which may have reminded him of London fogs and said: 'Pity!' He looked searchingly as he spoke at Sara's mother, who was the most romantic-looking woman he had seen in his life.

That evening Gracia wailed until midnight:

'I can't stand it any longer! May God strike me dead; If He's going to let the likes of him live, then let Him kill me instead!' Sara and Ofra stopped up their ears in their room and put their dolls to sleep with a lullaby.

> Daddy's work is far away
> He'll come back at close of day
> He'll bring games for us to play-a-y.

In the course of time Gracia's suffering became ritualized.
With the approach of every holiday or feast, the family
braced itself for her screams, her migraines, her slamming of
doors, her drawn-out wails that faded away in the end to an
incantatory *tranquil, tranquil,* her appeals to God in
Hebrew, French and Ladino. Glancing up at the grandfather clock that hung in the kitchen, where she was busy
straining steamed wheat to make noodles, her sleeves pushed
back and her arms caked with flour, Bukas would grumble:
'Look how late it is! Why hasn't she started yet?'

The whole neighbourhood awaited Gracia's screams: they
gave everyone the chance to say pityingly *miskenika,* poor
little one, allowed the women to despise their husbands and
remind them of all their sins, and the men to congratulate
themselves for not acting like that fool of a Zaki, who left his
wife high and dry, despite their little peccadillos. At such
times a kind of communal atonement took place, a ritual of
purification that reaffirmed what mattered in life and made
everyone feel his self-worth. The important thing, the neighbourhood held, was what went on behind a family's doors,
not in front of them – and so strengthened in their convictions, all sat down to eat, penitents if not perfect angels,
poured the children a drop of wine, and made sure that they
drank no more.

Once when Sara was sitting in the kitchen with Bukas,
kneading a small ball of dough which she had plucked from
the bowl, she inquired:
'Bukas, why doesn't grandfather let my mother get married again?'
'Who said she wants to get married?' said Bukas crossly.
'Just because you scream, does that make it so?'
Sara jumped up and hit her. Grandmother Amarillo
banged with her cane on the floor of her room. Bukas went
to complain. It ended with angry tears.
'Don't you ever dare tell me again my mother's a liar!'

'She's not only a liar, she's cross-eyed too,' said Bukas, as she left the room.

Little by little, however, Sara began to think that perhaps Bukas was right. There was something put on about her mother's holiday tantrums. Once Sara went up to her room before the Passover *seder* and saw her burning a piece of cork in order to blacken the already dark circles beneath her eyes. She and Ofra stopped paying attention to her attacks. Only Grandfather Amarillo still paced back and forth in his room, troubled and ill-at-ease: back and forth, back and forth, while his daughter-in-law wailed, until, spying Sara in the doorway, he would motion her inside and hand her a bill from the safe.

'Go buy yourself something, *miskenika*.'

There was an air of trumpery in grandmother's room: ancient, cunning trumpery, yet also brazen, improperly concealed. Grandmother was full of a malicious energy. She rambled querulously on and on, whether to herself or someone else no one knew.

'I'm sixty years old. That's a fact. Of all the neighbours only Luna Cardozo *no tiene* any shame, she says I'm seventy-two. What a lie, what a lie; God strike me dead if there's a word of truth in what she says. They've all become liars, *kazzabe'eva*. It's impossible to live with them. That Bukas is the biggest liar of all. *Mentirosa*. She told me she paid four mils for my handkerchiefs, but I saw it say five on the label with my own eyes. Why does she lie to an old woman? What for? When I don't get out of bed, nobody knows how I suffer. Everyone cheats me to my face. Gracia's a liar *también*.'

The business of prices was anything but simple. Grandmother Amarillo refused to believe a word about prices going up. The merchants, she insisted, were cheats, and the family was stupid enough to be cheated. To keep on her good side, it was a household rule never to tell her the real price of anything. Even this didn't satisfy her, though, and she would begin to mutter to herself, chewing the price with her ancient teeth. The family had been deceiving her in this way for years, doing everything to avoid her wrath, until one day she decided that it wasn't enough for prices to stay the same: the family deserved a discount. Propped up in all her trumpish magnificence in her huge bed, which resembled a taut-sailed schooner that never raised anchor, she demanded a discount. The family obliged her and knocked prices down even further. In grandmother's room bread now cost a quarter of what it did in the market. But Grandmother Amarillo still didn't believe them. Playing a cunning game of her own, she secretly sent Sara or Ofra to ask what things really cost. In their innocence the girls did as they were told. *Grandmother, he said half a piastre a rotel. He said a piastre and a half a bottle, grandmother.* The old woman nearly had a stroke each time. Stubborn, senile and stinking of pee, she would scream at Bukas until she was red in the face:

'You're a liar! A cheat! There's no God in your heart! I swear to God there's no God there!'

It would end with her groaning:

'It was never like this when I was *en mi cama matrimonial.*'

She meant her big double bed. Ever since she had left it for her alcove kingdom full of chamberpots, trumpery, pistachio nuts, muslin nightgowns, shawls and Turkish-delight, the world had never been run properly.

Grandmother Amarillo played cards with the girls and cheated with a straight face. They played rummy in her room, which always smelled of medicine and urine, the cards scattered over her bed. Grandmother Amarillo ate candy while she played. She refused to offer it to the girls and boastingly won every hand. Sara caught her cheating once or twice, but got a box in the face when she mentioned it. Ofra, on the other hand, either didn't or pretended not to notice, for the only way to get one of grandmother's sweets was to lose.

'How well you play, grandmother,' twittered Ofra, looking up with her baby blue eyes, while Sara whispered venomously in her ear: 'Asslicker!'

One time Grandmother Amarillo cheated so openly that it was impossible not to react. Sara screamed. Grandmother Amarillo screamed too. Grandfather Amarillo came to the room.

Que se pasa aqui?'

Grandmother Amarillo said that Sara was a snake: that's right, a snake, whose head should be crushed before it bit everyone. Grandfather Amarillo took one look at the cards, gathered them up, and threw them out of the window.

'Sodom and Gomorrah!' he said out loud, and left the room.

Ofra picked up the cards in the street and returned them to her grandmother.

Once Gracia sat on the terrace with a friend while Sara did her homework inside. Though she couldn't see her mother, she did see her long brown taffeta dress that hung down to the splendid floor tiles, the black tassels that dangled from it, and, above them, a black knitted shawl. She saw her mother's hand, too, which held a purple Japanese paper fan, and the railing of the terrace, which was beautifully worked into a pattern of lilies, acanthus and horse-drawn carriages, all held together by long, formal ropes of ivy that were also black grille work. In the spaces between the bars the smith had made a kind of anchor that hung suspended in air, over nothing.

'For giving them money, I forgave him,' Gracia said to her friend. 'What he did *con son cuerpo*, I forgave him too. Everything I forgave him, except what he whispered in their ears. I could have torn his eyes out for that.'

'Yes,' said her friend. 'You're right about that, Gracia. They can be forgiven everything except the whispers.'

One day a pleasant-looking, unassuming Arab arrived in the lane and asked for Elder Amarillo. It was the last house on the corner. Beyond the border that it marked lay an empty field, and then the great unknown. The Arab entered the house and shut himself up with Grandfather Amarillo in his office, talking Arabic with a Lebanese accent.

He was, it turned out, the father of the countess. He lived in a village not far from Beirut and was a fez-cleaner by trade. In his shop, he related with a modest pride, he had a special steam press: Judge Amarillo would scarcely believe what pleasure he got from adjusting a wrinkled fez on the machine and seeing how clean, smooth and ready-to-wear it came out, its tassel newly sparkling and springy. He had ten children, of whom one, his daughter Claudine, was never quite right in the head. The paintings for the exposition that she claimed were her mother's were actually her own, while the jewels, begging Elder Amarillo's pardon, were all stolen. This wasn't the first time she had run away from home or found some man to fall for her story. He was genuinely sorry

61

that she had done such a thing to the Amarillos. The news had come as far as his own village when he had already given up all hope of finding her. He had simply come to the Judge, as he put it, to help him shoulder the misfortune. Her madness had struck both their families, not just one of them, he said. Should Elder Amarillo ever visit Lebanon, he and his family must stay with them. As for Don Isaac Amarillo's children, he considered them his own.

Elder Amarillo insisted that the visitor stay for a while. They dined together, conversed till late in the night, and parted on friendly terms.

That evening Ofra asked with perfect nonchalance:

'What happened, have they found father?'

'They haven't and they never will,' said Bukas. And Gracia added:

'One lie has met another.'

Sara and Ofra broke into hysterical laughter in their room. They jumped on the beds, threw pillows at each other, and shouted at the top of their lungs:

'No Panama! No Nicaragua! No India! No England!'

And when the family tried to quiet them, with cajoling and threats, they screamed till they were hoarse:

'No father! No mother! No grandfather! No grandmother! No nothing!'

In the end a pillow broke open and feathers flooded the room. Sara started to bite them. Ofra fell on the bed and hurt her hand. Imperceptibly they passed from shrill laughter to tears. Bukas refused to sweep up the feathers until morning. They fell asleep among them, exhausted by the sensation of a bitter and all-knowing victory.

Translated by Hillel Halkin

'City of Many Days' is a chapter from the novel of the same name shortly to be published by Doubleday, New York.

YOU HID YOUR SOUL

You hid your soul from me,
and the sound of the high river
overflowing its banks
went silent in me.

My life is cut off from the song
and I stand in a cave ashamed
without sun
without moon
without candle.

You hid your soul from me
and the bread on the table is dry
and mouldy.

Translated by Chana Hoffman

TIME

We had a hidden treasure of time
tender as morning air,
a time of stories, tears, embraces
and holy days.
A time of Mother, Grandma and the aunts
sitting tranquil in a boat
of splendor,
gliding slowly-slowly
in a tiny boat of peace
with the moon and all the stars.

Translated by Edna G. Sharoni

Two Poems   *by* Hayim Be'er

TABERNACLE OF PEACE

In Kerem Abraham
Ada with the right hand of her righteousness
bakes cookies from the dust of the earth,
rejoicing in the world of His earth,
A little girl three or four years old
sitting in a sandbox in the morning
in the place where a century ago
the children of ancient and proud families
used to clear stones
and build unhewn stone walls under the guidance of the
    villagers
in the field of the missionary Mrs. Finn:
young Jews from the Old Settlement
who for their daily bread
earn three and a half piastres
from the wife of the English consul,
touching the Christian heart
by their strangeness and fragility,
and already several vines have been planted
and some mulberry trees
in the heat of the sun
in the yard of the Rachel Strikovsky Kindergarten
where I now see
Hebrew women yawning and sneezing.
holding their children by the hand
in the shade
beneath the mulberry trees,
for in Salem also is His tabernacle.

THE SEQUENCE OF GENERATIONS

I am a child
of six generations here
under the sun of lower Syria.
Mother and my aunts
during the World War
eat grass
and go begging for

colonial merchandise—
little girls trapped
in poverty,
waiting for Genral Allenby,
a commander who is more like Wellington
than Napoleon,
an Englishman who spent the last decade of his life
studying the lives of birds
and taking long trips,
getting down from his horse at Jaffa Gate,
and in the Street of the Patriarch
the heathens say to them
Return return O Shulamite,
eyes on them from every side.
Return that we may look upon thee,
and they run away and answer
What will ye see in the Shulamite,
hungry little girls in checkered blouses
who remind them of
the lady Mary, a Semitic woman
in Terra Sancta,
and I am a child
little by little
in the world of actions
building the family tree,
always as if walking
in happy light.
There is nothing more enchanting in life than this,
to sit in the crusader East
and to see the sheep scattered upon the hills
and only the Lamb of God
standing and weeping—
Dominus flevit – the Lord
in his Byzantine beauty
standing and weeping
on Mount Olives
as he comes from Bethany,
and on the threshing floor of Aravna the Jebusite
already the Mother of Zion hears
words of a husband to his wife
and laughs.
Praise is comely.

Translated by Stephen Mitchell

Ehud Ben Ezer

'The flowers that you didn't give me will never wither'

(Chapter six from *Nor the Battle to the Strong*, a novel)

The novel tells the story of the life and death of a young Israeli, Fullik Shomron, a student of philosophy at the Hebrew University in Jerusalem. It is written in a naturalistic manner with a partly documentary background of Jerusalem and Tel Aviv during the time of the so-called 'Lavon Affair' in the autumn of 1960. The more Fullik gets involved in his desperate love affair with Ofra, a fellow student, the more he tends to interpret political events in the country as his own personal affair. The following summer, while on reserve duty with his military unit, an inner feeling of rebellion causes him to run towards the spot from which shots are fired. He is killed. Even in his last moments his thoughts are concentrated on the necessity to break down the wall of Arab hatred. 'You are killing me by allowing me to kill you', he appeals to the Arabs in his mind.

I'LL send you a bunch of flowers and I'll write: 'The flowers that you didn't give me will never wither.' A woman's a very small god – one you can touch with your hands. 'Why'd you send me away, Ofra?' he heard himself say aloud, and looked around in embarrassment and started whistling to allay any suspicion that he'd been talking to himself. Madman. The hell with it. Even Kiki the cat means more to you.

Should he have told her his old story? For the first few years after his father's death, the pain of the change and of being uprooted from the settlement had been with him every day. But the years passed, and the wound healed over. The scar that remained was like the things about which Aristotle said that 'The past has a quality such as even the gods cannot change.' But, like the historian, each one of us re-writes the story of the past according to his sensations in the present. And so, especially tonight ... he remembered – noon of summer's day, bathed in sun, and he a boy of nine, running and skipping barefoot from the settlement's enclosure to the just-cropped field which extended as far as the Arab village, his heels trampling down the brown stalks of straw which pricked and tickled the soles of his feet while he sang the last part of the Symphony From the New World – ta ta ta tata tum, ta ta ta . . . He hadn't even known its name, but remembered it for years later as the first work he'd ever loved. He would have liked to remember more details about his father, but an unseen barrier stood between him and that paradise. The way to his childhood seemed blocked. And he said to himself that perhaps when he grew old those beautiful years of before the disaster would rise up in his memory again.

He wanted to get away from the city center, where many people filled the streets and sidewalks, streaming past lit-up shop-windows on their way to the cinemas. He was afraid he might meet someone who knew him, who'd see him wandering around on Saturday night without a girl. And he kept thinking of what each of the people in the street looked like while copulating. The men didn't interest him. They panted like animals. He followed a young couple, his eyes on the girl, studying the lines of seriousness, restraint and practicality which lent her face dignity. Maybe she was a student. Her swaying woman's walk was both insolent and dreamy, the heels lifting her thighs with a touch of careful hauteur which gave no hint whatsoever of the same body when it lay writhing and moaning in heat while the face grew savage and ugly and the legs opened wide and waved shamelessly in the air. And Ofra? Saint Ofra. He trailed along behind the couple until the man became conscious of his gaze.

In King Street he hastened his steps and headed down toward the railway station, where he went into a field where rocks lay scattered among dark shadows cast by olive-trees, opposite Mount Zion. He sat down on a large rock, facing the wall of the Old City and the dark mass of trees and the church on top of the hill. Now the newsreel'll be over and the second show will be starting, he said to himself – we could've made it to the movies, I could've stayed at her place. What's she doing this evening? Should I ring her? I could've asked her out dancing to a bar. We could've gone to 'Taboo', or 'My Bar', or to 'Bacchus', the students' club. But Falik doesn't know how to dance and he's never been to these places which are very expensive, and anyway he isn't properly dressed, doesn't even have a jacket or a tie. Jerusalem's beautiful? What's the good of that without Ofra?

So he went and rang her and his daring affected her and they met, and in the street he changed plans and suggested they go for a walk in the city and she agreed, and they walked down King George Street and as they passed Mount Zion she asked 'Where are you taking me?' and he said 'Come, let's sit down here, it's nice,' and took her to the same rock he'd been sitting on a short while ago, with the traces still fresh of his footprints and clods of earth he'd dug up and scrub he's squashed into the earth, but he didn't tell her a thing and said, as if discovering the place for the first time, 'Look at the beautiful view here, down there's the Vale of Hinnom, and there's that district, Abu Tur, have you been there?' and she said 'Sometimes I think that they built Mount Zion and the Wall just for me, only the moon never means anything to me.'

'Yes, Ofra, Jersualem is beautiful just for you, and the wall and the mountain were built to decorate the night when you look at them. I also think the moon has no meaning, I never liked it in my life. I sat on this stone before I rang you and I was sad but now you're with me and I love you, you're the only person in the world I care about, and I believe that you're still a virgin and waiting for me to be your first.' No, not like that, but – when I'm with you I long to say those words which the devil waited for Faust to say to the passing instant: 'Tarry a while, you're so beautiful.' And if you get tired we can go to my room which is closer to here than your apartment, we can go up through Talbiya and we'll get to Rehavia. Martin Buber lives there. He says that we exist only in the presence of someone with whom we can make real contact, and that's why I'm not willing to give you up. In basic training there was a sergeant-major called Makhlouf who shouted at one of the trainees in the mess hall and said he'd send him out at night to the top of the quarry hill to light a candle on his prick. This was the same Makhlouf who on their first night in the base, after the rapid march for equipment-orientation, had made the following speech: 'Now the army's looking after you so you can sleep well so's you can get up in the morning fresh and healthy like you'd just come out of your mother's cunt!'

What do you see in Uri Ben-Ami? – I saw you walking together in Ben Yehuda Street. He's an idiot but he happens to be close to the megaphones so his voice gets to be heard. The unification of the people is the rubbing-out of the individual. Freedom is the refusal to carry out an order and it's anarchy and the Lavon Affair and my father. The Arabs give us two alternatives – to unite out of fear or to disintegrate out of weakness. That's why I don't live the life I want to live but the life that Nasser wants for me and Lavon wants and Ben Gurion decides and Makhlouf shouts and the Shin Bet follows and even they don't act of their own free will but out of necessity and are dependent on each other like puppets pulling each other's strings. And if you oppose them they'll tell you there's no alternative, it's our State, and if not the Lavon Affair then Auschwitz. A training base is preferable to a concentration camp because better the live Israeli than the dead Jew. There on the wall sits a legionnaire who can solve my whole existential problem with one bullet.

Yohanan ben-Zakkai, who may have walked in this very field of rocks one dark night and who fled to Yavne, was a traitor. For two thousand years the traitor Jews fertilized their women in the diaspora, and secretly the blood of the Maccabbees and of the defenders of Massada passed from generation to generation until you arose, the last generation, fresh and healthy like you'd just come into the world from your mother's cunt in a training base in the State of Israel and whoever can't make the grade had better commit suicide. 'If the road at times gets too weary / And you sweat in the heat and the steam / If your pack and your gear get too heavy / And your home's far away like a dream . . .'

And your infrequent letters in the pale-blue imported envelopes with their sweet paper scent in the evening on returning from the exhausting exercises, in the rusty whitewashed barrack by the light of a bare light-bulb on a bed covered with a gray blanket and gear laid out on it army style in a line as straight as a rule with all the other beds: in the mornings we fixed the packs straight with a string stretched from one end of the barrack to the other; and if you had to go on sick parade you'd have to find two friends who'd give up their breakfast and help you carry your bed with all the gear on it to the company quartermaster's store and only then you got permission to go to the doctor. And when even that didn't help, all those who wanted to go on sick parade were ordered to bring their beds with all the gear to the infirmary at the other end of the camp. And then there was the special pack-and-gear punishment: having to go around all day, meals, rest-breaks and all, with full marching equipment strapped to your back. Some were sent to prison. But in Pulik's group, thank God, the most any of them got were pack-and-gear punishments and extra parades – not to speak of 'rondelles' on the double and being made to dig pits (Zadok the squad-commander gave them precise measurements: 'A meter by a meter by a meter by a meter') in which to bury a fart or a cigarette-butt, none of them was imprisoned or got sent to the madhouse or committed suicide and only one deserted from the army.

The letters had a taste of home and of a dream and of yearnings which pinched your heart to tears in this chaos where you were never alone or free even for a moment, always hungry and resentful and worrying about keeping your rifle clean, and tired and never managing to keep up with the cramped schedule. To sleep without sheets under army blankets which make you itch, and in your dreams you walk barefoot with a wheelbarrow along Lovers-of-Zion Street to Ichilov's shop bringing fodder for the chickens and the goat, and to wake up horny in the morning in the middle of a dream about Esther Munschein who was the ugliest girl in class and you haven't even remembered her name for years and she's getting undressed for you in a solitary house on the beach in Tel Aviv, and Tel Aviv's completely empty, no houses and no people, all hills of sand like the training area; Esther Munschein whose breasts swell at the touch of your lips and her dark nipples lengthen like little sausages before your eyes and your lips touch her red flesh, and it's she and not Ofra, pure, desired Ofra, who stands there looking at you in that dream moment, and you know that she can see that you're unfaithful to her and you can't control your awful desire to hold Esther Munschein, until you're woken by the instructor yelling at you to get up, throwing the blankets off you, and your clothes are wet and smell of fresh sperm, and you go out into the cold dark winter morning in your boots and short pants for the morning run of several kilometers, a prisoner of the glorious tradition, to run or to sing: 'It's not so bad, we'll make it sure, we'll make it yet to the radiant shore!' Not a break to rest or walk, it's good for you to run like this until your breath gets short and your legs hurt and your muscles are tight knots and you think you'll never be able to run all the way back to the camp, but you're not freezing cold any more, you're sweating and in a stupor.

You are back with three minutes to shave and a rifle that has to be cleaned meticulously (an extra parade at noon!) and boots that have to be polished and a shovel and eating gear (Makhlouf'll smear the black oil all over your face!) and the floor of the barrack that has to be scrubbed and a bed that has to be made and at breakfast-time you have to march in threes to the mess-hall and stand for a long while erect at attention with your mess-tins under your arm and then file in rank by rank on the command, tasteless coffee and a tiny Polish egg and a rotten tomato, and fight for a few slices of bread to put in your pocket so you'll have something to chew on during the day when your intestines squirm in hunger. And what do you actually dream about? Of putting some salt on a fresh-picked cucumber from the first crop of summer and eating it with its green peel, of going on a long exercise of individual infiltration, alone along orchard paths, and buying a quarter of a kilo of soft white cheese and half a loaf of fresh bread or some rolls in the co-op of a settlement far away, and gobbling it all up.

And the day when you understood that there was an order to punish you with extra parades night and day and on Sabbaths too even if you and all the others in your platoon had cleaned the last grain of dust in the barrack when you sprawled over the floor with shoe-brushes in your hands – just in order to break you all. And the despair that gnawed at you because there was no reward and punishment, only punishment and screams and endless speeches of squad commanders and platoon sergeants in the late hours of the night at the expense of your few hours of sleep – speeches designed to stupefy and degrade you. Your combined efforts to do the right thing and to get everything done quickly and efficiently and then to go to sleep is a sign of freedom and of initiative and that borders on mutiny. But the absurdity of the punishment which we, the commanders, dish out to you as we feel like it, is the only thing that's going to break you completely and make you into good obedient soldiers who don't ask questions. Don't look for logic in the army. If you start asking about the logic of every order then when the time comes to mount a charge against the Arabs you'll all finish up scattering in every direction. Right now you're nothing but miserable rookies full of piss, and until you get that infantry badge with the red background under it we're gonna make sure you wear your arses to the bone so's you don't disgrace the badge. A good soldier's obedient, like a robot, and well-trained, like an animal (a wild animal, but!) – and hell, I want to worship God, not think about the training base and Arabs all day. And when you get home on your first leave, your mother says: 'You should be proud to be a soldier in the Israeli Army. Your father never had that honor.' And one day in the bivouac you're called over by Zadok the squad-commander, who didn't finish high school, to explain what the P stands for on the topographic map, and you say to him – it's a phosphorus mine, the P stands for phosphorus. O.K., he says, well, seeing as you're so bright, go for a run around the platoon. And you run and sweat around the marching platoon and curse the moment you were tempted to show off your knowledge of chemistry. The bells started ringing in the Old City, beyond the wall, and Pulik left behind him the broken wings, which poked into the night like amputated black fingers, of the windmill erected by Montefiore in Yemin Moshe and walked past the King David Hotel and the YMCA tower and came to Café Alaska but didn't go in. He felt that if he rang from there everyone in the café would hear his pleas. He remembered the public telephone in Jaffa Road and retraced his steps and rang.

'Ofra, you know I wanted to ask you out to a movie tonight, well ... well, I thought ... 'Three Men in a Boat' with ... it doesn't matter, maybe to a bar? They say it's fun. They dance there. No? Pity. But you're sure you're not busy tonight? Studying? Well then ... all right. You know all this evening's been awful for me, I've been walking around the streets feeling rotten and I can't find anywhere to go. I thought maybe you'd like to come for a walk, oh, opposite Mount Zion, there's a nice place there. Oh, sure, you're studying. I'm really sorry. I shouldn't have said what I did at your place. O.K. Well, good night then. And ... Ofra, may I ring again next week? O.K., O.K., we'll see, sure. Good night, love ...' Ah, go to hell! I've done my bit.

He went down the steps of Nachlat Shiv'a and took a short cut up to King George Street opposite the Knesset and lengthened his steps to take the last stretch of the way almost at a run through the narrow streets of Rehavia over which weighty trees formed a thatch and cast a shadow of the dignity of Berlin and of professors from the Hebrew University; he went into his room and threw himself on the bed, bit the mattress and strained to cry. But to his great anger his tears betrayed him, and only the stale taste of straw filled his mouth. He spat out the stalk that had come out of the mattress, picked up a towel and went to wash his face.

The cool water felt pleasant, and he came back to the room whistling the opening of Vivaldi's 'Four Seasons'; opened, with his teeth, the bottle of milk which had been on the shelf and drank it down in one gulp. Then he lit a cigarette, but it tasted as bad as the straw and he put it out.

Suddenly he laughed. 'Tears wept alone are wasted tears. No one knows about them.'

And he paced around the room, this way and that. He felt light of wing.

'Ofra'le, a strong man is one who has no one to weep to.'

Make me strong.

Go to hell.

And he felt that now he absolutely couldn't go to sleep, that he had to do something, to explain, and meanwhile he kept on whistling with great delight as though each new note following upon the one before it revealed something new to him about his situation, and he was sorry that Ofra didn't share his feelings, and what was very clear to him was that only in a letter could he explain himself completely. He cleared a space on the table where he could write, among the pages of his paper on the great ideas in Plato's later dialogues. 'When you get my letter,' he wrote, and crumpled up the white sheet and threw it into the waste-paper basket. He took another sheet and stuck the end of the pen in his mouth, waiting and wondering how to begin, for surely it was possible to create a bridge of logic the necessity of which would unite him with Ofra in one copula and they would be one flesh. 'My dear Ofra, it's strange to be writing to you, the pain of silence stands still.' Should I apologize for apologizing? Bribe her by confessing my failure, which is the objective situation, and weave out of that the web of logical necessity in which she'll be trapped, if only she believes the original promises? Or is it better to pretend? But even that's a concealed apology.

'Silent people are strong people. I didn't want to write. I wanted my silences to oppress you more than all the paper prattle and meditations of weakness and outbursts of helplessness. Strength in a man is a magnet to which one is drawn. And I, I will wait for you within myself, strong and unbreakable, reserved, saying little – so that you'll long to decipher me. But now I'm miserable and I'm eating the end of my pen. Laugh, go ahead, laugh – but the first signs of this silence have you as their source. And you, will you understand? When one really thinks words out to the end, one can find among the thousands of possible combinations a few hidden threads which, if one only knows how to weave and arrange them together properly, have as much power to change destinies as have implements of war. I must find words which will bind you. I must find an irrefutable proof. And so, words conjoined with hope will always exhaust all the possibilities before us, and you are among these.

'But that's silly. Stronger than everything is silence. After all, you can't plaster with words something that's been cut off and rooted out like a limb from a living body. Silence, and magnets, laugh, go on, ha ha! – You're the distant one now, so that even my silence doesn't reach you. Look, I'll say it again: words are weapons, and I have to hew them and plane them so that they can hit you like slaps on your uncaring face, stab you like swords, strike you and smite you, so that you'll always carry within you the sense of giving in and the taste of guilty flight which is your life. Words of love? They're the ink of poisoners of wells. Ha – and you, – you were like God to me. And who will give you a moment of doubt? So you can start looking back: that's where they're waiting for you, like a spider in its web, to die.

'If I'm bad to you, you'll punish me, you'll fill yourself with contempt for me. You won't even stop to say hello to me in the street with your smile which always seems to promise that there'll be another time. But words aren't poison. Words must be able to caress like distant hands which cannot reach, to flatter you and hypnotize you with a magic snake-like sibilance, like the yogi's flute playing to the snake, to catch you, to envelop you—

'That's silly too. I'd better say nothing. You know that the proud heart stands alone. Weeping repels its witness, and he who repeats himself ends up without a listener. Strength in a man doesn't have to be a magnet. A little cat would do, as long as it's always beside you. No! I won't try to prove anything. Words prove nothing. Living sensations grow of themselves. It's only we who break them up with words which turn out to be even less real and melt away. Look, the letter I sent you attests to everything that's written in it. If I tear it up into little pieces that'll be the hardest apology of all. Your Fulik.'

He felt that if he sent the letter now all would be lost. He'd be giving himself away. But, he said to himself, words have an influence, and went out to drop the letter in the mail-box. What's she doing now? Maybe someone else has rung her up and taken her out? Have to go take a look in at 'Bacchus', 'My Bar', 'Taboo'. But if she's there, what'll I do? Must pass under her window. If the light's on, it's a sign she's really studying. A sign? And if it's dark? What's that mean? Is she out or in? Alone? Or not? No. Must ring her. And out he went again to the city center. In Café Pinati the telephone beckoned him from above the counter but there were two people sitting close to it so he went on up to the Central Post Office in Jaffa Road and circled around for a long time near the public telephone until the night clerk peered out at him suspiciously through the glass partition and asked:

'Don't you have a place to sleep?'

'No, it's all right,' he said, and dialled.

'Hallo, hallo?'

He heard her voice but didn't have the strength to answer her.

'I can't hear, who is it? Is that you, Dov? . . . hallo . . . hallo?'

Slam.

The bitch.

By the time he got back home dawn was already breaking, and the church towers above the wall of the Old City seemed bent in the grayness of the morning. What makes me mad more than anything else is that I never change. I don't develop. Why wasn't I born in Europe? First of all, I'd've got to see the world, I'd know languages, I'd be steeped in classic culture. But Auschwitz? O.K., so it's a good thing I'm here. But you have a heritage – the Bible? True, the Bible's good for the Prime Minister's quizzes and for the florid prose of Hebrew literature from Abraham Mapu to Uri Ben-Ami, who, if he were honest, would have to confess: 'In my native language I can't write a single sentence without sweat – to be funny and not artificial, sad but not repulsive, refined but not boring – and when I laugh at myself, I'm pathetic.'

He closed the shutters and threw himself on the bed and fell asleep in his clothes, and it seemed to him that he was dreaming that he was crying, and a pleasant warmth crept from his back and seeped through all his limbs. If I could get on a plane and land in Paris, and have a lot of money, and all the women I could want. There there's no shame in buying love.

Zvi looked at the lines in the palm of her hand. 'What do you want?' she asked. He got off the bed and started dressing. 'What's wrong?' – 'Nothing.' – 'I have no luck,' she smiled sadly, and the cat slipped into the room and wailed. 'That's the way it always is. I . . . you're not the first to find out, you . . . What's the matter, Kiki?'

'No. I didn't mean anything.' And, after a pause, 'I have to go to the university this morning. Take that cat away from me, I can't stand it.'

'No. I have to have somebody with me. Stay a little longer. We'll have coffee.' She stared at him stubbornly, as if trying to decipher something.

'It isn't morning yet.'

'It's already light outside. You know, I think I never loved anyone in my life. Does that sound strange to you?'

'You know what, a whole woman is too much for me.'

'But how could you have done it like that, without love? To rape me. It's frightening, what happened to us. I'm ashamed.'

That amused him. 'Seriously?'

She did not answer.

'Really, don't start again. As if you'd never seen . . .'

She got up and came towards him, her eyes wide.

'What? Seen what?'

'Nothing.'

'You must listen to me. This has never happened to me, I'm not like that . . .'

'I already told you, nothing!'

'Can you be trusted?'

'I'll say I got scratched by a branch.'

'You feel contempt for me, don't you? You think I'm mad?'

'But I didn't say that!'

'You thought it!'

He said nothing.

'And that's the same thing.'

'Yes. But now, well, I don't condemn you for what happened. You were a bit nervous, that's all. Now let me go. All right?'

'Zvi, you ... did you think, while it was happening, what did you really think of me?'

'Hell, Ofra'le, I'm not a psychologist! And I was glad that you, that I, I could help you, that it made me, well, how to explain, a lot better than I really am.' And he turned around to pick up his shoes.

'Zvi!' she screamed, 'you ... you pitied me?' She hurried after him. 'Is that all? Charity? All that I ...'

And suddenly she knelt down and started sobbing and kissing his feet which were pale brown in color and cold as marble to the touch. Shame filled him. His toes. 'Don't go, Zvi, don't go. Stay with me. I don't have a single person in the whole world.'

'Ofra'le, please, you're being silly ... What're you doing? Stop it! You don't have to debase yourself. If that's what you mean.'

'Just don't think that I ...'

Translated by Richard Flautz

Zelda

'I HAVE DRIVEN ALL THE WORDS...'

> I have driven all the words
> out of my heart
> because the day has ended
> and she will sleep
> till the Messiah comes.

Translated by Chana Hoffman

Moshe Tabenkin

The Parting

FIRST VOICE
My love
As shade to shade
In the darkness of my flesh
Sinking
   I see you vanishing
   I see you
   I see
   I

My rocking grief
Moves—
   In the foam of your flood, shell of nut,
   In the blast of your storm
   Feather hovering
   In clouds.

ANSWERING VOICE
My love
As shade to shade
In a glass booth, like a cage
A telephone rings—
   Like blood of fist beating a wall
   Like blood of fist beating,
   Like blood of fist,
   Like blood—

In the salt darkness of my eyelid
My ruined fortress
Submits—
   My lips' scarlet whitens to chalk.
   Their warmth is turned to snow.
   Then each his own way—
   And so the end.

Translated by D. Krook Gilead

Nathan Yonatan

Another Poem on Absalom

Cunning as a woman beautiful as a snake shy as an
    idol,
Always with his crew of cronies on horses in gold,
And now, tell me, where is the cunning of his women,
The beauty of his snakes, his shy idol?
The dreams of his kingdom – where are they?
A tree in the forest, that's all that's left of Absalom,
And the tears of a father, the old lover, man of wars:
Even his charioteer turns aside to weep;
Thus to break a father's back,
To make a joke of death, of everything!
Absalom my son my son Absalom
You couldn't wait,
You spoilt child, until we aged,
Until the crown brought us down in agony.
And your curls, what of your curls—
Didn't you know the danger that hides in such curls?
And why through the forest, of all ways—
Did you forget what happened to Jonathan?
Do you not know the terebinths?

Your father loved in you all that he was not,
See how this man trembles all over, why
Do you think I would not make you king—
Because of my concern for the people? Because
You were too young? If we'd only been able to speak, of it
    calmly
You'd have understood that I'm no longer the same David,
Your mother's sorrow, but just an aging king
Going joylessly to his death,
With one last intrigue concealed in his heart:
To save at least one of his sons
From the crown and the wars.
I wanted, my little fool, only you, Absalom.

Translated by Richard Flantz

Nathan Shaham

The Choice

BEFORE evening thick gloomy clouds began to spread across the sky, forming a black dome from horizon to horizon. The few rays of light which managed to penetrate this dense curtain, strengthened perhaps by having to struggle for existence, cast a brilliant dark radiance over the ploughed fields, like an unnatural glow. Visibility stretched to mist-draped distances and invaded hidden valleys that had looked like no more than black stains. Groves split into single trees, trees into separate leaves. Distant houses awoke to life. Black clumps of earth moved slowly and licked the fresh grass beginning to emerge near the water channel. Even the noise of the tractor and the shuffle of the shoes of the seed-drill skipping over hard clumps seemed to increase, welcoming this feast of fierce clarity. The tractor advanced slowly at the edge of the sown area, amid clouds of dust which gradually thinned out behind the seed-drill that was drawing behind it a strip of dark moist earth. The man on the tractor, intent on his steering, occasionally glanced back questioningly at the man on the seed-drill, who, eyes fixed on the openings in the floor of the seed-container, would nod to signal that everything was in order; the instrument was working, and seeds were dropping and embedding themselves in the earth.

Now, with everything in order, machines working, the seed-drill full, no interruptions or obstructions – time itself was a creative act. The man on the tractor pulled the levers automatically, glancing forward and then back, while the other man, occasionally looking at the reddish stain on the fringes of the black dome, walked about on the plank of the seed-drill to escape the dust thrown up by the tractor, and the work did itself. Every hour that passed meant a piece of earth sown.

They were clearly in a hurry, as they stopped to refill the seed-drill from the cart loaded with bags of seed, and then munched their evening meal standing up. Now, with the rain hanging over their heads, every minute meant an additional conquest of unsown soil.

'Off again?'

'Sure.'

Although the border was close and they had explicit orders from the army to stop work when it grew dark and to return home, they returned to their machines and worked on in the dark for a long time. Finally, before driving the tractor into a ravine where it would not be found by passers-by with harmful intentions, they loaded everything worth stealing from the cart onto the truck waiting for them beside it. When the sound of the engine died, the darkness was filled with the sound of the wind whipping at the canvas canopy over the tractor-seat and rubbing against last year's thorn bushes, now dry, along the sides of the ravine.

Now, with time their own once again, they moved slowly. They lit a match beside the meter of the seed-drill, peeped at the numbers, put a tin over the tractor's exhaust, locked the tool-box and hid it under the seat, and, after checking the cart again to see that they hadn't forgotten anything, got into the truck, started it, and drove off.

'It'll rain tonight yet.'

'Maybe.'

'Pity. If it'd only wait a few days. Till we finish the field.'

'Nothing we can do about it.'

'It'll be all mud here. Granny will get bogged. We won't be able to get to the tractor.'

'We'll walk.'

At that moment there was a suspicious explosive sound in the engine.

'You shouldn't have called her Granny. See, she's offended.'

'You're laughing, Yehuda, but I think it's happened.'

In another moment they had stopped. The purr of the engine had become a grating screech. Yoav silenced the engine and started cursing. When he saw his neighbour's calm he stopped.

'Well?' he asked.

'Stuck,' replied Yehuda, and calmly lit a cigarette.

By the dim light of the cigarette, Yoav saw Yehuda's serious face, its handsome lines covered with dust. For a moment he was put off by his calm. The prospects now before them bothered him, arousing in him a numb anger of protest against mechanics who let a damaged vehicle out of the garage, against the branch-head who had saved himself a trip by using two cars to change shifts, against the custom that family men worked morning shifts and bachelors evening shifts, against the Agricultural Centre, which had given their kibbutz these abandoned lands on the country's border so far from their homes, while other kibbutzim worked good lands close to their own fields – and against all such and other people and events because of whom they were now stuck here on the border, some forty kilometres from home, and fifteen kilometres from any settlement, in a broken-down vehicle, with the first drops of rain gleaming on the window by the light of the cigarette.

'Here it comes,' said Yoav, discouraged.

'Yes.'

He knew Yehuda wasn't thinking about what might happen to them during the night. His mind would be on his own grief, and on his wife lying in hospital. He'd be in no hurry to return home, to the room that would close in upon him in the silence of bitter memories.

For a moment he felt contemptuous of himself for getting worked up over such a little thing. He envied this man, only four years older than he, for his disregard for little mishaps. That's how one ought to live, he said to himself, with everything in its rightful place. He felt that he himself had not been tried by any worthwhile experience, apart from one battle he'd participated in by sticking shells into the smoking mouth of a mortar until the barrel grew red-hot and the order came to retreat.

Again he looked at Yehuda's quiet face. In him he saw the embodiment of his concept of real maturity, as he'd imagined it before his army days. This was how he'd always wanted to see himself – never moaning or complaining; a quiet smile ready for all the upsets of life. This maturity was strengthened, it seemed, by afflictions.

But he hadn't undergone any afflictions. And the little mishaps at work troubled him like real disasters. This was why he felt a deep respect, mixed with envy, for the serenity flowing from the quiet figure sitting beside him in the dim cabin. A man who bore the death of his little son so courageously would not sully himself with feeling distress over a minor incident like this. True, he'd seen people who'd taken their real disasters quietly but had got into a fury over a small injury, or an unintentional shove but Yehuda wasn't like them.

'There's a thing,' he said, now proud of his new disregard, as if for the first time getting the feel of this adventure. His fingers drummed on the steering-wheel.

'Quite dead,' said Yehuda, after going out, peeping into the engine, coming back, and settling himself down for a long session on the upholstered seat.

'Now what?' asked Yoav.

'We'll wait.'

'For what?'

'For something to happen.'

His hunger bothered him, but more than anything he wanted to be clean, to be rid of the dust, the smell of oils and fuel sticking to his clothes, his hair and the skin of his face.

'What can happen? Meir won't notice we haven't come back. He gave us a vehicle – we have the means to get back. That's all that matters to him: he's done his bit. He couldn't care less,' Yoav said, and sensed that he was complaining again. 'There's a thing . . .'

'If only Tirza were home . . .'

If Tirza, Yehuda's wife, were home, thought Yoav, she'd be coming back from the dining-hall now, expecting to see the light on in the room she'd left dark, with a kind of familiar surprise, a gentle hint of partnership in light and in darkness, for better and for worse, and she'd be preparing herself to bring him a little gift of respect and admiration: her delicate smile which paid tribute to the dusty weary face and lent to a return from the field something of the glory of a return from the battlefield, promising a night of love which was sure to shake a man out of his ashes. This smile is one of the secret rewards of work in distant fields. But now the window is dark. She looks at her watch. She walks, with quick steps, to look for Meir, head of the field-crops branch. Near his room she slows down, ashamed to display her love to others. Through the window she sees a picture of family bliss: Meir on all fours, his little daughter riding on his back, whipping his behind with a strand of wool 'Gee-up, gee-up, lazy horse!', his two bigger sons bent quietly over a chess-board, his wife combing her lovely hair in front of the mirror. Tirza hesitates; has she the right to impose her worry on this peaceful nest? Again she peeps at her watch, and knocks softly on the door. As she opens the door she says to herself that it'd be better to borrow a knitting needle and go home.

Finally she says half-heartedly: 'Is Yehuda here?' 'No, he isn't.' Meir answers, and goes on playing horse. 'I wondered,' she says, confused. And he looks up at her, puts his little daughter down on the bed, looks at her again, and asks, as if by the way: 'Isn't he back from the fields yet?' And she takes a deep breath, coughs a couple of times and says: 'No, I thought that . . .' And he says: 'What time is it? They should have been back by now.' And immediately regrets it. Then he smiles and says: 'We'll have to hop over and see what's going on there, maybe this rain . . .' And then, as she goes to her room to hide her concern and her gloomy speculations, Meir parts from his daughter who cries and demands 'Daddy! Daddy!' and goes to take council with some other members. They debate a little whether to 'make a big deal out of it' and notify the police, or whether to think, as usual, of the most pleasant possibility, and to take some light weapons, the lighter the better, and drive out to the fields with a towing cable, as a kind of proof that it's nothing, the truck's just got bogged in the mud, or something's gone wrong with the engine.

But since Tirza wasn't home, he wasn't awaiting anything, just letting time do what it would.

Yoav stole a glance at Yebuda, who was carefully toiling over his cigarette butt so as to use it up to the end. The burning part was very close to his lips and looked as if it was planted inside his mouth. He imagined lips of fire, and in so doing took his mind off his neighbour and thought of his loves.

'Well, if no one's going to miss me, perhaps someone will notice that *you* haven't come back,' said Yehuda, a smile of gentle mischief glinting in his eyes.

'I'm afraid not,' said Yoav.

'Why not? There'll be a girl waiting for you. She'll wait and wait, and then she'll get sick of waiting, swallow her pride, wander around a little near your empty room, see that it's dark, peep into the room of one of the other young workers: 'What's going on, are they letting you work a third shift now beside the border? And from there on things will move of their own accord, and in an hour or two you'll see a pair of headlights coming up the road towards us. We've been waiting for you, we'll say to Meir. – What do you mean you've been waiting? he'll say – why didn't you walk to some settlement and call us on the phone? – What? Walk! Fifteen

kilometres in the rain! – You call this rain? Meir'll say –
why, you could have been stuck here for hours on hours. And
how could we have known, anyway? – See, the fact is you've
come . . .'

'If you mean Leah,' said Yeav, 'no good'll come of her.'

'Why?'

'If she doesn't find me in my room, she won't think that
I'm in the field.'

'Which means?' asked Yehuda, without inquisitiveness.

'She'll think that I'm somewhere else,' said Yoav.

'Ah,' said Yehuda, and again a smile lit up his handsome
face. The cigarette flew out the window and vanished, and
he coughed in the darkness. After a moment he added:

'So there's problems, eh?'

There seemed to be a note of mockery in the voice. Yoav
wanted to protect his store of pride and hesitations. He
sensed that he had thoughtlessly let Yehuda into his most
secret affairs. Now he couldn't retreat. There was no alternative but to answer, as far as possible without either swagger
or self-contempt, courageously:

'Yes.'

In the dark cabin he heard the sound of a broken and
hearty laugh, which subsided in a sigh.

'Who's the second one?'

Before he was able to make up his mind if he could insult
Yehuda by refusing to answer a simple and friendly question, or if there was any point at all in keeping a pretence of
secrecy about something that everyone could see with their
own eyes, Yehuda asked: 'Nitza, if I'm not wrong, eh?'

'Yes.'

'Oh, that's quite something,' said Yehuda, as if approving
of his choice.

He was hurt by the lecherous tone, which didn't suit a
man whose wife was suffering from afflictions born of love.
He was also hurt a little for himself, for this was how one
spoke to someone whose feelings one didn't respect.

'Listen, friend, I have a suggestion. Put their names in a
hat, and be done with it. Why should you decide? Don't rely
on yourself.'

Now there was no doubt that Yehuda was mocking him.
He felt indignant, Man, he wanted to say to him, your
burden's heavier than mine, but don't force me to be
ashamed of what I have.

Twenty-three years, or rather twenty-two, since the day when he'd toddled on fat bent legs on the wooden floor of the old infants'-house, and to this day his life and the lives of the others of his age-group had been shaded by the achievements and standards of the first-born of the kibbutz. Shamed, he and his age-group had ridden along on three-wheelers, while those of the elder group flew past them on bicycles. And when they passed down the bicycles, throwing them aside like unwanted implements, the others were galloping on horses across broad fields and holding competitions with the fierce and brave sons of the Bedouin. They had grown up in the shade of the courageous silence which their seniors had brought with them from the Palmach camps in neighbouring kibbutzim. They studied history and mathematics while the others were coming home for short leaves, in vehicles riddled with bullet-holes. And even now he was being forced to defend his right to a serious life, as if this right could only be purchased by deeds or afflictions, to be attained only by the grace of sorrows.

'Did you give yourself the same advice?' he asked, and his resentment could be heard in his voice.

Again he heard that broken laugh with a sigh at the end of it. He sensed that Yehuda was looking at him. In the darkness, the solitude, the sense of isolation from their comrades, which was now more powerful because of the noise of the rain on the tin roof of the truck, at least a momentary solidarity was called for. Yoav felt ashamed. A girlfriend was not the same as a woman one loved, and he hadn't earned the right to speak lightly of Yehuda's life which was full of real grief, even if Yehuda had mocked the hesitations which were confusing him.

'In any case, it all begins *afterwards*,' said Yehuda, gravely.

Yoav felt like a blundering boy. Again Yehuda had taken the birthright to himself. Now he was letting him into his own secret, by hints, completely ignoring the childish desire to return insult for insult. 'It all begins afterwards.' He hadn't been mocking him at all. In his original, surprising style, stamped with the mark of his personality, he had laid out before him an entire outlook, a profound one, the fruit of the rich experience, schooled in afflictions, of a courageous man, one who knew himself. 'It all begins afterwards.' While he and his friends had *collected* corks, coloured glass, silver-paper and army badges – the seniors had *built* a doghouse, a dove-coop and then a real hut. Is the choice important? What's important are things in the sphere of doing. Here, a whole life was laid out before him: clear, in place, being built. A man like this Yehuda would never be capable of thinking regretfully about some decision which had denied him the right of choice, nor would he ever be sorry for what had not fallen to his lot. He'd be proud of whatever was in his power to do in the sphere he had limited himself to.

'Maybe, I don't know. One has to try,' Yoav mumbled philosophically.

'Try? No need to try. It tries you.'

'Hmm.'

'Yes, it's true.'

'I can imagine.'

'Yes, yes. Well then, we'll sleep here tonight.'

Now, when everything that could be said on the subject had been said, they grew silent. Yehuda lit another cigarette and Yoav leaned his head on the steering-wheel and closed his eyes. The rain grew weaker, and it seemed that a new possibility was opening up.

'We can lie in the back and cover ourselves with sacks,' Yoav suggested.

'The roof leaks.'

'Ah, I can't sit here all night.'

'Well, best give the old legs a shake and walk to the nearest phone.'

'When the rain stops we'll go.'

'Not we. I'll go. Someone has to stay here. What'll happen if Meir does finally move his bones and peep into my room to ask me how the sowing's coming on?'

'Why you then? I'll go.'

'Ho ho, I can say exactly the same.'

'True. But I . . . I'm younger.'

'Don't be funny! . . . What do you think I am?'

Then they planned their actions, to cover anything that might surprise them at any hour of the night: 'lines of movement', 'meeting-points', 'agreed signs', in perfect military style, as if they were two army units about to be separated by the night, but wanting to assure their unity.

When clearings of stars spread out over broad patches of sky, Yehuda pulled on his coat, fixed his revolver to his hip, wiped his nose, coughed, and shook his shoulders, preparing himself for the action which at least gave them some fresh hopes in this monotonous expectancy. A moment later he opened the door and cold air penetrated into the cabin. Quickly he was swallowed up by the dark. Yoav switched on the truck's headlights, picking Yehuda out of the sphere of black oblivion in front of the truck's bonnet. Yehuda, caught in the light, waved his hand at him, without looking back. For some time Yoav kept watching him, as he walked with the light step of a veteran scout, skipping from foot to foot, arms hanging down loosely, as if out for a stroll in the sticky mud. When his figure shrank and blurred at the rim of the weary beam of the headlights, Yoav pushed in the button and his world again contracted into the cabin of the truck, now filled with the sorrow of parting and monotonous guesses. For a while he played with thoughts about the terrifying action of time passing slowly and going to waste. Then he tried to sleep. He folded his legs on the seat, laid his head on his coat, and closed his eyes, drawing into them all the burning grains of dust covering his eyelids. As he rubbed his eyes urgently with both his fists, it occurred to him that at that very moment he was missing a revelation lighting up for him on the horizon in the form of two headlights gradually nibbling up the darkness until they knocked down the black wall which separated him from the world. He mustn't lose even a moment of good hope. After getting up and lying down several times, now forcing himself to sleep, now feeling his expectancy demanding that he at least make the minimum effort of keeping a look-out, since there was nothing more useful he could do to bring him closer to his goal, he gave up the weary conflict between the desire to sleep and his impatient expectancy for the unexpected, sat up confidently behind the steering-wheel, twiddled his moustache, fixed his gaze at the dark scene in front of him, and waited for fatigue to vanquish him and force sleep upon him against his will. At the edges of the picture glinted distant lights, the accepted signs of warmth and human solidarity, witnesses of the ordered process of life. Those which were alight bespoke rest, and those which were out – love. Above the settlements was a faintly glowing dome, like a silk canopy which makes people into a single society. Lights moving from one settlement to another occasionally turned towards him, throwing out beams of light, and disappearing into somewhere, and hope going with them. Other lights moved within the big glow of light in the neighbouring town, appearing and disappearing, like threads in a warp, weaving the lives of others into a single tapestry. He yawned deeply, and the innocent moan which burst from his throat sounded like the voice of a dear friend lamenting his bitter fate.

An animal passed, making a noise like human footsteps, and reminded him of the proximity of the border. A truck like this one, abandoned near the main road, would be a fine target for infiltrators returning from their robberies, to complete their pleasures. He didn't place much hope in his revolver, which was as good for battle as a nutcracker – he put his trust in the box of hand-grenades under the seat. To be more sure he set three of them and put them within reach of his hand, ready to dismantle them the moment the rescuing headlights appeared on the road, so as not to be ashamed when the driver – devil knew who it'd be – saw them.

After an hour, during which every light moving on the horizon brought first hope and then despair, like an eternity of silence and cold without beginning or end, he wearied of just gazing at the lights and the joys of others, at the dwellings of man and the stars in the sky. He compelled himself to lie down, to cover himself with his coat and close his eyes and not get up until he heard the sound of the car coming to release him from his prison.

If it weren't for Nitza, right now Leah would be knocking gently on the window of his hut. 'You asleep?' Then she'd open the door slowly, walk up to the bed, and sit down next to him. If he woke – she'd kiss him on the forehead. If he didn't wake – she'd wait a little while in the dark room, listening to his breathing, and then go out on tiptoe, the wooden floor singing under her feet. He's tired, poor fellow, he's worked so many hours today – she'd say to the night breeze, as if apologizing for a night of love wasted.

See, for the first time now he was paying a modest price for his scepticism. He didn't feel he'd done wrong. He was proud, modestly so, with no offense, of his ability to give happiness to two girls so different from each other. He knew that one day he'd have to put an end to the whole thing. 'Put their names in a hat,' Yehuda had suggested. And he'd got angry. But it seemed to him now that he'd really been waiting for chance to choose for him.

In his imagination he saw the figure of Nitza. Tall, lithe,

ballerina-like. The froggish mouth suddenly bursting into a rapid staccato laugh like the first burst of beans into the empty tank of the combine, trembling waves rippling over her bare arms to the many-changing landscapes under her shirt. This was a laugh which abandoned itself, wholeheartedly, without reservations, to really successful jokes and to plain good joy. Cra-zy, he said to himself and smiled in the darkness. Her hand, when she got up or sat down or climbed stairs, held her dress over her knees, as if an evil wind was constantly attacking her chastity. And the things she said! He remembered her coming to him one evening. She wanted to borrow a book. She refused to sit down, because she was going to leave any minute now, and she stayed for a long time. She stood by the door, her hand on the latch, and told him some childhood memories. 'I'm afraid to suggest you sit down in case you might remember that you're going to leave any minute now, but really, you can sit down, we hear just as well sitting down,' he said to her and smiled, and his smile must have been sly, like someone catching someone out, because she peered at him angrily and said: 'Is that smile meant to make me shake in the knees? Not me, I've got strong healthy knees.' And as she spoke she raised the hem of her dress a little, as if to verify her words, and bared a pair of round knees and the edge of the slope of a taut, planed thigh muscle. And when he approached her, his arms stiff beside his body, and stood very close to her, looking straight into her eyes, she slipped away from him with agility, sat on the edge of the bed, and said: 'What's the matter with you? It's just knees. In summer you see a lot more, and no one . . .' and she began chuckling. He came closer to her, put one leg on the bed, his elbow resting on his knee, his big tanned hand hanging limply right in front of her laughing face. 'Is that your style?' She raised her head and peered at him for a moment, and the hair which slid across her face fell to the sides of her head, like the tail of a colt bursting into a sudden gallop. She whispered: 'Want to fight?' He put his hands on her shoulders and said: 'No, to wrestle.' She lowered her head. 'In that kind of wrestling the woman always comes out the loser,' she said, this time quite in earnest, and there was no longer any room for his hands on her shoulders.

She'd come out the loser once and didn't want to repeat her mistake. At times she envied the person who had taught her a lesson, because he'd broken rules of behaviour which feelings repudiated. All the same, she let him tour her estate, revealing some of her secrets to him very willingly. The rest she kept for another time.

She had come to the local school at the beginning of her adolescence, wiser in the ways of the world than all her fellow-pupils, her life experience enriched by her parents' incessant quarrels. According to a prudent arrangement, such as only children are able to make without it smelling of charity, she used to spend her evenings in the rooms of her friends' parents, where she'd seen a calm and serene family-life which, as she told him once, both captivated her and bored her. He didn't need her declarations. He could see that that kind of life fascinated her, as the summit of a full and happy human life. Her refusals showed him how much she yearned for a stable life, without interruptions or adventures. He could see her as a devoted wife to some modest person who would be content with her dominating love and a trade which was a credit to him. Meanwhile she was messing up the minds of foolish young men with her promise of light abandon. With him too she played the role of a temporary visitor, intelligently and with good taste, but he could sense that she wanted to settle down for good. To Leah she offered a decent, broad-minded friendship, one based on a knowledge of life, and raised above the envy of village girls. But Leah refused to take part in the game, apparently knowing that the one who lied would be the loser.

His friends had hinted to him to have done with this frivolous game. The hell with it, he said to himself. Frivolity? It's a headache!

He had never seen himself as a husband, until one day some shells fell on the hill where they'd taken up their position, during one of the attacks on the enemy's border patrol. Being inexperienced, he had believed that these shells, which exploded with a mighty noise, had the power to kill everybody. And during those moments, before the dust and the smoke cleared away and a total silence spread over all, and it turned out that everyone was whole and unharmed, he had had time to think of a son of his own, one who would proudly bear the memory of his father who had been killed on the battlefield. That son had been sitting in Leah's lap.

'And you remember the hike to the spring, and how Mika fell into the mud?' They had been in the same class once, and later they'd been separated. Just before he went into the army they'd found themselves in the same class again. At first he'd been astonished by the treasures she'd stored in her memory, all the smallest details of their childhood, sad events, happy events, ridiculous events. And then he'd discovered that all these events were connected to him. Her love was a kind of storehouse, in which she'd collected all his childhood for him. She came, bringing her treasures with her. There, he was all of one piece: all those little characteristics and deeds, which everyone ignores, all wrapped up together like precious possessions. And only there, it seemed. Others, and Nitza among them, disintegrated him and made him into a mixed heap of unimportant characteristics in a male piece of body; a mixture of moustache, arrogance, innocence in the ways of the world, hearty selfishness and a willingness to give to others of what he had in abundance: love and contempt. Their glances fenced in the reckless character, and from under his skin they pulled out a bit of good diligence, and some lazy obedience which kicked out occasionally, to deny itself. They believed only they could give him a colouring of his own. They, through boundaries, and Nitza – through her talent of kneading his character. With Leah, he was a completeness, a clearness, and his life was a continuum of events which shaped his image. And this was a great possession, too great for him to allow himself to waste it.

He remembered her, always neat and organized – clean notebooks, combed hair, quiet speech. A mother's child. Everyone loved her a little, and everyone hated her a little. Some said that she was very clever, and some said she was stupid, because she didn't know what she was taught. And when they grew up, even the bodily signs she grew were modest and obedient.

After that they accumulated some memories which belonged just to the two of them, some very sweet and some very bitter. Now, at their second meeting, he saw that there were things which broke through her restraint. He remembered the snow. 'Snow!' she'd cried. And he, a little bewildered by her unexpected excitement, had said: 'Yes, snow. I've already seen snow once, in Jerusalem.' 'Snow, Yoav, look, real snow, all the fields are covered in snow!' Her eyes glinted with a strange mischief. Snow! The actualization of all dreams which were beyond realization, of

everything which was not natural to this climate, of everything strange and distant and unthinkable. He felt vaguely
jealous of the snow. He too wanted to be one of those forces
of nature which shattered her calm. But she gave herself to
him with great affection, as if all her pleasure came from just
his presence beside her, while everything else belonged to
him and was laid out for him alone, because like her he was
not content with little. Even though she was always there for
him whenever he wanted, he sensed that he had only come
halfway. Possibly if he had a distant dream beyond realization, she would now love him with the same avidity that
knew no satiety.

Yoav rubbed his freezing hands together, pleased about
how much time had gone by without his even peeping at his
watch, and then rolled up the sleeve of his shirt slowly, as if
expecting to be disappointed. The large hand had travelled a
fair way. He thought of Yehuda, who by now was surely
close to a settlement, perhaps even able to hear the sound of
distant human voices through the clear night air. In half an
hour or so he'd reach a settlement, the guard would suspiciously inspect his face, then he'd go to the office, pick up
the telephone, and from then on everything would be set and
there'd be nothing to do but wait for time to pass.

Thus he came to think of Yehuda. A man, one of us especially, needs a wife like his. Both ornament and moral
courage. A woman to raise the children of a man who might
fall in battle, whose work involves unforeseeable dangers. A
woman who can bear a tragedy without breaking. He remembered the sight of her face, aching in silence, over her
son's grave, then walking in the cypress-grove, with
Yehuda's arm around her, her head trembling, about to drop
on his shoulder and then jerking erect again, like the needle
of the oil-gauge when the mechanism is working properly.
He had walked behind them, afraid of catching up with
them, afraid of overhearing their conversation. And yet he
had heard, as they spoke to each other about everyday
things, in quiet and tremulous voices. He remembered his
admiration for them, for their emotion and their self-ne-
gation, and his strange envy for this real life, which had
stood the supreme test and not collapsed.

A woman like Tirza was what he wanted; one who would
not make him slack and lazy in his organized life and in his
secure happiness. It seemed to him that he'd been waiting

for trials and tests so as to find out which of the two were like her. But chance hadn't brought him any. Apart from small jealousies and insignificant insults, which he and the two girls had sometimes borne with ridiculous fortitude, no serious obstacle had yet risen in his path. And as for them, they had borne even the great insult of his double infidelity very lightly, as if the fluctuations of his feelings were not really real. If the freedom to enslave yourself to your instincts is dearer to you than a life which you put together and make with your own hands – so Leah's eyes would say to him – then I'm willing to wait until you mature or grow tired.

At noon, on their way to the field, they'd gone to the hospital. He'd wanted to leave them by themselves, to wait outside. 'Don't be stupid, come with me' – Yehuda had said – 'Tirza'll be glad to see friends.' He walked in behind Yehuda like an uninvited guest, stood shyly beside her bed and looked at her pale, delicate face. From under the blanket she drew out a naked white hand and he took it up carefully like a fragile object, wondering at the strange contrast between this petite delicate body and the tremendous strength contained within this firm and wise woman. On her lips there played that sidelong feminine smile, the essence of her charm, which now filled him with sorrow and pity, like a precious gift which was no longer wanted. 'How's things?' asked Yehuda, after she had taken her hand back and dropped it in his palm. 'Sad,' she said. 'That's very bad,' he said. Driving to the field he had thought about this laconic dialogue, which had contained all of the love, the devotion and the courage needed for family life of the kind he wanted.

He had almost fallen asleep when he again heard the dripping of rain, first in the field, like a snake's whisper, and then on the tin roof, like the scamper of mice. He raised himself, looked out through the window ahead, and thought worriedly about his friend walking in this rain.

Suddenly he noticed two eyes of light slowly dancing over the road in front of him, a long way away. He didn't believe his eyes. It had happened! A car was driving slowly, along the muddy road, and it could not possibly have any other goal but him. He signalled with the headlights of his truck. After a moment of tense expectancy he received a reply. The eyes of light closed and lit up again.

The lights approached, and after some time he heard the groans of the car sliding along the two deep mud tracks. Finally it stopped opposite him, its lights on, and somebody got out and came towards him at a run, because of the rain. At first he thought it was Meir, because he was wearing Meir's raincoat, but when he drew nearer he saw Giora, one of the young workers who were always ready for any adventure with vehicles.

'At last,' said Yoav apathetically. And then he asked with curiosity: 'How did you find out?'

'I don't know. Meir sent me,' said Giora. 'What's going on here?'

'And you didn't meet Yehuda on the way?'

'No.'

He began to feel concerned. By his calculations Yehuda hadn't had time to reach a settlement.

'How's that? Which way did you come?'

'By the side road.'

'Why'd you take the side road?'

He remembered. Giora's girlfriend lived in one of the settlements on the other road.

'All right, let's get to work. We'll catch up with him on the road.'

They wound a cable around the front bumper of the truck and tied it to the connecting-rod at the back of the other truck. Yoav got back into his cabin and Giora into his, and they drove off, in low gear, both trucks sliding along the slippery dirt road. Finally they came to the main road, after a number of minor incidents, such as the cable coming undone, an accidental plunge into a water-channel, and a swerve which smashed one of the beams of the bridge over the wadi. Drenched to the skin and looking as if they'd come out of a mud bath, their clothes plastered with sticky wet dust, they left the damaged truck at the crossroads as a sign of life for Yehuda if he happened to pass there, and made their way to the nearest pool of light. For some time they wandered around until they chanced to meet someone outside, and he showed them the way to the office hut. But Yehuda wasn't where they had decided that he should wait for them 'according to the plan'. They sat down on the wooden floor, wondering what to do, until someone came along and told them that someone like the person they'd described had really been there, but he'd already left the settlement. They drove quietly to the truck abandoned at the crossroads, signalling with their lights in all directions. The lights on the horizons remained fixed, and not one of them winked. After a short consultation they again tied on the truck and started driving home. Some time later their head-beams fell on a man walking along the side of the road. It was exciting to find him there in the midst of darkness, ready to walk on calmly all night in the thin drizzle. But he joined the meeting happily.

'The telephone wasn't working,' he explained, as he got in beside Yoav. 'I came back to the crossroads. I signalled to you. I didn't get an answer. I decided that you'd fallen asleep. So I started walking home. How did they find out?'

'I don't know, Meir sent him.'

'At home we'll find out.'

Close to the kibbutz the rain stopped completely. By the gate Meir was waiting for them.

'So Granny's had it, eh?' he said. 'Lay her away in the garage. She can spend the winter there. We'll be better off without her. We'll get a car that can also come back from the fields. Well, all right, go and wash. There's cold water. Actually, I wanted to transfer you to the morning shift, but what's the time? So, all right, you'll work afternoon. I'm sure you don't really want to get up at four, eh? We know you!'

On his way towards the dining-hall Yoav saw a white dress gleaming by the grain store. When he came nearer, it suddenly approached him. The girl threw her arms around his neck and kissed him on the cheeks.

'You crazy?' he cried, 'I'm filthy as a black devil. Now move a bit and see what you've done to your white dress.'

'Ah, it doesn't matter,' Leah laughed.

By the lamp-post they examined the damage. Pale stains clearly marked the protruberances of her body, separated from each other, standing out in their uniqueness, as if they'd awoken to life from under a covering of snow. Both of them roared with laughter, and when they turned away and walked from the lamp into the shade of the fig-trees which fenced them into a darkness of their own within the general darkness, he grabbed her.

'The dress is dirty anyway,' he said.

And when he fiercely shoved his naked body under the spray of cold water in the shower-rooms and sang at the top of his voice, he said to himself: Here, that's it, we'll start from this. A smile gleamed at him from the mirror when he remembered that 'Ah, it doesn't matter' of hers, at the moment when she'd abandoned her clean white dress to her feelings. Hell! An overcoming of a tiny injury, which the laundry would take care of, yet it was a hint of traits he wanted to dig up from within her. Hadn't she just pulled her name out of his hat?

And after they'd eaten in the kitchen, a group of field-crop workers and other passers-by standing around them, flooding them with questions and giving good bits of advice on what to do in case the same thing happened again, he came back to her room. She was sitting on her bed, in a dressing-gown, the table-lamp spreading a soft light over her lap, and her eyes warming him in her anticipation.

'Was it you who noticed we hadn't come back?'

'Yes,' she said proudly.

'Did you think God knows what had happened?' he asked, afraid that because of an over-estimation of the danger she had given her feelings away.

'No,' she said. 'I guessed right away you'd got stuck in the mud.' She placed her hand over his mouth, which had opened wide in a lengthy yawn.

'And how did you know we hadn't come back?'

'I saw it was dark in your room.'

'Ah.'

'And it was late.'

'Of course.'

'To make quite sure, I went to Nitza's room ...'

'You what?'

'I just knocked on the door and asked if you were there. And when I saw you weren't there, I went to Meir, and that's all!'

And when after she put out the light and the intoxicating rustle of cloth arose in the room, he mumbled something about the importance of seriousness and continuity, she wasn't surprised.

'I was waiting for that,' she said, simply.

And he said nothing, because he sensed that one doesn't argue with a woman's intuitive knowing.

Translated by Richard Flantz

SMOKE

Now is the time
That the birds sick with yearning sing.
Fall out of the mist
Into the feast of light amazed,
Murmur like a spring
Among the shadows of a late rose
In the autumn.
Suddenly a cloud from the west
And a mist like acrid smoke
Malignant.
Nailed to the bosom
Of an alien bush they recite
Their cold verse.

MY BIRD

Beneath heavens loaded with lightning
She smiles. She walks leaping
Like a wagtail. But in her eyes
As in the eyes of a singing thrush
Gold of bitter lemons.
Lord, my Lord, hold back your lightning
For I have no other.

VINE

In my dreams he used to appear in a worn
Khaki shirt, as in the old
Photograph: bent over his spade
Planting a vine in the first
Vineyard.
But when he suddenly appeared to me
In the alien village, he was
Dressed in black, the violet light
Of the lake gleaming

In his glasses.
Bent on the path, he blessed with a pale
Hand a crowd of children hurrying
Out of Sunday school.

I stood there older than my father
By ten years or more
Yearning for the sad look
Of his eyes.
For a brief moment I saw a child
Labouring at a vine
On a vintage day
And whispers with parched lips
'This vine
My father planted,
My father.'

Translated by D. Krook Gilead

Israel Hameiri

In a plane from Refidim to Lydda

I wouldn't have believed it. How the desert suddenly became
   distant,
And the dug-in vehicles of destruction grew smaller and
   smaller
And the earth began moving slowly, circling as in a dream,
And a strange, icy wind blew, and darkness came slowly
   down,
And stars appeared between the clouds, quite clearly stars,
Didn't want to believe it (or perhaps couldn't), and fell
   asleep
For a moment, and then came the hard, dry blow of landing.

Translated by Arthur C. Jacobs

Amos Oz

A Hollow Stone

I

THE next day we went out to assess the damage. The storm had ruined the crops. The tender shoots of winter corn had been wiped off the fields as if by a gigantic duster. Saplings were uprooted. Old trees lay writhing, kissed by the terrible east wind. Slender cypresses hung limply with broken spines. The fine avenue of palm trees planted to the north of our kibbutz thirty years ago by the founders when they first came to these barren hills had lost their crests to the storm. Even their dumb submission had not been able to save them from its fury. The corrugated iron roofs of the sheds and barns had been carried far away. Some old shacks had been wrenched from their foundations. Shutters, which all night long had beaten out desperate pleas for help, had been broken off by the wind. The night had been filled with howls and shrieks and groans; with the dawn had come silence. We went out to assess the damage, stumbling over broken objects.

'It isn't natural,' said Felix. 'After all, it's spring.'

'A typhoon. Here. A real tornado,' added Zeiger with mingled awe and pride.

And Weissmann concluded:

'The loss will come to six figures.'

We decided on the spot to turn to the Government and the Movement for help. We agreed to advertise for specialist volunteers to work with us for a few days. And we resolved not to lose heart but to make a start on the work right away. We would face this challenge as we had faced others in the past, and we would refuse to be disheartened. This is the substance of what Felix was to write in the kibbutz newsletter that weekend. And above all we must keep a clear head.

As regards clarity, we had only to contemplate the brilliant clarity of the sky that morning. It was a long time since we had seen such a clear sky as on that morning when we went out to assess the damage, stumbling over broken objects.

A limpid crystal calm had descended on the hills. Spring sunlight on the mountains to the east, benign and innocent, and excited choruses of birds. No breeze, not a sign of dust. We inspected each part of the farm methodically, discussing, making notes, taking decisions, issuing immediate instructions. Not wasting a word. Speaking quietly and almost solemnly.

Casualties: old Nevidomsky the night-watchman, slightly injured by a falling beam. Shoulder dislocated, but no bones broken, according to the doctor at the district hospital. *Electricity:* Cables severed at various points. First priority, to switch off the current before letting the children come out to play and inspect the damage. *Water:* Flooding in the farmyard and no water in the nursery. *Provisions:* For today, a cold meal and lemonade. *Transport:* One jeep crushed; several tractors buried in wreckage: condition impossible to ascertain at present. *Communications:* Both telephones dead. Take the van into town to find out what has happened in other places and how much the outside world knows of our plight. Felix saw to the dispatch of the van and proceeded to the nursery. From there he went on to the cowsheds and poultry houses. Then to the schoolhouse, where he gave instructions for lessons to be resumed not later than ten o'clock 'without fail'.

Felix was animated by a passionate energy, which made his small, sturdy frame throb. He stowed his glasses away in his shirt pocket. His face took on a new look: a general rather than a philosopher.

The farmyard was full of hens, unconcernedly scrabbling hither and thither, just like old-fashioned chickens in an old-fashioned village, as if oblivious of the fact that they had been born and bred in cages and batteries.

The livestock showed slight signs of shock: the cows kept raising their foolish heads to look for the roof which had been carried off by the wind. Occasionally they uttered a long unhappy groan, as if to warn of worse things still to come. The big telegraph pole had fallen on Batya Pinski's home and broken some roof tiles. By five past eight the electricians had already trampled all over her flower-beds rigging up a temporary line. First priority in restoring the electricity supply was given to the nurseries, the incubators for the chicks, and the steam boilers which would ensure a hot meal. Felix issued instructions for a transistor radio to be found and brought to him, so that he could follow developments elsewhere. Perhaps someone should look in on Batya Pinski and one or two invalids and elderly people, to reassure them and find out how they had weathered the terrors of the night. But social obligations could wait a little longer, until the more essential emergency arrangements had been made. For instance, the kitchens reported a gas leak whose source could not be traced. Anyway, one could not simply drop in on people like Batya Pinski for a brief chat: they would start talking, they would have complaints, criticisms, reminiscences, and this morning was the least suitable time possible for such psychological indulgence.

The radio news informed us that this had been no typhoon or tornado, but a merely local phenomenon. Even the nearby settlements had hardly suffered damage. Two conflicting winds had met here on our hills, and the resulting turbulence had caused some local damage. Meanwhile the first volunteers began to appear, followed by a mixed multitude of spectators, reporters and broadcasters. Felix delegated three lads and a fluent veteran teacher to stem the tide of interlopers at the main gate of the kibbutz, and on no account let them in to get under our feet. Only those on official business were to be admitted. The fallen telegraph pole was already temporarily secured by steel cables. The power supply would soon be restored to the most essential buildings. Felix showed himself to combine the qualities of theorist and man of action. Of course, he did not do everything himself. Each of us played his part to the best of his ability. And we would keep working until everything was in order.

3

Condensation on the windows and the hiss of the paraffin stove.

Batya Pinski was catching flies. Her agility belied her years. If Abrasha had lived to grow old along with her, his mockery would surely have turned to astonishment and even to gentleness: over the years he would have learnt to understand and appreciate her. But Abrasha had fallen many years ago in the Spanish Civil War, having volunteered to join the few and fight for the cause of justice. We could still remember the eulogy which Felix had composed in memory of his childhood friend and comrade; it was a sober, moving document, free from rhetorical hyperbole, burning with agony and conviction, full of love and vision. His widow squashed the flies she caught between her thumb and forefinger. But her mind was not on the job, and some of the flies continued to wriggle even after the were dropped into the enamel mug. The room was perfectly still. You could hear the flies being squashed between her fingers.

Abrasha Pinski's old writings were the issue of the moment. Thanks to Felix's energetic efforts the kibbutz movement publishing house had recognized the need to bring out a collected volume of the articles he had written in the thirties. These writings had not lost their freshness. On the contrary, the further we departed from the values which had motivated us in those days, the more pressing became the need to combat oblivion. And there was also a certain nostalgia at this time for the atmosphere of the 'thirties, which promised a reasonable market for the book. Not to mention the vogue for memories of the Spanish Civil War. Felix would contribute an introduction. The volume would also contain nine letters written by Abrasha from the siege of Madrid to the committed Socialist community in Palestine.

Batya Pinski sliced the dead flies at the bottom of the mug with a penknife. The blade scraped the enamel producing a grating yellow sound.

At last the old woman removed the glass cover and poured the mess of crushed flies into the aquarium. The quick, colourful fish crowded to the front of the tank, their tails waving, their mouths opening and closing greedily. At the sight of their agile movements, their magical colours, the widow's face lit up and her imagination ran riot.

Fascinating creatures, fish: they are cold and alive. A striking paradox. This, surely, is the longed-for bliss: to be cold and alive.

Over the years Batya Pinski had developed an amazing ability: she was capable of counting the fish in her aquarium, up to forty or fifty, despite their perpetual motion. At times she could even guess in advance what course an individual fish or a shoal would take. Circles, spirals, zigzags, sudden totally capricious swerves, swoops and plunges, fluid lines which drew delicate, complicated arabesques in the water of the tank.

The water in the tank was clear. Even clearer were the bodies of the fish. Transparency within transparency. The movement of fins was the slightest movement possible, hardly a movement at all. The quivering of the gills was unbelievably fine. There were black fish and striped fish, blood-red fish and fish purple like the plague, pale green fish like stagnant water in fresh water. All of them free. None of them subject to the law of gravity. Theirs was a different law, which Batya did not know. Abrasha would have been able to discern it over the years, but he had chosen instead to lay down his life on a faraway battlefield.

4

The illusion of depth is produced by aquatic plants and scattered stones. The green silence of the underwater jungle. Fragments of rock on the bottom. Columns of coral up which plants twine. And on top of a hill of sand at the back of the tank is a stone with a hole.

Unlike the fish, the plants and stones in the aquarium are subject to the law of gravity. The fish, for their part, continually swoop down on the stones and shrubs. Here and there they rub themselves against them or peck at them. According to Batya Pinski, this is a display of malicious gloating.

As a procession of blood-red fish approaches the hollow stone, Batya Pinski lays her burning forehead against the cool glass. The passage of the live fish through the dead stone stirs a vague power deep inside her and she trembles. That is when she has to fight back the tears. She feels for the letter in the pocket of her old dressing-gown. The letter is crumpled and almost faded, but the words are still full of tenderness and compassion.

'I feel,' writes Abramek Bart, one of the directors of the kibbutz movement publishing house, 'that if we have been unfair to the beloved memory of Abrasha, we have been even more unfair to the minds of our children. The younger generation needs, and deserves, to discover the pearls of wisdom contained in the essays and letters of our dear Abrasha. I shall come and see you one of these days to rummage (in inverted commas, of course) through your old papers. I am certain that you can be of great assistance to us in sorting through his literary remains and in preparing the work for publication. With fraternal good wishes, yours,' signed by some Ruth Bardor p.p. Abramek Bart.

The old woman held the envelope to her nose. She sniffed it for a moment with her eyes closed. Her mouth hung open, revealing gaps in her teeth. A small drop hung between her nose and upper lip, where a slight moustache had begun to grow during these bad years. Then she put the letter back in the envelope, and the envelope in her pocket. Now she was exhausted and must rest in the armchair. She did not need to rest for long. It was sufficient for her to doze for a minute or two. A stray surviving fly began to buzz, and already she was up and ready for the chase.

Years before, Abrasha would come and bite. Love and hate. Suddenly he would burst and collapse on her and at once he would be distracted, not here, not with her.

For months before his departure the tune was always on his lips, sung in a Russian bass, shamelessly out of tune. She recalled the tune, the anthem of the Spanish freedom-fighters, full of longing, wildness and revolt. It had swept their bare room up into the maelstrom of teeming forces. He would enumerate the bleeding Spanish towns that had fallen to the enemies of mankind, ticking them off one by one on his fingers. Their outlandish names conveyed to Batya a resonance of unbridled lechery. In her heart of hearts she disliked Spain and wished it no good; after all, that was where our ancestors had been burnt at the stake and driven out. But she held her peace. Abrasha enlarged on the implications of the struggle. Expounding its dialectical significance and the place of the war in Spain in the final battle that was being waged all over Europe. He considered all wars as a snare and a delusion; civil wars were the only wars worth dying in. She liked to listen to all this, even though she could not and did not want to understand. It was only when he reached the climax of his speech and described the iron laws of history and averred that the collapse of reaction would come like a thunderbolt from the blue that she suddenly grasped what he was talking about, because she could see the thunderbolt itself in his eyes.

And suddenly he was tired of her. Perhaps he had seen the tortured look on her face, perhaps he had had a momentary glimpse of her own desires. Then he would sit down at the table, propping up his large square head with his massive elbows, and immerse himself in the newspaper, abstractedly eating one olive after another and arranging the stones in a neat pile.

5

The kettle whistles fiercely as it passes boiling point. Batya Pinski gets up and makes herself some tea. Since the storm died down, close on four o'clock in the morning, she has been drinking glass after glass of tea. She has still not been out to inspect the damage. She has not even tried to open the shutters. She sits behind her drawn curtains and imagines the damage in all its details. What is there to see. It is all there before her eyes: shattered roofs, trampled flower-beds, torn trees, dead cows, Felix, plumbers, electricians, experts and talkers. All boring. Today will be devoted to the fish, until the premonition is confirmed and Abramek Bart arrives. She always relies unhesitatingly on her premonitions. One can always know things in advance, if only one really and truly tries and is not afraid of what may come out. Abramek will come today to see the havoc. He will come because he won't be able to contain his curiosity. But he won't like to come just like that, like the other good-for-nothings who collect wherever there's been a disaster. He will find some excuse. And then he'll suddenly remember his promise to Batya, to come and rummage in inverted commas and sort through Abrasha's papers. It's half past eight now. He will be here by two or three. There is still time. Still plenty of time to get dressed, do my hair and get the room tidy. And to make something nice to give him. Plenty of time now to sit down in the armchair and drink my tea quietly.

She sat down in the armchair opposite the sideboard, under the chandelier. On the floor was a thick Persian carpet and by her side an ebony card table. All these beautiful objects would shock Abrasha if he were to come back. On the other hand, if he had come back twenty years ago he would have risen high up the ladder of the Party and the Movement; he would have left all those Felixes and Abrameks behind, and by now he'd be an ambassador or a minister, and she would be surrounded by even nicer furnishings. But he made up his mind to go and die for the Spaniards, and the furnishings were bought for her by Martin Zlotkin, her son-in-law. When he married Ditza he brought all these presents and took his young bride away with him to Zurich, where he now managed a division of his father's bank, with branches in three continents. Ditza ran a Zen study-group and every month she sent a letter with a stencilled leaflet in German preaching humility and peace of mind. Grandchildren were out of the question, because Martin hated children and Ditza herself called him 'our big baby'. Once a year they came on a visit and contributed handsomely to various charities. Here in the kibbutz they had donated a library of books on Socialist theory in memory of Abrasha Pinski. Martin himself, however, regarded Socialism the same way as he regarded horse-drawn carriages: very pretty and diverting, but out of place in this day and age, when there were other more important fish to fry.

6

On the eve of Abrasha's departure Ditza was taken ill with pneumonia. She was two at the time; blonde, temperamental and poor of health. Her illness distracted Batya from Abrasha's departure. She spent the whole day arguing with the nurses and educationists and by evening they had given in and allowed the sick child to be transferred in her cot from the nursery to her parents' room in one of the shabby huts. The doctor arrived from the neighbouring settlement in a mule-cart, prescribed various medicines and gave instructions for the temperature of the room to be kept up. Meanwhile Abrasha packed some khaki shirts, a pair of shoes, some underwear and a few Russian and Hebrew books, into a haversack and added some tins of sardines. In the evening, fired with the spirit, he stood by his daughter's cot and sang her two songs, his voice trembling with emotion and fervour. He even showed Batya the latest lines dividing the workers from their oppressors on a wall-map of Spain.

He enumerated the towns: Barcelona, Madrid, Malaga, Granada, Valencia, Valladolid, Seville. Batya half-heard him, and wanted to shout what's the matter with you, madman, don't go away, stay, live; and she also wanted to shout I hope you die. But she said nothing. She pursed her lips like an old witch. And she had never lost the expression since. She recalled that last evening as if it had been re-enacted every night for twenty-three years. Sometimes the fish moved across the picture, but they did not obscure it: their paths wound in and out of its lines, bestowing upon it an air of strange, desolate enchantment, as though the widow were confronted not by things which had happened a long time previously, but by things which were about to happen in the future but could still be prevented. She must concentrate hard and not make a single mistake. This very day Abramek Bart will step into this room, all unawares, and then I shall have him in my power.

The cheap alarm clock started ringing at three o'clock. He got out of bed and lit the paraffin lamp. She followed him, slender and barefoot, and said 'It's not morning yet.' Abrasha put his finger to his lips and whispered 'Sssh. The child.' Secretly she prayed that the child would wake up and scream its head off. He discovered a cobweb in the corner of the shack and stood on tiptoe to wipe it away. The spider managed to escape and hide between the boards of the low ceiling. Abrasha whispered to her: 'In a month or two, when we've won, I'll come back and bring you a souvenir from Spain. I'll bring something for Ditza, too. Now don't make me late; the van's leaving for Haifa at half past three.'

He went out to wash in the icy water of the tap which stood twenty yards down hill from the shack. An alarmed night-watchman hurried over to see what was going on. 'Don't worry, Felix,' Abrasha said. 'It's only the revolution leaving you for a while.' They exchanged some more banter in earnest tones, and then, in a more light-hearted voice, some serious remarks. At a quarter past Abrasha went back to the shack, and Batya, who had followed him out in her nightdress, went inside with him again. Standing there shivering, by the light of the paraffin lamp she saw how carelessly he had shaved in his haste and the dark: he had cut himself in some places and left dark bristles in others. She stroked his cheeks and tried to wipe away the blood and dew. He was a big, warm lad, and when he began to hum the proud sad song of the Spanish freedom-fighters deep in his chest it suddenly occurred to Batya that he was very dear and that she must not stand in his way because he knew where he was going and she knew nothing at all. Felix said 'Be seeing you,' and added in Yiddish, 'Be well, Abrasha.' Then he vanished. She kissed Abrasha on his chest and neck and he drew her to him and said 'there, there'. Then the child woke up and started to cry with a voice that was almost effaced by the illness. Batya picked her up and Abrasha touched them both with his large hands and said, 'there, there, what's the trouble'.

The van hooted and Abrasha said cheerfully, 'Here goes. I'm off.'

From the doorway he added, 'Don't worry about me. Goodbye.'

She soothed the child and put her back in the cot. Then she put out the lamp and stood alone at the window, watching the night paling and the mountain-tops beginning to show in the east. Suddenly she was glad that Abrasha had cleared the cobweb from the corner of the shack but had not managed to kill the spider. She went back to bed and lay trembling because she knew that Abrasha would never come back, and that the forces of reaction would win the war.

7

The fish in the aquarium had eaten all the flies and were floating in their clear space. Perhaps they were hankering after more titbits. They explored the dense weeds and pecked at the arch of the hollow stone, darting suspiciously towards each other to see if anyone had managed to snatch a morsel and if there was anything left of it.

Only when the last crumbs were finished did the fish begin to sink towards the bottom of the tank. Slowly, with deliberate unconcern, they rubbed their silver bellies on the sand, raising tiny mushroom-clouds. Fish are not subject to the laws of contradiction: they are cold and alive. Their movements are dreamy, like drowsy savagery.

Just before midnight, when the storm had begun to blow up, the widow had woken and shuffled to the bathroom in her worn bedroom slippers. Then she made herself some tea and said in a loud, cracked voice, 'I told you not to be crazy.' Clutching the glass of tea, she wandered round the room and finally settled in the armchair facing the aquarium, after switching on the light in the water. Then, as the storm gathered strength and battered the shutters and the trees, she watched the fish waking up.

As usual, the silver-fish were the first to respond to the light. They rose gently from their haunts in the thick weeds and propelled themselves up towards the surface with short sharp thrusts of their fins. A single black molly made the rounds of its shoal as if rousing them all for a journey. In no time at all the whole army was drawn up in formation and setting out.

At one o'clock an old shack next to the cobbler's hut collapsed. The storm banged the tin roof against the walls and the air howled and whistled. At the same moment the red swordfish woke up and ranged themselves behind their leader, a giant with a sharp black sword. It was not the collapse of the shack which had woken the swordfish. Their cousins the green swordfish had weighed anchor and gently set sail into the forest as if bent on capturing the clearing abandoned by the silver-fish. Only the solitary fighting-fish, the lord of the tank, still slept in his home among the corals. He had responded to the sudden light with a shudder of disgust. The zebra fish played a childish game of catch around the sleeping monarch.

The last to come back to life were the guppies, the dregs of the aquarium, an inflamed rabble roaming restlessly hither and thither in search of crumbs. Slow snails crawled on the plants and on the glass walls of the tank, helping to keep them clean. The widow sat all night watching the aquarium, holding the empty glass, conjuring the fish to move from place to place, calling them after the Spanish towns: Malaga, Valencia, Barcelona, Madrid, Cordova. While outside the clashing winds sliced the crests off the stately palm trees and broke the spines of the cypresses.

She put her feet up on the ebony card table, a present from Martin and Ditza Zlotkin. She thought about Zen Buddhism, humility, civil war, the final battle where there would be nothing to lose, a thunderbolt from the blue. She

fought back exhaustion and despair, and rehearsed the un-
answerable arguments she would use when the time came.
All the while her eyes strayed to another world, and her lips
whispered, there, there, quiet now.

Towards dawn, when the wind died away and we went
out to assess the damage, the old woman fell into a half-sleep
full of curses and aching joints. Then she got up and made a
fresh glass of tea and began to chase flies all over the room
with an agility that belied her years. In her heart she knew
that Abramek Bart would definitely come today, and that he
would use his promise as an excuse. She saw the plaster fall
from the ceiling as the pole fell and broke some of the roof-
tiles. The real movement was completely noiseless. Without
a sound the monarch arose and began to steer himself
towards the hollow stone. As he reached the arched tunnel
he stopped and froze. He took on a total stillness. The stillness of the water. The immobility of the light. The silence of
the hollow stone.

8

Had it not been for Ditza, Batya Pinski would have married
Felix in the early nineteen-forties.

It was about two years after the awful news had come
from Madrid. Once again a final war was being waged in
Europe, and on the wall of the dining hall there hung a map
covered in arrows, and a collection of heartening slogans and
news-cuttings. Ditza must have been four or five. Batya had
got over the disaster, and had taken on a new bloom which
was having a disturbing effect on certain people's emotions.
She always dressed in black, like a Spanish widow. And
when she spoke to men their nostrils flared as if they had
caught a whiff of wine. Every morning, on her way to the
sewing room, she passed the men working in the farmyard,
erect and slender. Occasionally one of those tunes came back
to her and she would sing with a bitter sadness which made
the other sewing women exchange glances and whisper:
'Uh-uh, there she goes again.'

Felix was biding his time. He helped Batya over her minor
difficulties, and even concerned himself with the development of Ditza's personality. Later, when he had submitted to
the desires of the Party and exchanged the cowsheds for

political office, he made a habit of bringing Ditza little surprises from the big city. He treated the widow, too, with extreme respect, as if she were suffering from an incurable illness and it was his task to ease somewhat her last days. He would let himself into her room in the middle of the morning and wash the floor, secreting chocolates in unlikely places for her to discover later. Or put up metal coathooks, bought out of his expenses, to replace the broken wooden ones. And he would supply her with carefully-selected books: pleasant books, with never a hint of loss or loneliness, Russian novels about the development of Siberia, the five-year plan, change of heart achieved through education.

'You're spoiling the child,' Batya would sometimes say. And Felix would word his answer thoughtfully and with tact:

'Under certain circumstances it is unnecessary to pamper a child, to prevent it from being deprived.'

'You're a sweet man, Felix,' Batya would say, and occasionally she would add: 'You're always thinking of others. Why don't you think about yourself for a change, Felix?'

Felix would read a hint of sympathy or personal interest into those remarks; he would stifle his excitement and reply: 'It doesn't matter. Never mind. At times like these one can't be forever thinking of oneself. And I'm not the one who's making the real sacrifice.'

'You're very patient, Felix,' Batya would say, with pursed lips.

And Felix, either shrewdly or innocently, would conclude, 'Yes, I'm very patient.'

And indeed, after a few months or perhaps a year or two, the widow began to soften. She permitted Felix to accompany her from the dining hall or the recreation hall to the door of her room, from the sewing room to the children's house, and occasionally she would stand and listen to him for half an hour or so near one of the benches on the lawn. He knew that the time was not yet ripe for him to try to touch her, but he also knew that time was on his side. She still insisted on wearing black, she did not moderate her arrogance, but she too knew that time was on Felix's side; he was closing in on her from all sides, so that soon she would have no alternative left.

It was little Ditza who changed everything.

She wetted her bed, she ran away from the children's house at night, she escaped to the sewing room in the morning and clutched her mother, she kicked and scratched the other children and even animals, and as for Felix, she nicknamed him 'Croakie'. Neither his gifts and attentions, nor his sweets and rebukes, did any good. Once, when Felix and Batya had begun openly to eat together in the dining hall, the child came in and climbed on his knee. He was touched, convinced that a reconciliation was coming. He had started to stroke her hair and call her 'my little girl', when suddenly she wetted his trousers and ran away. Felix got up and ran after her in a frenzy of rage and reforming zeal. He pushed his way through the tables trying to catch the child. Batya sat stiffly where she was and did not interfere. Finally Felix snatched up an enamel mug, threw it at the elusive child, missed, tripped, picked himself up, and tried to wipe the pee and yoghurt off his khaki trousers. There were smiling faces all around him. By now Felix was acting secretary-general of the Workers' Party, and here he was, flushed and hoarse, with a murderous gleam showing through his glasses. Zeiger slapped his belly, sighing 'what a sight', until laughter got the better of him. Weissmann too roared aloud. Even Batya could not suppress a smile, as the child crawled under the tables and came and sat at her feet with the expression of a persecuted saint. The nursery teachers exclaimed indignantly: 'I ask you, is that a way to carry on, a grown-up man, a public figure, throwing mugs at little children in the middle of the dining-hall, isn't that going too far.'

Three weeks later it came out that Felix was having an affair with Zeiger's wife Zetka. Zeiger divorced her and early in that spring she married Felix. In May Felix and Zetka were sent to Switzerland to organize escape routes for the survivors of the death camps. In the Party, Felix was regarded as the model of the young leadership which had risen from the ranks. And Batya Pinski started to go downhill.

9

When Abramek comes, I'll make him a glass of tea, I'll show him all the old papers, we'll discuss the lay-out and the cover, and eventually we'll have to settle the problem of the dedication, so that there won't be any misunderstanding.

She picked up the last photograph of Abrasha, taken in Madrid by a German Communist fighter. He looked thin and unshaven, his clothes were crumpled and there was a pigeon on his shoulder. His mouth hung open tiredly and his eyes were dull. He looked more as if he had been making love than fighting for the cause. On the back was an affectionate greeting, in rhyme.

Over the years Batya Pinski had got into the habit of talking to herself. At first she did it under her breath. Later, when Ditza married Martin Zlotkin and went away with him, she started talking out loud, in a croaking voice which made the children of the kibbutz call her Baba Yaga, after the witch in the stories they had heard from their Russian nurses.

Look here, Abramek, there's just one more point. It's a slightly delicate matter, a bit complicated, but I'm sure that we can sort it out, you and I, with a bit of forethought. It's like this. If Abrasha were still alive, he would of course want to bring his own book out. Right? Right. Of course. But Abrasha isn't alive and he can't supervise the publication of the book himself. I mean the colour, the jacket, the preface, that sort of thing, and also the dedication. Naturally he would want to dedicate the book to his wife. Just like anybody else. Now that Abrasha isn't with us any more, and you are collecting his articles and his letters and bringing out his book, there isn't a dedication. What will people say? Just think, Abramek, work it out for yourself: what will people make of it? It's simply an excitement to the meanest kind of gossip: poor chap, he ran away to Spain to get away from his wife. Or else he went to Spain and fell in love with some Carmen Miranda or other out there, and that was that. Just a minute. Let me finish. We must kill that kind of gossip at all costs. At all costs, I say. No, not for my sake; I don't care any more what people say about me. As far as I'm concerned they can say that I went to bed with the Grand Mufti and with your great Plekhanov both at once. I couldn't care less. It's not for me, it's for him. It's not right to have all sorts of stories going round about Abrasha Pinski. It's not good for you: after all, you need a figure you can hold up as an example to your young people, without Carmen Mirandas and suchlike. In other words, you need a dedication. It doesn't matter who writes it. It could be you. Felix. Or me. Something like this, for instance: Front page, QUESTIONS OF TIME AND TIMELY QUESTIONS, collected essays by Abraham brackets Abrasha Pinski, hero of the Spanish Civil War. That's right. Next page: this picture. Just as it is. Top of the next page: To Batya, a noble and dedicated wife, the fruits of my love and anguish. Then, on the following page, you can put that the book is published by the Workers' Party, and you can mention Felix's help. It won't hurt. Now don't you argue with me, Abramek, I musn't get upset, because I'm not a well woman and what's more I know a thing or two about you and about Felix and about how Abrasha was talked into going off to that ridiculous war. So you'd better not say anything. Just do what you're told. Here, drink your tea, and . . . stop . . , arguing.

Then she sighed, shook herself, and sat down in her armchair to wait for him. Meanwhile, she watched the fish. When she heard a buzzing, she leapt up and swatted the fly on the windowpane. How do they get in when all the windows are closed. Where do they come from. To hell with the lot of them. Anyway, how can the wretched creatures survive a storm like that.

She squashed the fly, dropped it into the aquarium, and sat down again in her armchair. But there was no peace to be had. The kettle started boiling. Abramek will be here soon. Must get the room tidy. But it's all perfectly tidy, just as it has been for years. Close your eyes and think, perhaps. What about.

10

We were recovering hour by hour.

We tackled the debris with determined dedication. Buildings which were in danger of collapse were roped off. The carpenters fixed up props and blocked holes with hardboard. Here and there we hung flaps of canvas. Tractors brought beams and corrugated iron. Where there was flooding we improvised paths with gravel and concrete blocks. We rigged up temporary power lines to essential points until the electrical system could be repaired. Old paraffin heaters and rusty cooking-stoves were brought up from the stores. The older women cleaned and polished them, and for a while we all relived the early days. The bustle filled us with an almost ecstatic joy. Old memories were brought out, and jokes were exchanged. Meanwhile Felix alerted all the relevant agencies, the telephone engineers, emergency services, the Regional Council, the Department of Agricultural Settlements, the head-office of the Movement, and so on and so forth. The messages all went by jeep, because the telephone lines had been brought down by the storm. Even our children were not idle. To stop them getting under our feet, Felix told them to catch the chickens which had scattered all over the village when their coops had been damaged. Happy hunting-cries arose from the lawns and from under the trees. Panting, red-faced gangs came running eagerly from unexpected quarters to block the escape-routes of the clucking hens. Some of these sounds managed to penetrate through the closed shutters, windows and curtains into Batya Pinksi's room. What's the matter, what's so funny, the widow croaked to herself.

By the same afternoon all essential services were operating again. A cold but nourishing meal had been served. The nurseries were light and warm once more. There was running water, even if the pressure was low and the supply was intermittent. After lunch it was possible to draw up a first unofficial assessment of the damage. It transpired that the worst-hit area was the group of old shacks at the bottom of the hill, which had been put up by the original founders decades previously. When they had folded up the tents they had pitched on the barren slope and installed themselves in these shacks, they had all known at last that they were settling here and that there was no going back.

Years later, when the successive phases of permanent buildings had been carried out, the old wooden shacks were handed over to the young people. Their first inhabitants were a detachment of young refugees who had arrived from Europe via Central Asia and Teheran to be welcomed by us with open arms. They were followed by a squadron of underground fighters which later produced two outstanding military men. From this group of huts they set out one night to blow up a British military radar installation, and it was here that they returned towards dawn. Later on, after the establishment of the State, when the task of the Underground had been complete, the tumbledown huts became a regular army base. This was the headquarters of the legendary Highland Brigade during the War of Independence, where the great night operations were planned. Throughout the 'fifties the shacks housed recent immigrants, para-military youth groups, intensive language courses, detachments of volunteers, eccentric individuals who had begun to come from all over the world to experience the new way of life, and finally they were used as lodgings for hired labourers. When Phase C of the building programme was drawn up, the huts were scheduled for demolition. In any case they were already falling down: the wooden walls were disintegrating, the roof-beams were sagging, and the floors were sinking. Weeds were growing through the boards, and the walls were covered with obscene drawings and graffiti in six languages. At night the children came here to play at ghosts and robbers among the ruins. And after the children came the couples. We had been about to clear the site to make way for the new development when the storm anticipated us, as if it had run out of patience. The carpenters searched the wreckage, salvaging planks, doors and beams which might be re-used.

Felix's short, stocky figure was everywhere at once. It was almost as if he appeared simultaneously in different places. His sober, precise instructions prevented chaos, reduplication and wasted effort. He never for a moment failed to distinguish between essential and trivial tasks.

For seventeen years Felix had been a public servant, a secretary-general, chairman, delegate, and eventually even a Member of Parliament and a member of the executive committee of the Party. A year or so earlier, when Zetka his wife was dying of cancer, he had given up all his public positions and returned home to become secretary of the kibbutz. Social and financial problems which had seemed insoluble for years suddenly vanished at his return as if by magic. Old plans came to fruition. Unprofitable sections of the farm took on a new lease of life. There was a new mood abroad. A few weeks previously, ten months after Zetka's death, Felix had married Weissmann's ex-wife. Just two days before the storm we had received a small, stern-faced delegation which had come to prepare us to lose him once more: with new elections coming our party would need a strong man to represent it in the Cabinet.

The telephone was working again after lunch. Telegrams of concern and good will began to pour in from near and far. Offers of help and sympathy from other kibbutzim, institutions and organisations.

In our kibbutz a calm reigned once more. Here and there police-officers confabulated with regional officials, or an adviser huddled with a curious journalist. We were forbidden by Felix to talk to the press and the media, because it would be best for us to put forward a unanimous version when the time came to claim from the insurance.

At a quarter past one old Nevidomsky was brought home from the hospital, with his dislocated shoulder carefully set and his arm in an impressive sling, waving greetings with his free hand. At half past one we were mentioned on the news; again it was stressed that it had been neither a typhoon nor a tornado but simply a limited local phenomenon: two conflicting winds, one from the sea and the other from the desert, had met and caused a certain amount of turbulence. Such phenomena were of daily occurrence over the desert, but in settled areas they were infrequent and the likelihood of a recurrence was remote. There was no cause for alarm, although it was advisable to remain on the alert.

Batya Pinski switched off the radio, stood up and went over to the window. She peeped outside through the glass of the shutters. She cursed the kitchen team who had neglected their duty in the confusion and forgotten to send her her lunch. They should know better than anyone how ill she was and how important it was for her to avoid strain and tension. In point of fact she did not feel in the least hungry, but that fact did nothing to diminish her indignation: they've forgotten. As if I didn't exist. As if it wasn't for them and their pink-faced brats that Abrasha gave his life in a faraway land. They've forgotten it all. And Abramek's also forgotten what he promised; he's not coming today after all. Come, Abramek, come and I'll give you some ideas for the jacket and the dedication, I'll show you the havoc the storm has wrought here, you're bursting with curiosity and dying to see it with your own eyes, only you have no excuse, why should the director of the Party publishing-house suddenly drop all his work and come and goggle at a disaster like a small child. So come, I'll give you your excuse, and I'll also give you some tea, and we'll talk about what we have to talk about.

She leapt across the room, spotting some dust on the bookshelf. She swept it away furiously with her hand. She stooped to pick up a leaf that had fallen from a pot-plant on to the carpet. Then she drew Abramek Bart's letter from her dressing-gown pocket, unfolded it, and stared briefly at the secretary's signature, some Ruth Bardor, no doubt a painted hussy, showing her thighs, no doubt she's shaved her legs and plucked her eyebrows, and bleached her hair, no doubt she wears see-through undies and smothers herself in deodorants. God damn her. I've given those fish quite enough food for today; they'll get no more from me. Now here's another fly; I can't undersand how they get in or where they hide. Perhaps they're born here. Kettle's boiling again. Another glass of tea.

11

After the embarrassing episode in the dining-hall in the early 'forties, there were those among us who were glad that the affair between Batya Pinski and Felix had been broken off in time. But all of us were sad about the change that took place in Batya. She would hit her child even in the presence of other children. None of the advice or discussions did any good. She would pinch her till she was black and blue and call her names, including, for some reason, Carmen Miranda. The girl stopped wetting her bed, but instead started to torture cats. Batya showed the first signs of asceticism. Her ripe, heady beauty was beginning to fade. There were still some who could not keep their eyes off her as she walked, straight and dark and voluptuous, on her way from the sewing-room to the ironing-room. But her face was hard and around her mouth there played an expression of disappointment and malice.

And she continued to discipline the child with an iron hand.

There were those among us who were uncharitable enough to call her a madwoman; they even said of her, what does she think she is, a Sicilian widow, that cheap melodramatic heroine, that Spanish Saint, that twopenny actress.

When the founders of the kibbutz moved into the first

permanent buildings, Batya was among them. Zeiger volunteered to build her an aquarium in her new house. He did this out of a feeling of gratitude. Zeiger was a thickset, pot-bellied, hirsute man. He was always joking, as if the purpose of life in general and his own life in particular was amusement. He had certain fixed witticisms. His good humour did not desert him even when his wife did. He said to anyone who cared to listen: I am a mere proletarian, but Felix is going to be a comissar one day, when the revolution comes; I'd live with him myself, if he'd only have me.

He was a short, stocky man, who always smelt of garlic and tobacco. He moved heavily and clumsily like a bear, and there was an endearing light-heartedness about him even when he was accidentally shot in the stomach during illegal weapon-practice in the old days. We were fond of him, especially at festivals, weddings and parties, to which he made an indispensable contribution.

Ever since his wife left him, he had maintained a correspondence with a female relative, a divorcee herself, who lived in Philadelphia and whom he had never set eyes on. He used to call to Batya Pinski in the evenings, and she would translate her letters from English into Yiddish and his comical replies from Yiddish into English. Batya had taught herself English from the novels she read in bed at night. He always apologized at the end of each visit for taking up her valuable time. But it was he who dug the flowerbed in front of her new house, and raked it and mulched it and brought her bulbs and seedlings. His distinctive smell lingered in the room. Little Ditza loved to ask him riddles; he never knew the answers or if he did he pretended not to, and she always laughed at his amazement when she told him.

One day he came with aluminium frames, panes of glass, a folding rule, a screwdriver, and a sticky, smelly substance which he referred to as *kit* but which Batya taught him to call putty.

'An aquarium,' he said. 'For fish to swim in. It's aesthetic. It's soothing. And it doesn't make a noise and it doesn't make a mess.'

And he set to work.

Batya Pinski took to calling him Ali Baba. He willingly accepted this nickname, and responded by calling her 'the Contessa from Odessa'.

It was perhaps because of this nickname that little Ditza

began to address Zeiger as Pessah. Even though his real name was Fischel, we all came to call him Pessah, so that even in the kibbutz newsletter he was referred to as Pessah Zeiger.

Firmly but carefully he fitted the panes of glass into the soft bed of putty. At intervals he employed a tool which fascinated both Batya and Ditza: a diamond glass-cutter.

'How can we thank you for this beautiful present?' Batya asked when the aquarium was finished.

Zeiger pondered for a moment or two, breathed out a gust of onion and tobacco, winked to himself, and suddenly shrugged his shoulders and said *'Chort znayet'*, which is to say, the Devil only knows.

The fish were brought in a jar and put into the aquarium with a great deal of fuss. Ditza had invited all her friends to a 'fish-party', which did not please Batya. That evening Zeiger brought, in addition to the letter from his relation in Philadelphia, a small flask of brandy.

'Won't you offer me a drink,' he said.

Batya poured him a drink and translated the letter and his reply.

That evening we were celebrating the Allied victory. The Second World War was over, and the monster had been vanquished. We flew the Zionist and Socialist flags from the top of the water-tower. In the nearby British army camp there was a firework display, and in the small hours of the morning the soldiers came in army lorries to join in the singing and dancing. The girls of the kibbutz saw fit to consent for once to dance with the British soldiers despite their smell of beer. The dining-hall was decorated with slogans and with a large portrait of Josef Stalin in uniform. Felix delivered a passionate oration about the pure new world which was about to be built on the ruins of the defeated powers of darkness. He promised us all that we would never forget those who had sacrificed their lives in this struggle, here and on distant frontiers. Then he pinned the victory badge printed by the Workers' Party on to Batya's lapel, shook her hand and kissed her. We rose to our feet, sang the Zionist anthem and the 'Internationale' and danced all night. At ten past three Zeiger seized Batya's arm, dragged her almost forcibly out of the corner of the dining-hall where she had been sitting silently all evening, and saw her to her room. His voice was hoarse and his white shirt was clinging to his back, because between dances he had taken it upon himself to act the clown, as if this had been an old-fashioned Jewish wedding. When they got to Batya's door Zeiger said:

'That's it. You've had more than enough. And now, good night. He turned to go.

But she ordered him to come inside and he obeyed her. She took off his sweaty shirt. When he asked if he could wash his face, and she said neither yes nor no, but instead she switched on the light in the aquarium and turned off the overhead light. He began to apologize or to plead but she cut his stammering short by pressing him to her, sweaty, steaming, unwashed and embarrassed, and conquered him in silence.

12

In a small village run on sound principles there are no secrets, nor can there be any.

Just before six o'clock in the morning the neighbours saw Zeiger emerge, subdued, from Batya Pinski's door. By seven o'clock the news had already reached the sewing-room. There were those among us, including Felix and his wife Zetka (who had previously been married to Zeiger), who saw a positive side to this new development: after all, the whole situation had been unnatural and full of unnecessary tensions. Now everything would be much simpler. Martyrdoms, Mediterranean tragedies, emotional arabesques were irreconcilable with the principles according to which we guided our lives.

Even these people, however, could not accept what ensued with equanimity. Zeiger was the first, but he was not the last. Within a matter of weeks news had spread of various peripheral characters finding their way to Batya Pinski's room at night. She did not even turn up her nose at refugees, or at eccentrics like Matityahu Damkov. Her silent, noble melancholy had become something better left unnamed. And her face was becoming ugly.

Within a year or two even little Ditza was going around with soldiers and birds of passage. We were unable to devote our full attention to this unhappy episode, because the struggle to drive out the British was reaching its climax, and then regular Arab armies invaded the country; they reached the very gates of our kibbutz, and we repelled them almost empty-handed. Finally all was calm again. Hordes of refugees poured in from all directions. Zeiger's relation, a middle-aged woman, also came, as a tourist, and dragged him back to Philadelphia with her. We were all sorry to see him go, and there were some who never forgave him. Felix accepted a central Party position and only graced us with his presence at weekends. As for Batya, her last embers died. Ditza ran away again and again to the pioneering camps and the newly-emerging settlements in the desert; again and again she was brought back. Her mother took to her room. She announced that her condition would not permit her to work any more. We did not know what this condition was, but we decided not to ask too many questions. We left her alone. We were all relieved when Ditza finally married Martin Zlotkin, the son of the well-known banker. Batya accepted the marriage and the presents of expensive furniture from the young couple calmly. It was the fish which were now in the centre of the picture. The electric kettle was always on the boil. It seemed as though it was all over with her, when the matter of Abrasha's literary remains came up, and it was decided to publish his collected essays together with his letters from Madrid. It was just as Felix had promised at the victory celebrations: we would not forget our comrades who had sacrificed their lives. And Felix it was who, despite all his commitments, did not forget, and made the kibbutz movement publishing house finally tackle the job. The widow waited day by day. The fish swam across the picture without blurring it. They were cold but alive, they were not subject to the law of gravity, since they could hover effortlessly in the water. Last night's storm will bring Abramek Bart; but it's two o'clock already, and he hasn't come yet. A man like him will be able to understand the delicate matter of the dedication; he won't make any difficulties.

But I can't receive him in my dressing-gown. I must get dressed. I must tidy the room, if its not tidy enough already. I must get out the best china, so that I can serve the tea properly. And open the shutters. Let some fresh air in. Freshen up the biscuits, too. But first of all, get dressed.

She went to the basin and washed her face repeatedly in cold water, as if to mortify her flesh. Then she ran her bony fingers over her face and hair in the mirror and said aloud, there, there, you're a good girl, you're lovable, don't worry, everything's all right.

She made herself up slightly and brushed her grey hair. For an instant she caught a glimpse in the mirror of the old witch the children called Baba Yaga, but at once she was replaced by a noble, lonely woman unbowed by her suffering. She preferred the latter, and said to her: No one else understands you, but I respect you. And the book is dedicated to Batya, a noble wife, the fruits of love and anguish. Just as she pronounced these words she heard the squeal of brakes in the open space in front of the dining-hall. She leapt to the window, still dishevelled because she had not had time to put the hairpins in place; she flung the shutters open and thrust her head out. Abramek Bart, director of the publishing house, got out of the car and held the door open for the Secretary-General of the Movement.

Felix appeared from nowhere to greet them both with a warm yet businesslike handshake and serious expression. They exchanged a few words and walked off together to inspect the damage and the work of reconstruction which had been proceeding tirelessly since early in the morning.

14

She finished getting ready. She put on her claret-coloured dress, a necklace, and an unobtrusive pair of earrings, dabbed a few drops of perfume behind her ears, and put the water on to boil. Meanwhile the blue daylight poured in through the open windows. Children and birds were shrilling joyfully. The streaming light seemed to dull the water in the aquarium. The old Spanish tune came back to her lips, and a warm, deep voice emerged from her chest. The song was compulsive and full of longing. In the old days, in the distant 'thirties, the Spanish freedom-fighters and their sympathizers all over the world had been forever humming it. Abrasha could not stop singing it the night he left. A decade or so later, during the Israeli War of Independence, it had taken on Hebrew words. It was sung round the campfire among the old shacks by pale-faced soldiers who had recently fled from Europe. Night after night it had drifted among the kibbutz buildings and had even reached Batya Pinski:

The first dish to be served
Is your beloved rifle
Garnished with its magazines ...

She suddenly made up her mind to go outside.

Bursting out among the fallen trees and broken glass she saw the sky peaceful and clear over the hills as if nothing had happened. She saw Matityahu Damkov, his bare back glistening with sweat, mending a waterpipe with silent rage. And further away she could see the empty spot where the wooden shacks, the first buildings of the kibbutz, had stood. Workers were rooting among the wreckage. A few goats were peacefully grazing.

She reached the open space in front of the dining-hall at the very moment when Felix was escorting his guests back to their car. They were standing by the car presumably running over the main points of their discussion. Up to that moment Felix had kept his glasses in his shirt pocket; now he put them on again while he jotted down some notes, and at once he lost the look of a general and regained his habitual appearance of a philosopher.

Finally they shook hands once more. The visitors got into the car and Abramek started the engine. As he began to manoeuvre his way among the beams and scattered planks, Batya Pinski darted out of the bushes and tapped on the window with a wrinkled fist. The Secretary-General was momentarily alarmed and covered his face with his hands. Then he opened his eyes and stared at the terrifying figure outside. Abramek stopped the car, wound the window down a fraction and asked:

'What's up? Do you need a lift? We're not going to Tel-Aviv, though. We're heading north.'

'Don't you dare, Abramek, don't you dare leave out the dedication or I'll scratch your eyes out and I'll raise such a stink that the whole country will sit up and take notice,' Batya screeched without pausing to draw breath.

'What is this lady talking about?' asked the Secretary-General mildly.

'I don't know,' Abramek replied apologetically; 'I haven't got the faintest idea. In fact, I don't even know her.'

Felix immediately took command of the situation.

'Just a minute, Batya, calm down and let me explain. Yet, this is our Comrade Batya Pinski. That's right, Abrasha's

Batya. She probably wants to remind us of the moral obligation we all owe her. You remember what it's about, Abramek.'

'Of course,' said Abramek Bart. And then, as if assailed by
sudden doubts, he repeated, 'Of course, of course.'

Felix turned to Batya, took her arm gently, and addressed
her kindly and sympathetically:

'But not now, Batya. You can see what a state we're all in.
You've chosen a rather inconvenient moment.'

The car, meanwhile, was disappearing round the bend in
the road. Felix found the time to see Batya back to her room.
On the way he said to her:

'You have no cause to worry. We'll keep our promise.
After all, we're not doing this just for your sake, there's no
question of a personal favour to you; our young people need
Abrasha's writings, they will be the breath of life for them.
Please don't rush us. There's still plenty of time; you've got
nothing to worry about. On the other hand, I surmise that
you didn't get your lunch today, and for that you have
reasonable grounds for complaint. I'll go to the kitchen right
away and tell them to send you round a hot meal: the boilers
are working again now. Don't be angry with us, it hasn't
been easy today. I'll be seeing you.'

15

There was still the aquarium.

Now the fish could get the attention they deserved. First
of all the old woman inspected the electrical fittings. Behind
the tank there was concealed a veritable forest of plugs and
sockets, of multicoloured wires, of switches and transformers
which kept the vital systems alive.

From a tiny electrical pump hidden underneath the tank
two transparent plastic tubes led into the water. One worked
the filter, and the other aerated the water.

The filter consisted of a glass jar containing fibres. The
water from the bottom of the tank was pumped up into the
filter, depositing the particles of dirt, uneaten food and algae
on the filter, and returned to the tank clear and purified. The
aërator was a fine tube which carried air to the bottom of
the tank, where it escaped through a perforated stone in a

stream of tiny bubbles which enriched the water with oxygen and inhibited the growth of algae. These various appliances kept the water clear and fresh, and enabled the fish to display their array of breathtaking colours, and to dart hither and thither with magical swiftness.

A further electrical fixture without which the aquarium could not function was the heating element, a sealed glass tube containing a finely coiled electric wire. The glowing coil kept the water at a tropical temperature even on rainy days and stormy nights. The light and warmth worked wonders on the grey-green forests of water-plants in the depths of which the fish had their home. From there shoal after shoal emerged to pursue a course which was unpredictable because subject to unknown laws. The quivering tails suggested a heart consumed by longing, rather than mere pond-life. The fish were almost transparent; their skeletons were clearly visible through their cold skins. They too had a system of blood-vessels, they too were subject to illness and death. But fish are not like us. Their blood is cold. They are cold and alive and their cold is not death but a liveliness and vitality which makes them soar and plunge, wheel and leap in mid-course. Gravity has no power over them.

The plants and stones emphasize this by contrast. The sight of a school of swordfish swimming gently through the hollow stone arouses a grave doubt in the widow's mind: is death a possibility, and if so, what need to wait, why not plunge in this very instant.

She pressed her burning forehead against the glass. It felt as though the fish were swimming into her head. Here was peace and calm.

Breadth distracts the mind from depth. Depth also exists. It sends wave upon wave of dark stillness up towards the surface. And now the surface of the water reflects the crestshorn palm-trees.

The daylight fades and the windows darken.

Now she will close the shutters and draw the curtains. The kettle will boil again. More tea – this time in one of the china cups she has brought out specially. The fish are clustering round the underwater lamp as if they too can sense the approach of night.

A blue-tinged crystalline calm descends on our hills. The air is clear. The day's work is done. May she repose in peace.

May the fish swim peacefully through her dreams. May she
not be visited in the night by the crest-shorn palm-trees. A
last procession passes through the hollow stone. Darkness is
coming.

1963

Translated by Nicholas de Lange

Uzi Shavit

Two Variations on Spring 1974

I

Blossoms appeared in the land, and
The neglected grapevines climbing in the ruins of Kuneitra
Gave forth fragrance, while
Even the prickles of dead thorns on Mount Hermon
Were unsheathed suddenly, sharp and miraculous, and the
        trails of aircraft
Began sprouting out of soft, white snow, like wounds
Whose bandages have fallen off.

2

How strange that spring is
High in the mountains: no blossom, no voice of the turtle,
A white waste changing slowly
Into a brown waste, and some small birds
Tuning up lightly each morning
Between the fence wires
On the white snow.

Translated by Arthur C. Jacobs

Elisha Porat

A Diagonal View

I

I POSITION the camera on the roof of the old outpost. I've been looking for the perfect observation point ever since yesterday. What I need is a clear, infinite field of vision. A stretch of road, of course, not too short; long enough for Captain Bar-Oz, on entering the kibbutz, to be seen on all sides. It would be better to set the range of visibility slightly further back. Perhaps I'll begin at the junction of the main road. Captain Bar-Oz is to arrive in a fast car from the direction of Tel Aviv. But he may, in fact come by way of Hadera. Hadera is a smaller town and will rouse greater confidence in the audience. Before screening the junction, together with the road sign, of course, to help the average viewer find his bearings, one could flash on a few shots of Hadera: busy cranes, to the side of the water tower and the darkness of the old orange groves, piling up cubes one on top of the other, the violet morning-glory hedges climbing through the tops of the cypress trees, struggling up to the sky, long, cracked cement water-ditches. That will do. Now the camera concentrates on the car which is dropping Captain Bar-Oz off at the junction. The pace can be accelerated a little: Captain Bar-Oz appears to be ejected from the car door, his knapsack thrown out after him to the side of the road by an invisible hand. His face cannot be seen as yet but his movements are strange. He is in such a hurry that he forgets to thank the driver. Here one should stop for a moment to consider whether he shouldn't be placed in a ceremonious convoy of cars. Kibbutz cars, yes, cheerfully decorated; tubes of musical instruments stick out the windows and the riders' faces express endless rejoicing. No, here real cruelty is called for. There will be no convoy of joy. No ringing of carriages of delight. He must arrive alone, accompanied only by his meagre knapsack. Something in his clothes must indicate that he has been away a long while. At this point, the camera must be carefully aimed to capture the discrepant sense of estrangement between Captain Bar-Oz and the stones of the road, and the shady avenue of carobs, and the fields and orange groves which he sees through the gaps in the trees. But it is a queer, imposed estrangement as it is obvious that he is familiar with the entire scene from childhood. The camera should follow him slowly, surrounding him on all sides and giving the audience the feel of the covering of foreignness enveloping him, that unfelt, transparent covering, moving one small step ahead of him like the pillar of fire in the desert. Now I have doubts. The best thing would be to take a consecutive series of aerial views, at a low altitude, over his head, let us say from a helicopter quietly lingering in the air, making no sound. A helicopter hovering above. But without all the damage the engine can cause: strong air waves and the fear of decapitation by the shining blades. Incidentally, that's a good idea. An accidental beheading, short and brilliant, accompanied by the jet's clamour pouring in a torrent through the tail-pipe. I must think about that. Perhaps I'll leave it to the end. If there is no other, more convenient solution. And if Captain Bar-Oz finds himself in irrevocable complications so that I can't get him back to the beginning. And if the viewers, bent tensely forward, say that the end is no end. Then I'll surprise them. I'll think up a beautiful end. A jet end. Perhaps I could attach a small, even minute, camera to the propeller blades. A camera which would activate itself at the precise moment, not a second too soon, a jet decapitation-camera. Ingenious ideas, perhaps I'll use them later. I bring the camera back to Captain Bar-Oz. What defeatist thinking. To foresee such calamities for him from the very moment of his ejection on to the inner road. When the entire world is here, at the end of the road, waiting for him, longing for him, yearning for him terribly!

Well, I must accept my limitations. I don't have a helicopter. I have only a portable camera, positioned on the roof of the old cement outpost. Now I can descend, go up to Captain Bar-Oz, kiss him, shake hands with him, break through the aura of alienation which is surrounding him. I can get even closer. I can forget my job as photographer, give the camera to one of the children who have been swarming about here for hours, and exchange tears with him. The rare but very real tears of men. Of course one mustn't weep for a soldier returning from the front, or a prisoner from captivity or a shadow from the land of shadows. The tears won't show up on film. There's nothing to worry about. I'll see to it. But who wouldn't contribute a few seconds of weeping in honour of Bar-Oz, of his return. And while I'm preparing the camera for a quick descent down the iron ladder crumbling with rust, I change my mind, that is to say, the angle of filming. I'll simply sprawl on the road, a few steps in front of Bar-Oz and film him from below upwards. His uniform, faded from so many washings, his ranks hanging on his shoulders in a strange voluntary abandonment, his eyes fixed on a distant point in space; and over his head the dark tops of the carob trees, the wild and meaningless darting to and fro of the small, grey songbirds. The carobs are in flower now, their blossoms give off a horrible odour, the stench of a floorcloth or of the vapour rising from an obstructed sewer. But the camera does not capture smells. Only shapes. And the fetid carob flower, if you look at it closely, is of interest. As always, the wonderous complexity of nature, its usual mocking ways, in the flowers, the songbirds crowding together, in the prisoner returning from the land of shadows. Now will come a slow, lingering but enlarged shot of the meeting of his shoes with the earth that he loved so much. I'll press the camera tightly to the asphalt, lean on it with all my weight until a precise picture emerges, with no movement distortion. The sole's crashing tread, the strangeness crackling between sole and heel, the alienation trampled on almost as an afterthought. Then a flash up to his face. To the bite of his lips. To a kind of secret blinking of his eyes. To a bead of sweat starting down his pale face. And for a poetical touch, I could light up the curls under his hat, and linger over the few grey threads which have begun to threaten his hair.

I have a proposal which I'm looking into now, the problem is the reception. That is, the reception for the lost captain. And if I divide it for filming purposes into points, this would be the order: the origin of the message, receiving the message, the couriers, the message bringers and the obsessive distribution which takes hold from the moment the message arrives. Here I have a brilliant thought. I must organize, via the film, a concentric distribution. That is to say, the circle of those who know of Captain Bar-Oz's sudden return, makes a strange skip over a dark centre. The message, on its path of distribution, plays strange tricks on the eye, passing over small pockets of people, especially over one central pocket. His closest family stand there. Or to be more exact, his parents aren't there. Neither are his brothers. His friends aren't there. They are dispersed on all sides of the circles of distribution. At the centre of the dark space one woman stands alone. His wife. Oh, if only it were possible to move the camera at the speed of thought. From world to world, and under the world and over the world. And perhaps to all the kinds of worlds. There is only one professional question: will the camera really film what can be guessed at in the mind? Or perhaps not, perhaps such figures do not leave their mark on celluloid.

When I finish organizing the distribution, I will begin activating a great movement in all the circles. A movement towards a meeting. A sudden flow, new circles kiss the old, a hidden commotion like in burrows. Here one should stand a large camera with as wide an angle as possible and hang it, like the sun, over the kibbutz. A few hours of hard lighting and then a quick interpretation. In such cases the developing makes me really excited. My heart beats faster, streams of perspiration crawl on my palms and a sort of quick but monotonous tune buzzes in my left ear. The fingers involuntarily tap out a strange beat on the table. No, I reject that idea. Its too general, encompassing too much. I'll lose Captain Bar-Oz so, whether under the thick tops of the old fiscuses by the culture hall, or among the women's colourful kerchiefs. Strange how the kerchiefs suddenly appear on festivals or on days of mourning. Masses of them. It's a pity, with my black-and-white, however sophisticated, the kerchiefs are a great loss. Their colourfulness is really frightening. And the way they are worn is so expressive. How they gather and crowd, all at once, like a herd of frisky lambs, round the dark patch; the woman stands there: his wife. That's where he should be standing too. Pushed by hundreds of aiding hands, flowing with good will. But we'll come to that later. The dark patch will not let go of us. I'm preparing a special roll for it.

2

I urgently need the children now. I gather them around me. I give them short, simple instructions. Take cameras, I tell them, many small cameras, and put them into all the surrounding rooms. Put them also in the tree trunk and on the old benches. And even into the sprinklers. To the children's question of 'and in the woodpeckers' hollows?' I answer, yes, in the woodpeckers' hollows too. They are of special interest. The children disperse like lightning, raiding the rooms, the lawns, the pavements. Thousands of small cameras begin to click, Captain Bar-Oz is now being filmed from every possible angle. Thousands of minute eyes are following him. Every step he takes, every hair pulled out, every twitch of a muscle. The children hide in the bushes, behind the wall closets, beyond the balcony screens, like little foxes. Their eyes are the eyes of foxes in ambush. A queer scene: from beyond the gate a strange troupe enters the kibbutz: I am at its head, that is, with my back to front, the helpless camera fastened to my shoulder, my stomach, my hands latched on to it in a kind of fear and anxiety. Behind me, that is in front of me, since I am walking backwards (like a stumbling reluctant crab, scrambling and halting, probably falling into potholes) walks Captain Bar-Oz. The distance between us remains unchanged, as if set by someone other than ourselves. Not large, but strictly maintained. I try to regulate my paces to his. And he, although he is not looking in front of him at all, knows with a wonderful sense of degree, not to shorten the range between us. Not to shorten it beyond the seemingly agreed upon, beyond this dryness. And round us, unseen, hidden in the transparent air, all the children of the kibbutz are ready and alert, like springs yearning to uncoil. Prisoners of my command, dispersed like tiny spy cameras, all their mechanisms clicking. Trembling, a dryness in their mouths, and a great shout balled up in their throats. They lie in ambush and see his wretched knapsack on his shoulder, his clothes almost disintegrating from washings and the lump of estrangement dancing before him like a gay troupe of monkeys tied to its master by a hidden collar chain. An immense curiosity seizes my mind: will the cloud of estrangement leave tracks on the film? Or does that too leave its mark only on my cornea, unable to penetrate the barriers of the indifferent lenses? But I don't have time now to stop and answer myself. The lost captain's dogged, harsh movement makes me run in front of him. And I am already skipping backwards in a bad posture, so uncomfortable. My whole body aches. This is where I should break away from him. I am thinking of taking off to a better, a higher, filming position. But now it is impossible. He continues to walk. He has even increased his pace somewhat and the field is completely blocked. From above, giant tree tops, crowded roofs and a deep shadow. I put my trust in the children whom I shook off in all directions. Profiles, half-lengths, diagonal shots which could be wonderful, right from the insides of the woodpeckers' hollows. I feel as if I'm a prisoner in the pace of his advance. Because he still hasn't bestowed a single glance on me and we haven't exchanged half a word, and despite all the manly embracing and kissing, not one tear has fallen. He dictates a fast pace of filming and skipping backwards. And so we move for a while, film and skip, skip and film.

Now, just before my fall, I halt the film, raise the question and put it on the cutting table. The tension is great. Children hiding in the gardens. The square in front of the dining-hall is about to burst with anticipation. Masses of the men who have put on their sunglasses and women who have donned their coloured kerchiefs, are locked in their rooms. Just behind the doors. Waiting for the hidden signal to pour outside and be swept into colourful streams gushing to the large square. The heavy rag smell of the carob blossoms stands in the air and the burdensome sound of the bees swooping down to the nectar drowns almost every other noise. There are no screeches of planes in the air, no call-signals from the radio sets. There are no tidings heard anywhere. The calm is so suspect that my heart-beats, even here by the cutting table, suddenly jump. One moment, I'll just take advantage of this tension-ridden pause before the decisive event, to flash on a few background stills for relief: here is the lost captain as Amos, a smiling baby whose fat, creased limbs are entwined between the wooden poles of his cot of hastily-put-together boards. And then the boy Amosi, in a white, sweet-smelling shirt, with a stiff, overstarched collar. Now the camera moves. The picture of the boy will come closer and closer until it fills the entire frame. Of course there are difficulties. The downy moustache suddenly appears, before its time. Unseen wrinkles show up. And badly healed scars of childhood are especially, exaggeratedly exposed. But these are the usual ills of enormous enlargement. There is no getting around them. The quick flashes on the screen light up the faces of the viewers. The faces assume a strange pallor. As if they already know the end of the boy with the downy upper lip who is now crossing the lawn with his meagre satchel swinging from his shoulder. The material of his clothes is so worn, and what has he left?

I mustn't linger so long at the cutting table. I must run and take shots in the field. And I can already hear voices buzzing and shouting, where is that photographer who was just here, where has he disappeared to? I hurry. I have a very short way to go. At this point Captain Bar-Oz is already crossing the lawn. The paved dining-hall square is no longer far away. I attach myself to him as before, a crab-like attachment, embarrassing. Here I'll have to put some-thing in. I feel that there is a gap in the series of takes. The Captain has been abandoned and somebody must fill it in. When I return to the cutting table I'll fill in all those dark spaces. Amazing close-ups of his face. The pallor of his skin will compete with that of the screen. The backwards walking was dangerous from the start. It's a miracle that I've reached to the edge of the lawn. I should thank God that I haven't failed thus far. But now it's coming. A small hole, an unim-portant bump, and I'm still attached to the captain's walk, the camera pressed hard to my chest. The heel slips, the foot searches for firm ground, turns, and I go after it. Thrown forward on my back, struck backwards, stunned, momen-tarily dizzy, and then I see, with my eye in the camera pro-truding out of me, that Captain Bar-Oz does not stop walking. He continues straight over me. His shoes throw a shadow over the lens. The air-brush of his trousers blows over me like a breath of wind. A wonderful shot. From the bottom of hell. From the lowest possible place. His heel slips on the straps. I am ground under your feet, I want to cry to him. I am dust under your heels, photographer dust. I forgot, there's no sound-track. There's no reason to shout. I pull myself up to overtake him. Someone must warn him. Not about the pits on the way, those are unimportant. But the dark patches outside the circles. I fear a serious develop-ment. I do a quick change of film under pressure. Faster than the change of magazines under fire. This is the special roll. I've kept it for this moment. It's just as well that I fell and the filming stopped for a moment. I am ground under your feet which do not stop moving. I am dust under your heels that do not turn back. I am crushed beneath you. Oh, would I were in your place.

The earth splits open with an immense roar, a river of people breaks through and flows and streams to the square. Colourful, singing, moving and dancing. The air explodes from the howls of the children who are set free in a split second. They break out of their hiding-places with wild jumps, as if my fall was a signal to them. A benevolent human river surrounds Captain Bar-Oz and he is carried and pushed on the waves of hundreds of well-wishing arms. His clothes disintegrate on him from the patting, the embracing and affectionate caressing of those around him. His knap-sack is removed, passed from hand to hand, goes round the whole circle. Its old strap is torn and thrown somewhere outside the dancing circles. I scurry around the crowd like a madman. I'm looking for an observation point. I'm dying to position the camera so that it will have a free, infinite field of vision. I need clear, long shots: the square empty, before everything; the square half-full, something beginning to happen, and a last precise shot, the square seething with the crowd. But there is no vantage point round the celebration anywhere. The roofs are far, the carob foliage is heavy and obstructive. I've no choice. I must apologize, send the entire crowd back to its burrows, the children back to their dens. And while the square is empty, stand a painter's ladder on it, or a blacksmith's iron tower. I climb to the top of the tower, slipping in haste, give a hidden signal with my finger, and the earth splits open around me again.

Oh, if only I had a small helicopter now. A jet-copter with tiny cameras welded to its blades. From its jet tail-pipe a yellowish cloud of the carob odour would be ejected. The heavy smell mists over and envelops the whole crowd and as though anaesthetizes it with its druglike aroma. There is his closest family. She stands there: the woman, his wife. It is to her he makes his way constantly, indefatigably. For her he sheds his disintegrating clothes. For her he discards his wretched knapsack. Now I'm filming him from right above his head in a long, continuous series of wonderful aerial views. His covering of alienation melts. I can see it with my eyes. The people touch and touch him again. Touch his torn clothes, shoes, hands, flesh. There is no barrier stretched between the crowd and his heart. Someone wants to tear out his heart and embrace it. But to him these are all obstacles that have to be set aside. He is drawn towards her alone. Now the last circle breaks open and he penetrates the dark patch. My special film works frantically. I pray for it to last. I put the brakes on the blades of the helicopter, slow down. Now everything is shot in slow motion. He falls into her arms, she into his. Some sort of turbid vapour disturbs the functioning of the camera. The penetration of light is somehow impeded. Wait, she actually falls out of his arms. I curse the obstructing vapour. What is he doing to her with such force? Embracing her? Strangling her? The dark patch turns quite black. The crowd presses on to them and a whirlpool of screams, bodies aloft, cries and frantic runs covers the square. I jump into the whirlpool with my jet decapitation-blades. It's too late. There's no need. They're ahead of me. She is already being carried outside the circle. What a pity, none of my schemes worked out. The crowding interfered again. Now I leave everything and run to my dark room. A strange excitement is bubbling in me. I identify the perverse lust for interpretation. When I enter I rush to the window. I must close it tight. The yellowish cloud of the thick carob smell is threatening to choke me.

Translated by Judy Levy

Two Poems   *by* Yona Wallach

WHITENESS

this whiteness will drive me out of my mind
like the unicorn in a tapestry I saw
a unicorn so white on grass and flowers
driving a virgin crazy with its distant grace
this white may drive me crazy

BECAUSE OF LOOSE NERVES

because of loose nerves
every scratching noise can
be more than the end of honey
you pass the sanctuary of butterflies
at night and thousands commit suicide
against your lamps

behind you, you leave
blood escaping
people, skin peeled away
bleeding
for something else
here things blend
like little box houses
on foggy nights
here the honey is less sweet
and will not stop
the faces
the faces terrible their eyes
moving, shifting places
it's not easy with a sin like this
to escape when you're leaping from row to row
and you're the only one who can
offer a meadow of hornets
never mind

Translated by Leonore Gordon

Nathan Zach

All this isn't mine. I reflect
With surprise. Whose, then, is all this?

I don't know. It's a legacy perhaps. No relative
Or kinsfolk have left me anything. Well then?

Perhaps I'll go away from here, if all this is not mine.
Perhaps I'll go away from here, soon.

I don't believe in the honesty of the question.
And I reflect upon myself with surprise.

Translated by Arthur C. Jacobs

Abba Kovner

Because We Are Strangers Before You

And how they rise . . . surround come near flinch
and stay in the curtain. And I, as you know, have nothing
but one white page

and how they swarm. With gaping mouths
they tremble on a narrow pier. This is not land,
I say, brothers! And all, all of them are here

and how they just are. The shoemaker and the wagoner and
　　the tailor
even the singing tailor. Only their heads are exchanged.
Their nails dig deep in my side. And they break out of the
　　sea.

While my hand still sways over my eyes, they demand:
if you weren't cast up as the land for our sakes
who's the ark for?
and you—

and how they stare. There's no sea
sailing, I say to them, brothers – no
ship on my breast. Nor on my forehead.

Ghosts, you cursed ones, leave me alone!

And how they submit. The whip in front of the shoemaker
　　in front of
the wagoner the feed bag and the tailor the singing tailor;
wrapped in seaweed and salt

she is also before you:
Here I am. Let me go
please let me.

　　　Translated by Shirley Kaufman with Judith Levy

From *The Little Book* (1973)

S. Yizhar

The Prisoner

SHEPHERDS and their flocks were scattered on the rocky hillsides, among the woods of low terebinth and the stretches of wild rose, and even along the swirling contours of valleys foaming with light, with those golden-green sparks of rustling summer grain under which the clodded earth, smelling of ancient soil, ripe and good, crumples to grey flour at a foot's touch; on the plains and in the valleys flocks of sheep were wandering; on the hilltops, dim, human forms, one here and one there, sheltered in the shade of olive trees: it was clear that we could not advance without arousing excitement and destroying the purpose of our patrol.

We sat down on the rocks to rest a bit and to cool our dripping sweat in the sunlight. Everything hummed of summer, like a golden beehive. A whirlpool of gleaming mountain-fields, olive hills, and a sky ablaze with an intense silence blinded us for moments and so beguiled our hearts that one longed for a word of redeeming joy. And yet in the midst of the distant fields shepherds were calmly leading their flocks with the tranquil grace of fields and mountains and a kind of easy unconcern – the unconcern of good days when there was yet no evil in the world to forewarn of other evil things to come. In the distance quiet flocks were grazing, flocks from the days of Abraham, Isaac, and Jacob. A far-off village, wreathed with olive trees of dull copper, was slumbering in the curves of hills gathered like sheep against the mountains. But designs of a different sort cast their diagonal shadows across the pastoral scene!

For a long time our sergeant had been carefully peering through his fieldglasses, sucking his cigarette, and weaving plans. There was no point in going further, but to return empty-handed was out of the question. One of the shepherds, or at least one of the boys, or maybe several of them, had to be caught. Some action had to be taken, or something be burned. Then we could return with something concrete to point to, something accomplished.

The sergeant, of medium height, had thick brows which met over his deep-sunken eyes; his cap, pushed back on his balding head, exposed a receding forehead and damp, limp wisps of hair to the wind. We followed his gaze. Whatever it was that he saw, we saw a world of green-wool hills, a wasteland of boulders, and far-off olive trees, a world crisscrossed with golden valleys of grain – the kind of world that fills you with peace, while a lust for good, fertile earth urged one to return to back-bending work, to grey dust, to the toil of the burning summer: not to be one of the squad which the sergeant was planning to thrust bravely into the calm of the afternoon.

And, in fact, he was about ready to take action because just then we noticed a shepherd and his flock resting in the levelled grain in the shadow of a young, green oak. Instantly a circle was described in the world: outside the circle, everything else; inside, one man, isolated, to be hunted alive. And the hunters were already off. Most of the platoon took cover in the thickets and rocks to the right, while the sergeant and two or three others made an encircling movement down to the left in order to surprise their prey and drive him into the arms of the ambush above. Amidst the tender, golden grain we stole like thieves, trampling the bushes which the sheep had cropped so closely, our hobnails harshly kissing the warm, grey, sandy soil. 'We 'took advantage' of the 'terrain', of the 'vegetation', of the protection offered by 'natural cover', and we burst into a gallop towards the man seated on a rock in the shadow of the oak. Panic-stricken, he jumped to his feet, threw down his staff, lurched forward senselessly like a trapped gazelle, and disappeared over the top of the ridge right into the arms of his hunters.

What a laugh! What fun! Our sergeant hadn't recovered before another bright idea struck him, astonishingly bold and shrewd: take the sheep too! A complete operation! Drunk with satisfaction, he slapped one palm against the other and then rubbed them together as if to say, 'This will be the real thing!' Someone else, smacking his lips, said: 'Boy, what a stew that will be, I'm telling you—' And we willingly turned to the task, roused to a genuine enthusiasm by the flush of victory and the prospect of reward. 'Come on! Let's get going!'

But the noise frightened the sheep. Some tossed their heads, some tried to flee, others waited to see what the rest would do. But who knew anything about handling sheep? We were ridiculous and that's just what our sergeant said, and he claimed that 'schlemiels' and idiots like us could only mess up a good thing. Raising his voice, he began calling the sheep with a br-r-r and gr-r-r and a ta-ah-ta-ah and all the other noises and signs used by shepherds and their flocks from the beginning of time. He told one of the men to get in front of the sheep and to bleat, while some of us paired off on either side, brandishing our rifles like staffs and striking up a shepherd's tune, and three or more brought up the rear the same way. Thus, with a show of energy and wild laughter, we might overcome our hesitation, and be, in fact, soldiers.

In the confusion we had forgotten that behind a rock on the slope, huddled between two rifle butts and two pairs of spiked boots, sat our prisoner shivering like a rabbit – a man of about forty, with a moustache drooping at the corners of his mouth, a silly nose, slightly gaping lips, and eyes ... but these were bound with his *kaffiyah* so that he couldn't see, although what he might have seen I don't know.

'Stand up,' he was told as our sergeant came over to take a good look at his prisoner. So you thought we wouldn't get a thing?' crowed the men. 'We did, and how! With us there's no fooling around! Didn't have to waste a bullet: "Hands up" – he got the idea right away.'

'You're terrific,' agreed the sergeant. 'Just imagine: the shepherd *and* his flock! What won't they say when we get back! It's really great!' Only then did he look at the prisoner: a little man in a faded, yellow robe, breathing heavily behind the cloth over his eyes, his battered sandals like the flesh of his hoof-like feet. On his hunched shoulders sat doom.

'Lift the blindfold, but tie his hands behind him. He'll lead the sheep for us.' It was one of those crack commands which the intoxication of battle always inspired in our sergeant, and a spark of joy passed among us. Good. The men unwound the black cord of the shepherd's *kaffiyah*, took his hands and bound them with it good and tight, and then good and tight again for safety's sake, and yet again for the third time. Then the blindfold was pushed above the nose of the frightened man: '*Nabi el'anam kudmana!*' he was ordered. 'Lead the sheep ahead of us!'

I don't know what our prisoner thought upon seeing daylight again, what he felt in his heart, whether his blood whispered or roared, or what stirred helplessly in him. I don't know – but he immediately began clucking and grunting to his sheep as if nothing at all had happened, dropping from rock to rock through the brush with accustomed ease, the bewildered animals behind him. We followed after with hoarse yells, our rifles slapping our backs as we stampeded along and descended with wanton abandon to the valley.

We were so absorbed that we did not notice the silhouettes of other shepherds on the ridges of the hills, now gathering silently to peer at us from the distance as they rounded up their flocks; nor had we looked at the sun which all this busy hour had slipped lower and lower, getting more golden, until, turning the corner of a steep slope, we were struck by an intense blinding light: the smoky, enflamed disc seemed a mute admonition from space! But, of course, we had no time for all that: the flock! the prisoner! The sheep were bleating and scattering in all directions, while he seemed to shrivel up within himself, dazed and stupefied, his mind a ruin in which everything behind him was lost and all before him, despair. And as he walked he grew quieter, sadder and more confused and bewildered.

It's too long to tell in detail how we made our way through valleys and past hills in the peaceful ripeness of summer; how the frightened sheep kept tripping over their own feet; how our prisoner was enveloped by dumbness, the silence of an uprooted plant – his misery so palpable that it flapped about his head in a rhythm of terror, rising and falling with the blindfold (tied to his brow with a brute twist of disdain) so that he was pathetic but also ludicrous and repulsive; how the grain turned more golden in the splendour of the sun; how the sandy paths followed their course between hills and fields with the faithful resignation of beasts of burden.

We were nearing our base of operations.

Signs of the base, an empty Arab village, became more frequent. Interrupted echoes. An abandoned anthill. The stench of desertion, the rot of humanity, infested, louse-ridden. The poverty and stupefaction of wretched villagers. The tatters of human existence. A sudden exposure of the limits of their homes, their yards, and of all within. They were revealed in their nakedness, impoverished, shrivelled, and stinking. Sudden emptiness. Death by apoplexy. Strangeness, hostility, bereavement. An air of mourning – or was it boredom? – hovered there in the heat of the day. Whichever, it doesn't matter!

On the rim of the village, in those grey, greasy trenches, the other citizen-soldiers of our Home Guard company wandered aimlessly – their food no food, their water no water, their day no day and their night no night, saying to hell with what we'll do and to hell with what will be, to hell with everything that was once nice and comfortable, to hell with it all! We'll be dirty, we'll grow beards, we'll brag, and our clothes, wet with sweat, will stick to our unwashed bodies, infested with ulcers. We'll shoot stray dogs and let their carcasses stink, we'll sit in the clinging dust, we'll sleep in the filth, and we won't give a damn! It doesn't matter!

Nearing the trenches, we walked with heads high, proud of our loot! We fell smartly into step, almost dancing along. The bleating sheep were milling about in confusion. The prisoner, whose eyes had been covered again, dragged his sandals with clumsy uncertainty as we good-naturedly railed at him. We were happy and satisfied. What an adventure! What a job! Sweaty we were, caked with dust, but soldiers, real men! As for our sergeant, he was beside himself. Imagine our reception, the uproar and beserk laughter that broke loose like a barrel bursting its hoops! Someone, laughing and sweating profusely, pointing at the unseeing prisoner, approached our sergeant. 'Is that the prisoner? Want to finish him off? Let me!'

Our sergeant gulped some water, wiped his sweat and, still grinning, said, 'Sit down over there. It's none of your business.' The circle which had formed around howled with laughter. The trenches, the troubles, the disorder, no leave, and all that – what were they compared to all this?

One man was taking pictures of the whole scene, and on his next leave he would develop them. And there was one who sneaked up behind the prisoner, waved his fist passionately in the air and then, shaking with laughter, reeled back into the crowd. And there was one who didn't know if this was proper or not, if it was the decent thing to do, and his eyes darted about seeking the support of an answer, whatever it might be. And there was one who, while talking, grabbed the water jug, raised it high over his head, and swilled the liquid with bared teeth, signalling to his audience with the forefinger of his left hand to wait until the last drop had been drained for the end of his slick story. And there was one wearing an undershirt who, astonished and curious, exposed his rotten teeth; many dentists, a skinny shrew of a wife, sleepless nights, narrow, stuffy rooms, unemployment, and working for 'the party' had aggravated his eternal query, of 'Nu, what will be?'

And there were some who had steady jobs, some who were on their way up in the world, some who were hopeless cases to begin with, and some who rushed to the movies and all the theatres and read the weekend supplements of two newspapers. And there were some who knew long passages by heart from Horace and the Prophet Isaiah and from Chaim Nachman Bialik and even from Shakespeare; some who loved their children and their wives and their slippers and the little gardens at the sides of their houses; some who hated all forms of favouritism, insisted that each man keep his proper place in line, and raised a hue and cry at the slightest suspicion of discrimination; some whose inherent good-nature had been permanently soured by the thought of paying rent and taxes; and some who were not at all what they seemed and some who were exactly what they seemed. There they all stood, in a happy circle around the blindfolded prisoner, who at that very moment extended a calloused hand (one never knows if it's dirty, only that it's the hand of a peasant) and said to them: '*Fi, cigara?*' A cigarette?

His rasping voice (as if a wall had begun to speak) at once aroused applause from those with a sense of the ridiculous. Others, outraged by such impudence, raised their fingers admonishingly.

Even if someone were moved to think about a cigarette, it all ended in a different way – in military style. Two corporals and a sergeant came over from headquarters, took the prisoner, and led him away. Unable to see, he innocently leaned on the arm which the corporal had just as innocently extended in support. He even spoke a few words to guide the prisoner's groping steps. And there was a moment when it seemed as if both of them were labouring together peacefully to overcome the things that hindered their way and helped each other as if they went together, a man and another man, close together – until they had almost reached the house, when the prisoner repeated: '*Fi, cigara?*' These few syllables immediately spoiled the whole thing. The corporal withdrew his arm that had been interlocked with the prisoner's, raised his eyebrows angrily and, almost offended, shook himself free. 'Did you ever see such a thing?'

It happened so suddenly that the sightless man stumbled and tripped on the front step of the house, lost his balance and, almost falling, plunged headlong into the room. In a desperate effort to right himself, he sent a chair flying and collided with the table. There he stood, helpless, clumsy, overwhelmed by the force of his own violence and the fear of what was to come. His arms dropped to his sides and he stood stupefied, resigned to his fate.

A group of officers, their faces frozen in severe formality, had been ceremoniously seated at the table. But the prisoner's sudden entrance completely upset their quiet preparations, disturbed the atmosphere, confused the sentry at the door, confused the corporals and the sergeant; in short, everything had to be put back together again and grudgingly reorganized from the very beginning.

The officer sitting in the middle was tall and muscular, with stubby hair and a fierce face. On his left sat none other than our sergeant. One could see now that he was quite bald; the hair above his forehead was still dark but what little hair he had at the temples was turning grey. Perspiring freely, a crumpled cigarette in his mouth, he was the hero of the day and only at the beginning of his glorious adventures. Near the wall, conspicuously removed from the others, stood a pale young fellow glancing about through half-lowered lashes like someone quite convinced of a particular truth but curious to see by precisely what means it stands to be revealed.

'What is your name?' the tall officer began his interrogation abruptly but the prisoner, still stunned, paid no attention. The lips of the young fellow leaning against the wall puckered with assurance: this was just what he had expected.

'What is your name?' repeated the tall officer, drawing out the syllables,

'Who? Me?' The prisoner trembled and reached for his blindfold with a faltering hand. Halfway there, he dropped it, as if it had been singed by flame.

'Your name?' the officer asked a third time in a tone that emphasized his patience.

'Hasan,' he rasped, bowing his head, frustrated by his blindness.

'Hasan what?'

'Hasan Ahmed,' he answered, now on the right course, and his head nodded affirmatively.

'How old?'

'Oh, so-so. Don't know exactly.' He twitched his shoulders and slid his palms together uncertainly, wanting to be of help.

'How old?'

'Don't know, my lord,' he said, moving his thick lips. For some reason he chuckled and his drooping moustache performed a little caper. 'Twenty, maybe thirty,' he said, eager to co-operate.

'Well, what's going on in your village?' The tall officer spoke with a restraint which, more than it emphasized his calm, betrayed the coming storm – the restraint of an original cunning deceit, a kind of slow circular descent that is followed by a sudden swoop to the heart, a strike at the jugular.

'In the village they are working, my lord.' The prisoner sketched a picture of country life, sniffing the trouble that was to come.

'Working, you say? As usual?' The interrogator was moving in like a spider when a trembling thread of the web announces the prey.

'Yes, my lord.' The fly had edged away from the intricate web.

It was clear he would lie at this point. He had to lie. It was his duty to lie, and we would catch him by his tongue, the dirty dog, and we would show him. And just as we understood that with these tactics he would reveal nothing, so we knew that this time he wouldn't fool us. Not us. It's his turn to talk!

'Who is in your village?' The hawk hovered over its prey.

'Eh?' The prisoner did not follow the question and licked his lips innocently, like an animal.

'Jews? English? French?' The interrogator continued his questions like a teacher setting out to trap a slow pupil.

'No, my lord, no Jews, only Arabs,' he answered earnestly, with no hint of evasion. Once again, as if the danger were over, he tugged absentmindedly at his blindfold. The interrogator was glancing about the room: take a good look! It's beginning. Just see how an expert does it!

'Are you married?' He was started on a new, oblique attack. 'Any children? Where is your father? How many brothers? Where does your village get its drinking water?' He wove his delicate web painstakingly, and the prisoner struggled to satisfy him; he fumbled uselessly with his hands and made superfluous, meaningless gestures, bobbing his head and rolling his tongue, getting involved in petty details which threw him into confusion and annoyed his interrogators: some story about two daughters and a son, and how the son, neglected by his sisters, went out of the house and, as a result, fell sick and passed from the world. As he mumbled along, the prisoner innocently scratched his back ribs up and down, first with his thumb and then with a knot of four fingers, stammering as he tried to find the right words – he was unbearable.

There was a pause. The sentry shifted his weight from one foot to the other. From the expression on the face of the young fellow leaning against the wall and from the way our balding sergeant got up from the table, it was suddenly clear – not that the prisoner had nothing more to say, but that nothing would help but a beating.

'Listen here, Hasan,' said the interrogator, 'are there any Egyptians in your village?' (Now he'll talk! Now it's going to begin. Now he's sure to lie.)

'There are,' answered the prisoner, so simply it was disappointing.

'There are,' echoed the interrogator resentfully, like a man who has been paid in advance by his debtor. He lit a cigarette, deep in thought, contemplating his next move.

Our sergeant paced back and forth across the room, rearranged his chair, tucked in his shirt-tails, and with evident dissatisfaction turned his back to us and stared out the window. The young fellow by the wall, looking very wise, was passing his hand downward over his face, pinching his nose at the end of each stroke. You have to know how to handle these situations!

'How many are there?'

'Oh, so-so. Not many.' (Now he'll start lying. This is it. Time for a beating.)

'How many?'

'Ten, maybe fifteen, about that.'

'Listen, you Hasan, you'd better tell the truth.'

'It's the truth, my lord, all the truth.'

'And don't lie.'

'Yes, yes, my lord.' His hands, outstretched in surprise, dropped to his sides.

'Don't think you can fool around with us,' the tall interrogator burst out. He felt it was the right moment to say this. 'How many soldiers are there?'

'Fifteen.'

'That's a lie.'

The bald sergeant turned to us from the window. His eyes were smiling. He was enjoying that last sweet moment of anticipating all the joy still to come. To prolong it, he lit the cigarette held in the corner of his tightly-pressed lips. The other five men in the room regarded one another with the same wide-eyed pleasure. The sentry at the door shifted his weight again.

'I swear, my lord, fifteen.'

'No more?'

'The truth, no more.'

'How do you know there are no more?' The interrogator intended to make clear that he was nobody's fool.

'No more.'

'And if there are more?' (How can one answer such a question?)

'No more!'

Suddenly a clumsy kick from too short a distance landed on the man at an awkward angle. The unsuspecting prisoner staggered and collapsed upon the table with a loud exclamation, more of surprise than of pain. The whole scene suggested some kind of unfairly-matched game rather than a cross-examination, something unexpected, unnatural.

'Now talk and see that you tell the truth!'

'My lord, I swear by my own eyes, I swear by Allah, fifteen.'

The young man by the wall was afraid that so gross a lie might be believed. He held a long stick which he drew through his fingers with the grace of a knight drawing his sword. Then silently, he placed it on the table.

The barrage of questions continued without a break. The kicks landed like lightning, more naturally and freely, cool, deliberate, increasingly skilful. If at times they seemed unavailing, they nonetheless continued.

Because if you want the truth, beat him! If he lies, beat him! If he tells the truth (don't you believe it!) beat him so he won't lie later on! Beat him in case there is more to come. Beat him because you've got him at your feet! Just as a tree, when shaken, lets fall its ripest fruit, so a prisoner, if you strike him, yields his choicest truths. That's clear. And if someone doesn't agree, let him not argue. He's defeatist, and you can't make wars with that kind. Have no mercy. Beat him! They have no mercy on you. Besides, a *goy* is used to blows.

Now they came to the question of machine guns in the village. A crucial point, this. Here you have to lay it on or you won't get anywhere. And if you don't, Jewish blood will be spilt, our own boys' blood, so this point must be completely clear. They questioned him again and again until it became nauseating, and they gained nothing but the certainty that he was lying. Then he was ordered to describe the village's fortifications. And there he got completely confused. He had difficulty with the description, the abstraction, the geometry, the mathematics. He tried to convince his questioners with gestures, freeing his arms from his sleeves and waving them about while he shuffled back and forth. But the cloth over his eyes reduced everything to a blur of confusion. It was clear to everyone in the room that all his talk was nothing but a tissue of lies.

'You're a liar,' exclaimed the discouraged interrogator. 'I can see in your eyes that you're lying,' and he raised a menacing fist in front of the prisoner's blindfold.

This got nowhere. It had become boring. Everyone was fed up. The cross-examination blundered along, without enthusiasm, and the kicks fell listlessly. There was sudden surprise when the stick came whistling down on the prisoner's back, a disinterested, routine blow from an obedient hand.

O.K. And now about the guns. The prisoner kept insisting that their barrels were no longer than the distance from his shoulder to his palm. He struck his left palm like a hatchet against his right shoulder and then against his wrist: from here to there. He beat himself incessantly, unstintingly, to remove any trace of doubt. Even then he was uncertain whether he had done enough or must continue, and around his mouth was the expression of a blind man who has lost his way.

The questions petered out. At the door the sentry, shifting

his weight from one foot to the other, was looking up at the sky, possibly searching in the glimmering light for something that was not in the dirty, gloomy room. He feared that something terrible was about to take place. It was inevitable! Take the stinking beggar, they would tell him, and get rid of him!

'Well, that's that,' said the interrogator, slumping back in his chair, eager to relax now that it was over. He stubbed his cigarette impatiently on the floor.

'I'd better finish him off,' volunteered the sergeant, flicking his cigarette through the doorway with a quick snap of his forefinger.

'He's a complete moron,' concluded one of the corporals.

'He's only pretending to be,' said the other.

'He needs somone who can handle him,' said the young man by the wall, curling his lips in a sneer at this offence to truth.

The prisoner, sensing a respite, licked his thick lips, stuck out a thick hand, and said: *'Fi, cigara?'* Of course nobody paid attention to the stupid fool. After waiting some time, the idiot dropped his hand and remained rooted to the spot, sighing softly to himself: Oh, Lord God.

Well, what now: to the village quarry or perhaps a little more torture to open his mouth? Was there any other way to get rid of him? Or ... perhaps one could give him a cigarette and send him home. Get out and let's not see you again!

In the end someone telephoned somewhere and spoke to the captain himself, and it was decided to move the prisoner to another camp (at least three of the men in the room wrinkled their noses in disgust at this unfit procedure, so civilian, so equivocal), a place which specialized in interrogating prisoners and meted out to each just what he deserved. The sentry – who had been uneasy throughout the cross-examination without knowing what to do – went to get the dusty jeep and the driver on duty. The young man who came was griping, angry that he had been called out of turn. Not that he objected to leaving: it would be nice to get back to civilization for a while and to see some human faces, but it was the principle, the principle of the thing! Another soldier, charged with an order whose execution had been delayed for lack of transport, took his place alongside the driver. Now he was assigned another duty: accompany the prisoner! (Thus shall they go through the streets of the town: the machine gun in front and the prisoner behind!) He sat and loaded his machine gun. With two jobs, the trip – God forbid! – couldn't be counted as leave!

The prisoner was pushed and shoved like a bundle into the jeep where the only place left for him was the floor. There he was dropped, kneeling like an animal. In front of him were the two soldiers and behind, the sentry whose pocket held the official order, travel authorization, and other essential papers. The afternoon, begun long ago among mountains, oaks, and sheep, was now drawing to a close. Who could foresee how it would end?

The jeep left the mouldering village behind, passed the dry river-beds, and spurted ahead at great speed through the fields, bouncing on all fours. Distant details of the landscape kept shifting to close view. It was good to sit and watch the fields now bathed in a rosy light trailing small, golden clouds, a light that seemed to envelop everything – all those things which are so important to you and me but mattered not at all to the driver and his comrade in the front seat. They smoked and whistled and sang. 'On Desert Sands a Brave Man Fell' and 'Beautiful Green Eyes' in turn. It was difficult to know what the man who lay on the floor of the jeep was feeling because he was blind, stunned, and silent.

A cloud of dust, billowing up behind the jeep like a train of smoke, caught the rosy light in its outlines. The uneven gullies and shallow furrows of the fields made the husky jeep dance. The fields stretched to infinity, abandoned to the twilight, to something distant and dreamlike.

Suddenly, a strange thought pierces one's mind: *The woman is lost beyond a doubt.* And before there's time to wonder where the thought came from, one understands, with the shock of lightning, that here, right here, a verdict is being rapped out which is called by so many different names, among them: fate.

Quick, escape this rotten mess! Join the harmonizing of the other two up front or journey towards a far distance with the deepening twilight. But the circle of that unexpected thought grows larger and larger: This man here at your feet, his well-being, his home, three souls, the whole fabric of life, have somehow found their way into the hollow of your hands, as though you were a little god sitting in the jeep.

The abducted man, the stolen sheep, those souls in the mountain village – single, living strands that can be joined or separated or tangled together inextricably – suddenly, you are the master of their fate. You have only to will it, to stop the jeep and let him go, and the verdict will be changed. But wait ... wait ...

An inner force stirs in the young man on the back seat of the jeep and cries out: Wait! Free the prisoner!

We'll stop the jeep right here in the gully. We'll let him out, free his eyes, face him towards the hills point straight ahead, and we'll say: Go home, man, it's straight that way. Watch our for that ridge! There are Jews there. See that they don't get you again. Now he takes to his heels and runs home. He returns home. It's that easy. Just think: the dreadful, oppressive waiting; the fate of a woman (an Arab woman!) and her children; the will-he-or-won't-he-come-back?; that what-will-become-of-me-now? – all would end well, one could breathe freely again, and the verdict would be a return to life. Come, young man, let's go and free him.

Why not? Who's preventing you? It's simple, decent, human. Stop the driver. This time no more lofty phrases about humanity; this time it's in your hands. This time it's not someone else's wickedness. This time it's an affair between you and your conscience. Let him go and you'll save him. This time the choice (that terrible and important choice of which we always spoke with awe) is in your two hands. This time you can't escape behind 'I'm a soldier', or 'It's an order', or 'If they catch me, what will they do?' or even behind 'What will my comrades say?' You are naked now, facing your duty, and it is only yours.

So stop, driver! Send the man away! No need for reasons. It is his right and your duty. If there is a reason for this war, it must show itself now. Man, man, be a man and send him home. Spit on all this conventional cruelty. Send him away! Turn your back on those screaming slogans that paved the way for such an outrage as this! Free him! Hallelujah! let the shepherd return to his wife and his home!

There is no other way. Years might pass before he is set free, by some magic, to return to the hills to look for his wife and family; meanwhile, they have become fugitives fleeing misery and disease – mere human dust. Who knows what can happen in this meanwhile, and where? Perhaps, in this meanwhile someone will decide to get rid of him, to finish him off for some reason or even for no reason at all.

Why don't you make the driver stop? It's your duty, a duty from which there is no escape. It's so clear that it's hard to wait for you to act. Here you must rise and act. Say a word to the driver. Tell him and his companion that this was the order. Tell them a story, tell them something – or don't even bother. Just let it happen. You are going to face the sentence, that's for sure. Let him go!

(How can I? He's not mine. He's not in my hands. It's not true that I'm his master. I'm only a messenger and nothing more. Is it my fault? Am I responsible for the hard hearts of others?)

That's enough. That's a shameful escape. That's the way every son-of-a-bitch escapes from a fateful decision and hides himself behind 'I have no choice,' those filthy and shopworn words. Where is your honour? Where is this independence of thought you boast about? Where is freedom, hurrah for freedom, the love of freedom! Free him! And what's more, prepare to be sentenced for this 'crime'. It's an honour. Where are they now, all your words, your protests, your rebellions about pettiness, about oppression, about the ways to truth and freedom? Today is your day of payment. And you shall pay, my son. It's in your hands.

(I can't. I'm nothing but a messenger. What's more, there's a war, and this man is from the other side. Perhaps he is a victim of the intrigues of his people, but, after all, I am forbidden and have not the power to free him. What would happen if we all started to set prisoners free? Who knows, maybe he really knows something important and only puts on that silly face.)

Is that what you really think? Is he a soldier? Did you catch him with a sword in his hands? Where did you find him? He's not a fighter; he's a miserable, stinking civilian. This capture is a lie – don't blind your eyes to that. It's a crime. You've questioned him, haven't you? Now set him free. Nobody can get anything more out of him. And are you willing to suppress the truth for one more detail? The truth is to free him – now!

(It's so difficult to decide. I don't dare. It's involved with so much that's unpleasant: talk to the driver, persuade his companion, face all the questions, get into a rotten mess, and all because of a good-for-nothing wretch named Hasan, and what's more, I'm not sure it's good to free him before he's been thoroughly questioned.)

Vanity! Someone with only a fraction of your feelings about truth and freedom would stop right here and send the man home and continue on his way, quickly forgetting the whole thing: short and simple, a man of action. And he wouldn't thank himself for being good! But you, with all your knowledge, arguments, proofs, and dreams, it's clear that you won't do it. You're a noble fellow, you'll meditate, enthuse, regret, reconsider, you'll be submerged in a sea of thoughts: oh, why didn't I do it? And you'll cast the bitterness of your unfulfilled existence over the whole world: the world is ugly, the world is brutal. So make up your mind, and do it this time. Stand up to the test. Do it!

(I feel sorry for him. It's a shame they picked me for the job. I would do it if I weren't afraid ... I don't know of what. If only I were alone with him here. It's bothering me like a desire almost within reach, and I can't begin. When I think that I'll have to explain, get all involved, go to people and argue and prove and start justifying myself, I simply can't. What can I do?)

Listen, man! Can you actually think of weighing these pitiful trifles against another's life? How would you look at this thing if you were the one crouched on the floor of the jeep, if it were your wife waiting at home, and all was destroyed, scattered to the winds like the chaff of the wheat?

The prisoner has already said all he can say, told all he can tell. What more do you want? And even if he has lied a hundred times, who is he and what is he? He is only a miserable nothing, a subdued, shrivelled creature, a mask wrapped in a cloth, someone shrunken and stooped like a worthless sack, frightened, dissolving into nothingness, for whom being kicked is second nature (kick him – he's an Arab; it means nothing to him). As for you, his little god, it's your duty to free him, even if he himself laughs at you, even if he (or someone else) sees it as a sign of weakness on your part, even if your friends make fun of you, if they try to restrain you, even if they bring you up for court-martial, for twenty court-martials! It's your duty to break free of this habitual swinishness. Let there be one person who is ready – even at the price of suffering – to get out of this heap of filth which was piling up in the days when we were good citizens and which is now the celebrated, the accepted, the official way of the world, embraced by those bearing the proud title 'soldier'. And all that was frowned upon is now allowed!

Oh, Hasan Ahmed, you with a wife named Halima or Fatima, you with two daughters, you whose sheep have been stolen and who has been brought God knows where one clear afternoon, who are you and what is your life, you who can cleanse from our hearts all this filth – may it rot forever in darkness!

Of course you won't free him. That's clear. Beautiful words! It's even not cowardliness – it's worse than that: you are a partner to the crime. You. Hiding behind a stinking what-can-I-do-it's-an-order. This time you have the choice, and it's at your disposal. It's a big day. It's a day of rebellion. It's the day when, at last, you have the choice in your hands. And you hold the power to decide. And you can return life to a man from whom it has been taken. Think it over. You can behave according to the dictates of your heart, of your love, of your own standard of truth, and – most important of all – of the freedom of man. Free him! Be a man! Free him!

It's clear that nothing will happen. It was certain that you would evade it, that you would turn your eyes away. It's clear that all is lost. Too bad for you, prisoner, he does not have the strength to act.

And maybe, even yet ... you, you right, here, it will only take a minute: Driver, stop! Hey, Hasan, get out and go home! Do it! Speak! Stop them! Talk! Right now! This is the moment! You can become at last a man, the kind of man you've always wanted to be ...

The glimmering plain was a thin, bright foil; thousands of acres shone like a magic loaf. There were no river beds, no hills, no ascents or descents, no trees, no villages. Everything was spread out to form a single, golden matrix, round and gleaming, strewn with moving pinpoints of light, a vast expanse stretching to infinity. And yet behind us (but no one is gazing there) in the misty evening over the mountains, there, maybe, there is a different feeling, a gnawing sadness, the sadness of 'who-knows?' of shameful impotence, the 'who-knows?' that is in the heart of a waiting woman, the 'who-knows?' of late, a single, very personal 'who-knows?' and still another "who knows?' belonging to us all, which will remain here among us, unanswered, long after the sun has set.

Translated by V. C. Rycus

THE FIRST BATTLES

The first battles grew
Fearful love flowers
With almost lethal kisses, like shells.
In the fine buses of our city
The soldier lads were driven away:
All routes, 5, 8, 12,
Finished at the front.

RAIN ON THE BATTLEFIELD

Rain falls on the faces of my friends;
On the faces of living friends, who
Cover their heads with blankets,
And on the faces of dead friends, who
Don't cover themselves up any more.

ON THE DAY OF ATONEMENT

On the Day of Atonement 1967 I put on
My dark festival clothes and went to the Old City of
    Jerusalem.
I stood a long time in front of the lowly shop of an Arab,
Not far from the Shechem Gate, a shop that had
Buttons and clasps and cotton-reels
Of all colours, and zips and buckles.
A rare light and many colours, like an Ark of the Law,
    opened.

In my heart I told him that my father
Also had a shop like that with buttons and cotton.
In my heart I explained to him all the decades
And causes and events, that set me here now,
While my father's shop lies burnt there, and he is buried
    here.

As I was finishing it was time for the Closing Prayer.
And he too pulled down his shutters and closed his door
And I with all the other worshippers went home.

Translated by Arthur C. Jacobs

Three Poems   *by* Anton Shammas

SITTING ON THE RAIL

Sitting on a Tel Aviv rooftop in the sun
On a cold day. Old pensionaries. A limp
Crane tries to lift the town
And the day fallen down into a cup of coffee.

Two cries for help, you and I,
In this sinking city,
Sit on the rail
Fishing for quiet with love-hooks.

I HAVE A DRAWER

I have a drawer full
Of lullabies. It's locked. I stand before it
And grow, hoping one day to reach
The key my mother hung
On her death peg.

LOVELIER THAN A WOMAN

Lovelier than a woman hanging her clothes
On the rack of my passion – a woman
Hanging her clothes out on the line at night.
Mr. Moon peeks from under her dress
And climbs the rusty fence and up her rusty arms—
Then he sits in the middle of the sky,
Smokes his pipe like an old guy in retirement,
Nodding as he contemplates the world situation.

*Anton Shammas' Hebrew poems were translated by Betsy
Rosenberg.*
*'Lovelier Than a Woman' was rendered by her from the
Arabic
in collaboration with the poet himself.*

Samih El-Kassim

Cinerama

1

In the next room clothes of a woman and a man
Scattered as in haste
And a whisper of tunes and strings of words
And in the window a strange bird nods its wings
Saying: I am the lover and the beloved.
And was gone. And didn't say. And didn't say
When my end will come.

2

No start of a song did they leave me to sing.
No splendour for my eyeballs.
Their laughter flows
When they hear me coaxing the winds
To uproot mountains.
O ancient dead – who will restore me
To the days of their might for but a split moment.
Fade, imaginings!

3

In my aloneness I'll let the sadnesses
Shake the ashes of my sorrows
Expel the smoke
From the spanks of my embers, revealing
My human account without deceptions
Then bells will sound inside my heart.

Translated from the Arabic by
Sasson Somekh and
Richard Flantz

Siham Da'oud

THREE POEMS

*　　*　　*

When the wind travels with the train
And the oranges fall asleep on my arm
The tears escape from my mother's eyes
And on the windows of my wounds
The waiting will kill me.

*　　*　　*

Descending I saw you from a new land
And I saw the lover who came and was rain
When I came back from the funeral a pomegranate
　　grain.
Your history I am
And the circle of the sun, the rains, the east winds,
And my cross is still here, not journeying,
Taking from my hips and from your skin
An offering for the birds, a nail
To shield us from the west wind.

*　　*　　*

When I ran towards you, bare,

Without longings,
The lines of your face, changed the hue of
　　the oranges
But I wrote to you from my lung!
They will not take the greenness from the
　　olives
For my tear, like the colour of your eyes,
　　is green.

*Translated from the Arabic by Sasson Somekh
and
Richard Flantz*

A. B. Yehoshua

Missile Base 612

AND in the night he knows a brief spell of pre-dawn wake-fulness, as though someone had pushed him off the mattress to the rug, seized him by the collar and plucked him off the floor, dumped him in a chair to face the gray TV screen gleaming in the dark, where now a vague reflection of his face begins to shimmer. And sleep-worn but wide awake, he sticks a bitter pipe between his teeth, wants to say something, would even give a little lecture.

Some minutes pass and he starts prowling about the dark flat, wanders in and out of the kitchen, the lav, the child's room; opens the bedroom door and stands in the doorway, casting a shadow over his wife's body which lies aslant the twin bed. He lingers, waiting to hear if she will mumble something in her sleep, moan perhaps, then retreats, turns back to the living room, goes to the radio and fumbles between low distant music, readings from the Koran, and faraway signals; drops into an armchair and broods on the impending divorce and how he'll have to take the whole place apart, and presently his strength fails him, his breathing grows harsh, he kneels on the rug, tugs at the sheet, smells people's footmarks, and falls into a deep sleep again.

In the morning when the light floods through the large balcony-door, nothing is left of all his early awakening except a red bulb in the radio which had got stuck between two stations.

And then he gets up, puts the kettle on, washes, dresses, folds the mattress, sheets, blanket, removes the traces of the night and goes to wake the kid. These past weeks he has been lifting him out of bed as he is, carrying him still half asleep into the kitchen, placing him on a chair and talking at the drowsy child while sipping his coffee.

He hasn't exchanged a word with his wife for months. The first shots were fired long ago, the cause obscured; now it's open war. Once they could squabble a whole day long, not letting go of each other, even forgetting to go to work sometimes; and till deep into the night, in hot fury, occasionally smashing a piece of crockery coming to hand. Now it's each to himself. Urgent messages are passed through the child, who has grown older lately, graver, whom the new silence in the house is grinding down.

Each of them cooks for himself, and they take turns to eat. On the stairs, at chance encounters, they stiffen for a moment, bow their heads – the gestures of stubborn knights. If she would die, he sometimes thinks, late in the evening and she not home yet from one of her unaccountable night journeys, he laying out the mattress for another solitary night in the living room, waiting in vain for the sound of key in front door, falling asleep in a rage and waking before dawn to find her in her bed, sleeping peacefully, slantwise, unstirring. And in the morning he is alone, dressing his son, giving him breakfast, taking him to school, driving to the university, looking for hitchikers to draw into conversation. But it's the spring vacation now and there are no students at this time of morning, and when he gets stuck in a line of cars at an intersection, two cleaning women from the university spot him, make a dash for the crawling car, and he stops, lets them in, not acknowledging their thanks, and fiercely, almost savagely, he gallops off with them through this freakish spring – a drab spring blowing with dank breezes, hangover of a winter that hasn't been much of a winter either but cold clear skies and sickly buds shriveling on their branches.

He crosses the university campus slowly, deliberately, looking for someone to accost; arrives at the nearly empty library, spreads his papers over a desk by the window, goes to take out Aristotle's *Metaphysics* from the reserved section, and in utter silence, with unutterable slowness, not concentrating, he starts to read the ancient, difficult text which he will have to explain to his students next year, his eyes continually straying from the lines to the gray world beyond the window. This sabbatical is also crumbling fast, a year without students, adrift in the library. It's been three years since he published anything. His friends say he's finished, dead. He ought to have tackled something long ago. And again he jumps up to look for someone, anyone, to flip newspaper pages in another room, wander through corridors, return to his desk, read another page or two before he is up and out again, walking in a cloud of tobacco smoke to the bursary to see if they've calculated his salary correctly, from there to his mailbox to find only a slender volume of poetry sent him by an old schoolmate who each year, come spring, publishes at his own expense a batch of wishy-washy love poems. He tears off the wrapper, glances at the inscription, turns a few pages and is filled with weariness. Then back to the corridors to resume his aimless rambling, to follow a slight, delicate girl student, stop with her to study the notice board, holding his breath, watching her furtively, it's been a long time, he's ready to fall in love, desperately, at a hint. Eventually he retreats; back to the reading room, to his book, listlessly, with growing reluctance, to discover after twenty pages that he hasn't taken in anything; and he starts anew, forces himself to summarize each passage like a first-year student. His gaze fixes itself on some grains of sand beating against the window; a few miraculously gain entrance, land by his plodding pen.

Towards noon he returns the book to the reserved section.

'Shall I keep it for this afternoon?' asks the elderly woman librarian, already used to seeing him show up suddenly towards nightfall.

'No, I'm flying to Sinai this afternoon to lecture at a missile base,' he informs her casually, with a smile, hoping to rise in her esteem.

'So for when?'

'Tomorrow morning, as usual.'

She does not even look up.

'Yes, I'll be back tonight . . .' he prods her gently.

But the woman just gives him an absent smile, hasn't listened very closely, or perhaps it doesn't strike her as anything particularly wonderful, these shortened distances.

Yet he himself had been amazed when a girl from the army's lecturers pool rang up a week ago to inform him of this lecture. Be at the airport at three, they'll fly you back after, she had told him. As far as I'm concerned, he had said, I don't mind staying the night. But she insisted: No, they'll fly you back. But I wouldn't mind staying once I've come that far. She had refused to give in, though, as if in all that desert there really was no place for him. Ah well, how could she have known that at home he sleeps on a mattress in the living room?

He had been transferred to this unit of itinerant lecturers early in the winter. Before that they used to call him up twice a year, summer and winter, for a fortnight of guarding two huge electrical transmission towers planted in the middle of some field. The long nights of guard duty had been a growing ordeal, the hours dragging out endlessly till at last, around midnight, time would stop completely. And in a trance of fatigue, his mind vacant, his rifle tossed into the corn, he would slip through the crisscross of iron bars, sit down inside the tower like a caged ape, listen to the monotonous hum of electric current overhead, and wait helplessly for the frozen sky to start moving again.

One morning a young lecturer on reserve duty had given them a talk about official Israeli policy. After the lecture – which he had considered rather crude – he had made inquiries about the lecturers' pool and the qualifications needed to join it. Eventually he had gone there, introduced himself complete with academic degree and a tentative list of subjects, and had been accepted at once to his own surprise. Now he would be called on to give a lecture once every week or two, wandering between various outfits, training camps, strongholds, remote spots he never knew existed. And the country spreads itself before him as he goes on his wanderings, skipping up hill and down dale and speaking, preaching to soldiers.

And all at once – a different audience; no longer a dozen philosophy students with metaphysical texts in front of them, fencing with him, waging stiff battles over every word, but motley crowds, boys and men who assemble on command and are placed in front of him, his words wafting over them as a gentle breeze. And he is treated with respect, is offered coffee or soft drinks. invited to meals, and when he displays an interest they show him their new weapons too – a bridge-laying tank or a bent-barrel gun. Sometimes, when he happens to arrive at some front line position in the afternoon and his listeners must be routed out of bed first, he mounts the observation posts on his own initiative, to peer through giant binoculars at the other side, watch the tiny enemy popping up here and there in the dunes, filling sandbags at leisure.

And he speaks. In field, outpost, mess hall; under a blue sky, under a canvas roof, on the top of a hill or in a bunker underground; early in the morning, at noon, and after supper; repeats the same two or three lectures over and over again, jokes and all. The ease with which the words spout from his mouth surprises even him. He does still preserve a tiny quiver of anticipation, every time anew, but it ebbs swiftly after the first few words. And the soldiers' faces before him – a many-colored multitude. Dozing, yawning, tense, laughing, irritated. And he always still relishes the thought that presently he'll wind up his lecture, answer last questions and be free to leave them, and it's they who'll be left to the long night of guard duty. In vain he tries to keep a face or two of his ever-changing audience in mind. The landscape, on the other hand, does stay with him – the view of a distant hill, a dry river bed, a mud track hugging a security fence. And the weapons too. The tanks, the swivel-guns, the infra-red sights of machine guns. And nowadays, missiles as well. He hasn't seen the missiles yet.

3

He leaves the university at midday, and the sky is a gray whirlpool. Mercilessly he cuts through the small flock of girls waiting for a lift, races homeward. All at once it strikes him again as something marvelous that he's going to be in Sinai this very day, and back tonight.

Arriving, he delves into the mailbox downstairs as if in breathless expectation of long-awaited, unknown tidings; inspects his wife's letters and returns them to the box, runs quickly over his own unimportant stuff and tears it up as he climbs the stairs. He enters the silent flat, makes straight for the kitchen, warms up the food he's prepared for himself earlier in the week, its charred flavor getting nastier every day. Then he clears the table, washes up, enters the bedroom to collect his army gear and is startled to find her still asleep in the half-light, at the same nocturnal slant across the bed, her expression peaceful as though time has stood still. What's happened? He feels a fleeting urge to wake her, to ask, but what's it to him, after all. If she were dead and done with, but her deep breaths ripple through the room. A glass of water stands at the bedside and sleeping pills show up white in the darkness. He collects his army clothes – khaki pants, old leather jacket, gray shirt, high boots; undresses, moves around a little in his underwear, makes some noise, but she doesn't move, her uncovered feet pale marble. Briefly, absently, desire stirs. But the sun piercing the clouds kindles cracks between the lowered blinds, casts arrows of light at him. He raises the blinds partly to see the sky swept clear, glances at the quiet street, at the children returning from school. He waits awhile and then his son appears round the corner too, alone, trudging uphill, weighed down by the heavy satchel. And with a surge of love for him he lowers the blind softly, puts on his clothes, sticks an old hat on his head, takes his army bag and rushes out.

He meets the child downstairs, flushed, worn out by his school day, bruised here and there with the fights he's been getting into lately. He pulls him close, smooths his hair, adjusts disheveled clothing and showers instructions upon him. What to eat, what to do, what to tell his mother if she asks about him. He has flown to Sinai to lecture at a missile base and he'll be back tonight. The kid doesn't take in either the flight or Sinai, only the missiles. A smile lights up in his eyes. Real missiles? You bet. But don't wake her up. If anyone phones tell them Daddy's out, Mummy's asleep. That's all. The kid listens, keeps nodding his head, saying yes, all right, all right, already looking forlorn. And now the lecturer takes him in his arms, kisses him, and the boy stands still, lowers his head, odd how he freezes these days, blushes even when kissed by his father. And now the sky clouds over again too, and a few drops fall and cease at once, as if by way of experiment, and he hurries to his car, on his way to the airport.

4

He watches Tel Aviv tilt slowly sideways, seesawing, as though straining to turn over, then clouds drop swiftly on top of it, and then it starts to sink, is covered by the sea; gray-green, turbulent sea, nipped by winds, whipped to feathery crests. Now it's all sea as far as the skyline. And what is left of the sky? A welter of murky light. A dubious spring.

He opens his old student-case-turned-army-bag and inspects its contents. The poetry volume he has received this morning and stuffed in here at the last moment, headache pills, sleeping pills, pep pills, tobacco pouch, a rotting apple from his previous lecture, razor blades, and finally the pages of his lecture in a crushed roll, notes written in outsize script. 'Zionism in Confrontation with Other Ideologies', 'The Israeli as Jew', 'The Face of Israeli Society under Drawn-Out Struggle'. He invariably picks his subject at the last moment, going by his mood, by the noise around him, the quality of the light on the upturned faces before him, the distance home. Sometimes he comes, talks fluently for an hour without interruption, and departs as soon as he's finished. At other times he stirs up a discussion, trumps up imaginary problems, and start arguing with stubborn composure.

And meanwhile the plane keeps steadily on its western course, the engines at full power, the coastline long vanished, as though they were heading for Europe, not for the desert. Yet before long it will veer, start the broad curve backwards, inland.

He is the only civilian aboard. The soldiers have removed their caps, shoved their weapons under the upholstered seats, settled down to rustle newspapers, solve crossword puzzles, converse in low voices. The girl sitting next to him, a small delicate girl-soldier, huddles against the window with her evening paper as if afraid he'll touch her, just wants to talk a little, exchange a few words, without hope, without expectations. He is still unsure of his liberty. His relations with women are clumsy. He gives up in advance.

Over her head he watches the slow return of the land avidly. Dunes, houses, fields, last orchards strung out over sallow hills. The sky is clear, and the sun which had been hidden all morning is there, sailing ahead of them in its full glory. The throb of the engines and the dry summery heat are sleep-inducing, and all around him heads drop, eyes, glaze over druggedly. He tries to sleep a little himself but is still too eager, his eyes searching the slow-moving desert landscape below him for novelties. The pipe is heavy in his hand. Gently he catches the evening paper slipping at him from the other seat, then the feather-light body of the girl-soldier who seems to have relaxed her guard, leaning against him drowsily as the plane dips; a hairpin drops into his lap. softly his lust awakens, and all of a sudden he conceives a provocative, subversive lecture – at a missile base of all places, before the pick of the army.

And now they are deep into the desert, the soldiers are coming to life, the girl beside him pulls away too, opens her eyes and blinks away a tear. He holds out the paper and she smiles vacantly, touching her hair which has come loose.

'When are we going to get there?' he asks, handing back the hairpin as well.

She throws a swift glance at the aimless, amorphous mass of desert:

'We're there already . . .'

It's true. The roar of the engines is falling off, the plane has begun to lose height, and as they hover above the runway he still sees nothing but wasteland, his eyes on the window drinking in every detail, thrilled to discover the row of bright hook-nosed fighter-bombers.

'Phantoms . . .' he identifies them with that curious excitement that all weapons rouse in him these days.

'Just painted dummies . . .' The delicate girl-soldier smiles, stares at him as though only now really noticing him. 'Have you never been here before?'

'Well, yes, in '56 . . . just for a few hours .. somewhere around here . . .'

'In '56?' she repeats, puzzled. 'What happened in '56?'

'The Sinai Campaign. I was dropped here by parachute, on one of these hills.'

The plane comes to a stop and there is a general bustle of rising, donning caps, slinging up guns, crowding to the exit. A stewardess, who has kept herself well out of sight during the trip, stands by the door dressed in a colorful uniform, bestows a personal smile on each passenger, bids them goodby as though they were vactioners arrived at a holiday camp. He inches forward behind the girl-soldier, his eyes on the nape of her neck, but once on the field he loses her, as usual, with not even a parting word.

5

A desert airfield, people milling about, a kind of Wild West. Dozens of vehicles by the fence like a line of hackney coaches waiting for fares. Station wagons, jeeps, vans, lorries, half-tracks, even an old tank sent especially to pick up two soldiers.

Tired, needled by a thin headache, his dead pipe bitter in his mouth, he wanders about the emptying field, the old briefcase in one hand and in the other the reels of a motion picture he's been given at the airport to pass on to the local education officer. It is the film in a thin black suitcase which attracts the attention of a dark skinny soldier to him. He approaches at a slouch, carrying a bulky transistor radio held together by string, and intoning an Egyptian hit parade in a shaky whine. He holds out a scrap of paper with the lecturer's name slightly misspelled in a soft, feminine handwriting.

'Yes, that's me . . .'

The soldier crumples the note and drops it as though relieved of a heavy burden, leads the way to a big empty truck, and with the transistor on the seat between them pouring out its tunes they drive slowly across a large bustling camp.

And already he is questioning the driver.

'Going straight to the battery?'

'No, only as far as command.'

'And where's the battery?'

'Not far . . .'

'Figure I'll make it back tonight?'

'Sure.'

'And who're the men there?'

'Regulars.'

'All high school graduates?'

'Not all . . . What you lecturing about?'

'Oh, I don't know . . . I'll make up my mind when I get there . . . maybe I'll let the men choose .'

He always prefers not to reveal his subjects in advance. They appear old-fogyish at first sight, heavy, off-putting . . .

'Give 'em a talk on drugs,' the driver suggests magnanimously. 'Know about drugs?'

'Drugs?' says the lecturer, faintly amused.

'Yeah. Couple of weeks back I brought them a lecturer on drugs . . . Guys loved it . . .'

'So what do you want another lecture for?'

'Why not? . . . it's interesting . . . like maybe about other kinds of drugs . . .'

The lecturer smiles to himself, a trickle of sweet smoke escaping his lips.

'Do the men take drugs?'

'Bet they'd like to . . .'

And all around a land of great drought, hills and copper mounds and army garbage, shacks, structures, and vehicles driving about, to the left and right of them, crossing in front, overtaking every which way. And from time to time they are made to stop at a rope barrier, one end held by a dark-skinned fellow, the driver's counterpart, lolling in a frayed wicker chair, a soldier twisted and paralyzed with idleness.

'Where you going?'

'Lemme through.'

'Where you going?'

'None of your bloody business. Lemme through . . .'

'Where you going?'

'To 612. So lemme through, dammit . . .'

But the other makes no move, sprawls full length, a wicked little grin on his face.

'What you got there?'

'None of your business. Lemme through.'

'What you got there?'

'Lecturer.'

And the rope drops before them.

6

And the truck rolls on, reaches a small service base, turns around a square and pulls up beside a piece of sculpture hatched by an unequivocal military mind. The torn rust-eaten tail of an Egyptian aircraft whose dim, slightly furry cracks gape at the missile which smashed into it and which has been resurrected here now, painted gaily and inscribed with biblical verses torn out of context.

'This is where I'm to drop you . . .' The driver bangs the radio to silence it and flits away, drawn like a butterfly to a bunch of soldiers kicking at a ball in a far corner of the camp. Ah, well, he is used to being transferred like this, handed on from one person to the other, one car to the next, sometimes left in a dim barrack, a communication trench, a storeroom, to wait till his listeners are rounded up for him.

He alights from the truck, strolls about the grounds, still with briefcase in one hand and film in the other; wanders between two rows of reddish prefabs, in the glaring light, stark summer light from an azure sky; inspects his surroundings as one who doesn't belong to this desert, this dull expanse of low shapeless hills, the incoherent mixture of a great dead hush and camp-noises – the roar of tanks, shouts, and windblown commands.

He takes a turn round the sculpture, taps the missile lightly and hears the echoing hollowness, peels a strip of metal from the shattered tail and is amazed at the ease with which the aircraft crumbles up between his fingers. Fifteen minutes pass and he is still alone. No one is coming for him. He approaches the playing soldiers, watches the brown bodies shiny with sweat pursue the ball in silence, in seeming fury. By now he can no longer even pick out his driver, who has doffed his shirt too and joined the game. He stands there puffing at his pipe and presently there is a faint stirring on the barren ground between his feet, a thin flurry of sand starts up as though a storm were about to arise from the earth. And as always in moments of waiting he already bemoans the time lost, confident that if he were seated in the library now he would be able to concentrate. The outline of the hills sharpens slightly. No one comes. They have forgotten him. Though why should he care, he is going back tonight whatever happens, they'll simply have to get him out of here. Still, he *would* like to deliver his lecture, feels a desire to speak, to speak without interruption, break a silence of several days. He returns to the truck, sounds a few brief blasts on the horn, walks over to one of the barracks, starts knocking at doors, one door, another, a third, and finds himself face to face with a gray elderly colonel who appears to have surrounded himself with missiles: models of missiles glowing in the afternoon light, diagrams of missiles on the wall, photographs of them in action. An ideology of missiles.

The man hasn't noticed his hesitant entry, sits bent over a manual, absorbed in his reading.

'Excuse me . . .' holding the call-up order.

The colonel looks up, removes his glasses, reaches for the order with smooth, almost effeminate hands, barely glances at it.

'No, that's not here . . . you want Ginger . . .'

'Ginger?'

'The education officer . . . Lecturers are her domain .'

And he points at the barracks across the road, hands back the order.

The lecturer retreats slowly, looking at the little missiles set out like toys on the shelves, longs to touch them, does touch them with his fingertips.

The colonel watches him curiously.

'What do you lecture about?

And he flounders on the doorstep, sticks his pipe in his mouth, chews the stem, removes it. Well, he hasn't quite made up his mind yet – as though anyone cared, as though there were some intrinsic flaw about his subjects – well, let's say, something about Jewish identity, or some brief outline if Israeli society under drawn-out struggle. Or maybe, for instance, Zionism in confrontation with other ideologies, with the New Left for example. Depends on the audience. He won't mind just letting them ask him questions, anything that may occur to them, and he'll do his best to answer.

The officer appears somewhat taken aback, as though these subjects of his were rather peculiar, as though there were something original or faintly shocking about them to give him some grounds for concern.

'Do you still want to get back tonight too?' he asks.

'They promised I would . . .' He is seized by a sudden fear they mean to detain him. 'The last plane . . . Do you think I won't make it?'

'You will.'

And now he's in a hurry, shuts the door behind him, crosses the grounds, stops at a door, knocks, pushes it open, enters a darkened, chaotic room, something between office and a girl's sanctum, and discovers by the light from the door, in the faint musty smell, a bed and a tangle of fiery red hair. A girl, a giant of a girl, a great redhead lying on her stomach under a blanket. Her clothes are all over the place, shirt and blue skirt, underwear in a heap beside a military phone. Filthy coffee cups, an empty wine bottle, a carpet of sunflower seed shells on the floor.

Wearily he touches her. He could have lifted the blanket and lain down silently by her side till this evening would end and the hour of his departure came, but he only touches her, lightly, embittered.

'You Ginger? . . .' he asks, his own reflection looking at him out of two large blue eyes open on his face, and hands her the crumpled call-up order. 'I'm the lecturer. I'm due at 612.'

He already says '612' as if it were a familiar place, as if

he'd moved among the batteries here for years.

She smiles, takes the order, stuffs it under her pillow unread.

'So you've arrived . . .'

'I arrived half an hour ago. I've just been hanging around here, and I've got to get back tonight. We'll never make it this way.'

'We will.'

Again she smiles at him, a wide provocative grin, still under her blanket, naked no doubt. He smiles back, embarrassed, unnerved by his own smile. Such a giantess. Even if he had the time she'd be impossible for him. Stuck there in the silence he waits for her to emerge out of her blanket.

But she lies there still, her eyes laughing.

'We will, if you'll let me get dressed.'

The blood rushes to his face as he turns to leave the dim room, the carpet of shells whispering underfoot. He leaves the door open, goes to the square, paces up and down beside the sculpture, very excited; and sees the flash and dazzle of white springing up there in the darkness he has left behind. She continues dressing at her leisure while he is already on his way back to her, not taking his eyes off, boldly, openly. And when she appears in the doorway, in a childish, much too short skirt, in sandals, zipping up a windbreaker with faded captain's insignia, he is already there beside her, eyes raised to her face:

'Mind if I just make a phone call?'

'Homesick already? . . .'

'No . . . something . . . it's just . . . I only . . .'

She puts him on her still warm bed, gets him a line and goes out. And at home the child picks up the receiver, and is joined by all the roar of the desert.

'Yoram, it's Daddy,' he shouts into the trembling, breathing line.

But the boy fails to recognize the distorted voice.

'Daddy's away, Mummy's asleep,' he hears the steady, disciplined voice through the turmoil.

'This is Daddy . . . Can't you hear me?' he cries desperately.

But the child is gone and the roaring desert is gone with him and the line goes dead, and someone in the middle of another conversation, very near apparently, lips soft cajoling words of love at him.

And the redhead in the doorway, a pillar of fire, stands calmly observing his struggles with the phone.

'Finished?'

7

Actually he ought to go home at once, to the child wandering about there by himself, ought to shake the sleeping woman who must be out of her mind. Instead of which he climbs into the battered, dirty jeep driven up by the girl, its floor strewn with yet more sunflower shells, mingling with machine gun bullets, food tins whose wrapping has come off, gummy sweets sticking to military documents, a huge white brassiere between cans of lubricant. A mixture of war apparatus and feminine paraphernalia. And only now sitting close to her, bending to put the briefcase and film between his feet, does he notice that she isn't so young anymore; the slightly bowed shoulders, the resignation to her oversize self. Maybe she signed on as a regular imagining that here, in this reddish desert, she'd be less conspicuous. His glance travels coolly over the large thighs, the pale flesh not taking a tan, yet affecting. What's growing here? This young generation, he thinks, amazed and faintly repulsed, his eyes on her enormous feet against the pedals. She waits for his eyes to complete their inspection and then smiles at him sadly, as if all too familiar with her self; lifts a hand to smooth her hair, glowing crown of thorns, then starts the jeep savagely.

But drives slowly, as though sleepy still, circles the sculpture twice as though lost in thought, then turns onto a pot-holed road that lies straight as an arrow in front of them. And beyond the dusty windscreen lies the dreary desert, low bleak hills, sand dunes; a stale, vapid landscape with its stubborn bushes growing under a layer of dust. This wearisome, war-worn desert, good for nothing except strategical vantage – even the approaching twilight hour cannot soften it.

'This landscape . . . so depressing . . .' he says, to break the silence, to make contact. For a moment she appears not to have heard, but then the jeep comes to a stop, in the middle of the empty road. She eyes him quizzically.

'You find the landscape depressing?'

This sudden braking, the direct question, as if it were a personal matter – his, or hers; as if there were any particular significance to what he says.

'Why does it depress you?'

He smiles, taken aback, the sun full in his face. They are alone in the sun, in space, all the army camps have long vanished behind them, and only the slow whirring of the engine accompanies the stuttered words he forces out in explanation. She listens tensely, her glance shifting from him to the scenery and back, as if anything could be done about it, as if the scenery were open to change or amendment.

'I suppose I've got used to it . . .' she says apologetically, 'I find it beautiful . . .'

And then softly, with absurd politeness:

'I'm sorry . . .'

'It's not your fault . . .' he laughs, shrinks in his seat, graceless, knowing himself to be graceless. In his embarrassment he discovers a whole sunflower seed among the debris of shells, picks it up, cracks it, chews absently, waits to be in motion again, and slowly they drive on, still in second gear, crawling along the rough road as though they had all the time in the world, and it is nearly six, and he still has a lecture to give and get home again.

Another silence, and she still smiling at him, as though she wanted something from him, this titanic redhead bent over the wheel, her hair brushing the canvas roof flapping in the wind, while he stares at the hills round him, avoiding her eyes. A distant memory flickers through his mind.

'Have you never been here before?'

'Yes I have . . .' he replies quickly.

And once again the jeep stops, as if she couldn't talk while driving, as if his words called for careful study, at a standstill.

'I was here in '56.'

'When?'

'In the Sinai Campaign.'

'Lecturing too?'

'No, of course not!' He grins – the idea! 'I was dropped somewhere around here, on one of these hills. Maybe even that one there . . .' pointing at a hill on the near skyline which is slowly turning crimson.

She listens thoughtfully, her hands in her lap. He is never going to give that lecture.

'Every lecturer who comes here goes on about some battle or other he took part in . . . Once we had one – told stories, talked my head off, in the end it turned out he was talking about the First World War.'

'The *Second* . . .' he corrects her.

'The *First*,' she insists. 'Me too, I thought he must mean the Second World War. He didn't seem that old . . .'

He doesn't answer, looks away, beginning to lose his patience. The girl's muddleheaded.

'I didn't hurt your feelings, did I?'

Her voice, very gentle.

'No.' Startled, he looks at her sitting beside him, hands loose in her lap, smiling sweetly at him. And with a jolt the jeep starts again and the pipe slips from his hand, drops to the floor, rolls under the pedals. He bends but she forestalls him, picks it up, but instead of placing it in his outstretched hand she thrusts it between his lips in an intimate gesture, and he smells her, covertly, the smell of a big queer animal. So that's her game, is it?

And now he is faintly excited. And they drive on in silence at the same slow nerve-racking pace, approach the crimson hills, and he's afraid to say a word or she'll stop again and this journey will never end, while by now he is bent on giving this lecture, passionately, an ache in his chest. The twilight, the lengthening shadows, the emptiness around. In this desert, this Sinai – this is where he wants to speak. Where are they? The people, the nation. To stand before them, hear the buzz, the murmuring, the creaking of chairs or stones. Briskly to pull the sweater over his head, fling it over a chair or on the ground, remove his wristwatch, place the notes in front of him, and start speaking as a first caress, in a sweet voice soon to harden. To envelop them, penetrate the veil of lethargy and seep through their attention, drive in the words at an ever-quickening rhythm, and see them surrender, eyes shining, mouth opening in surprise, in resistance, then in a smile of pleasure. Till he is quite becalmed, starts retreating, drawing himself out of them, lightly smoothes over final questions, dabs at the sweat, leaves a few question marks, a few vague promises for the future, smiles self-consciously, gathers up the notes, the watch, pulls on the sweater and gets out.

The jeep picks up speed with a humming of air through the wheels. He looks at the approaching hills, first clouds looming in the distance.

'Is the Canal visible from here? . . .' he asks unthinkingly, half to himself, and at once regrets the question. But she hasn't heard, or at any rate doesn't stop but drives on, only turns the wheel a bit, leaves the road, sweeps onto a dirt-track and without slowing down, without shifting gear, in one rush, starts climbing a hill, at an ever steeper angle, regardless of any track, straight up as if aiming for the sky. Flintstones catapult from the plunging wheels. A bare waste all round, no sign of a house, a missile, a man.

'This it?' Wearily he climbs out of the jeep, looks for the missiles, but he's already used to finding his listeners hidden behind ridges and down dry riverbeds.

'Not yet. You wanted to see the Canal.'

'Oh, never mind, thanks, it's getting late,' and he turns back to the jeep.

'Come here . . .'

Calls him like a dog.

And the sense of freedom gripping him suddenly—

8

An unexpectedly strong wind is blowing here. He holds onto his hat, bows his head, but the wind tugs at him, winds come from every side and pounce on him as though they had lain in wait. Ten past six already. The sky has darkened, the light grown murky. The last plane back is at nine. She'll have to see that he gets there, this redhead. First he's had to wake her up and now she chooses to go gallivanting about the hills with him. She's taken a fancy to him, apparently. He follows her over the rocky hillside polished by the winds to a pale sickly pink. Great big strides she takes, bobbing up and down, hunched with long habit of minimizing her tall stature. Her hair blazes in front of him. But a few hours ago he was still sitting in the university reading room, a feeble, woolgathering intellectual; and now here he is – far from human habitation, hundreds of miles to the south, on a hill of stone, clambering after this pillar of fire who does as she pleases. What does she want of him? Could she want him to make love to her in the short time left to his lecture? Perhaps other lecturers before him had made love to her here. He shivers, his eyes on her strong feet, sapphire flashing white over rock.

They reach the top in a few minutes. It isn't a very high

hill, there are higher ones around, but it looks out straight at a gap in the mountain ridge ahead and a wide horizon beyond. Breathlessly he catches up with her, and she points out the Canal to him, far away to the west. A brief, alarming glitter of blue. The sun is going down over the coasts of Egypt. And distant objects – rocks, hillocks,, bushes – seem to float in the air by a trick of the falling light. She is standing very close to him, a full head taller, his hair grazing her captain's bars. Her freckled face smiles at him again.

'Still depressed by the landscape?' – as to a small child she speaks to him.

'Less so . . .' He laughs, knocks out his pipe hard against a stone. Could he touch her? He steps up on a low rock to poise himself over her, suddenly thinks of his wife and son.

'Maybe it's here they dropped you?'

Maybe.

A brief silence.

'What're you going to lecture about?'

'If we ever get there, you mean?' he asks, irony in his voice, and resignation.

'Why shouldn't we?'

And once again he flounders through his catalogue of subjects. His eyes on the ground, he starts listing the various possibilities in a low voice. The face of society in drawn-out struggle, or – The Israeli's Jewishness, or even – Zionism in confrontation with other ideologies. To provoke a discussion or something. Occasionally they just ask questions, anything that comes into their mind, and he answers.

She hears him out evenly, her eyes on the setting sun, as though his words didn't touch her, as though they swerved and fell on the rocks about her. He grins, stoops to pluck a leaf from a scorched, dusty balsam bush at his feet, notices a scrap of torn fabric, and further down a couple of rusted windworn jerrycans, the loose chain of a tank, a soot-blackened square of canvas, empty food tins, smashed munition crates – the relics of a vanquished army camp coming to light on the stony soil as on a strip of exposed ocean floor.

'Have they heard all that stuff before?' he asks with a surge of unreasonable despair.

She climbs up on a rock, looks down kindly at him, acts as though she still had all the time she might want, and all of a sudden he feels as though an eternity had passed since he came here, and he looks at the horizon and a sense of peace comes over him as well. Forget about the lecture and touch her, just touch her and the words will come later. And promptly he is gripped by excitement, stoops over the bush again to break off a sprig, to smell, to chew something, rouse himself, and then he notices that the bush at his feet isn't a bush at all but a heap of half-buried old clothes growing out of the earth. A crumbling tunic, a riddled, rust-eaten water canteen attached to an outworn military belt, a pair of mildewed trousers. He kicks at them lightly and starts, flinches, looks again, appalled. These are the remains of a human body, how come he didn't notice before? An ancient Egyptian soldier hidden in the sand, a hastily buried corpse, pale gray bones marking out a vanished form.

He looks up at her, and she, casually:

'That used to be the lecturer on Zionism ... didn't hit it off with the men ... annoyed them ...'

Vainly he scans her face for a smile. Still grave, she points at the tumble of canvas and smashed crates.

'And that's the lecturer on Israeli society. Failed to convince them. Too sanguine ...'

And now he laughs – a brief, muffled snort. He glances about him, leans towards her, searches her face for the smile, but she remains grave, only her eyes twinkle. Not muddleheaded after all then. He is drawn to her, points to a large smudge in the dark wadi.

'And who's that?' – teasingly.

'That one preached Jewish ethics,' she flashes back at once, 'Put everybody to sleep, including himself, and when he woke up ...'

She stops, falls silent.

The lecturer puffs at his pipe, and the smoke twirls blue in the light dying on their clothes. He hugs his briefcase closer to him, already grown restless, shivery. A star lights up in the sky and all of a sudden he loses confidence.

'Funny sort of lecturers ...' he says, trying to keep up the note of banter – here on this barren hill exposed to the vast landscape, to the distant strip of water in the west still glowing with daylight – 'dressed in those old ragged greatcoats ...'

At last she smiles.

'Yes, that's how they always come here, dressed in their oldest clothes. They figure they're being sent to the back of beyond. Show up to lecture in high boots, old briefcases, funny hats ...'

He touches his own, reddens.

'Yes . . . hat is a bit funny . . .'

Now he'll take her. Just a little courage. To hold her, suppress the slight nausea and seek the smooth tender place in her flesh, draw her mouth to him for a first kiss. He isn't going to get to that missile base tonight anyway.

He takes his hat off, throws it down, approaches her, but she slips away, starts downhill to the jeep, now a blurred mass in the fast-falling darkness. She bends down beside one of the wheels, picks something up. Stone? Skull?

'And this one imagined he could answer any question . . .'

And laughing wildly she gets in, starts.

9

And the missile base turns out to have been only a short distance away all along, on a hill dug up as an anthill, well camouflaged, none of it visible except a pinpoint of light floating high on top of a tall aerial. But as soon as they halt at the gate in the gray dust he hears the rumble – as if the entire anthill were throbbing. And beyond the barrier he sees the slowly rotating radar scanners, the huge camouflage nets, and blank, egg-shaped domes from within which one can eavesdrop on the depths of space. And meanwhile the redhead is already scolding the guards for dawdling – impatiently, loftily, as if they were to blame for her wasted time. And then they are driving uphill again furiously, raising a cloud of dust, and the throbbing around them increases, large dug-in generators producing a din and a great blast of air.

And all of it lightless, not a glimmer of light. All the lights are hidden and buried. And here finally are the missile pits, real missiles, not quite as big as he'd imagined. And the girl maneuvers along twisting roads, always aiming upwards. And now metal screens flow on both sides of them as the jeep gathers momentum, and metal-roofed communication trenches, metal steps dropping down into the earth, and gradually the ground itself becomes plated in iron. They draw up just below the crest of the hill, next to an enormous thundering generator, and she leaps out nimbly, opens some door, is sucked in by a great spill of light, leaves him standing outside, briefcase in one hand, suitcase with film in other; and after a few seconds she pops out again, comes and shouts something at him over the fearful racket, but he doesn't catch a word, smiles in utter confusion, draws nearer to her. In the end she leans over him and wrenches the suitcase from his tight grip, takes it away. The O.C. has gone off somewhere and she's going to look for him. She opens the door again and ushers him into the brilliance now, and all at once the night seems dispelled and he finds himself in the middle of a bright noonday.

10

It is the blue camouflage paint on the windows and the yellow light of bare bulbs reflected in them that has created the momentary illusion of deep, spring-sky noon.

But then it turns out to be nothing but a military office after all, or maybe Operations itself, for the walls are covered with maps and charts. Two sergeants are playing chess, the board on a camp bed between them. They glance up wordlessly as he enters, then look away again, exchange a brief smile but say nothing. Ah well, he is familiar with the slight numbness, the curious embarrassment that comes over soldiers when suddenly confronted with a lecturer. He puts his briefcase on the floor among a litter of old magazines and tattered thrillers, and sinks into a plush Egyptian armchair, piece of loot from one war or another.

Silence. Only the dull roar of the generator outside.

Crushed by the silence again he rises, starts fidgeting about the room, inspecting the roster, the missile set-up, charts marked with black circles and computer codes for every hill and mountain. Arrows point straight at the heart of Egypt, at the Nile meandering on its way into the depths of Sudan.

Now the two men are watching him.

'Won't you sit down . . .'

'That's all right . . . thanks . . .' – a little uneasy, as though caught red-handed, but continuing to look at the charts nevertheless, defiantly, as if to show he takes orders from no one, as if busy trying to make out some underlying principle there. At last he retreats, comes over to them, looks down benignly at their chessboard, stands there. A long silence.

'What's the range of these missiles?' he asks softly.

And they, evidently familiar with the question—

'Depends on your target.'

'No, I mean ... just like that ... without any target ...'

'Without a target? ...'

And he smiles to himself, gives it up, goes on watching the game; then off again, back to the charts, tries estimating their scale himself.

And then the O.C. bursts into the room: a tall young officer, skull-capped, good looking, one of those boy-soldiers, lords of the front line, who rush about the trenches always in a hurry, never sporting their rank; comes in and finds a dark, silent, square-set civilian puffing a pipe before the telltale charts, his fingers roving about Sudan.

'Yes? ...' laying a hard hand on his shoulder.

'I'm the lecturer ...' says the lecturer, grabbing the officer's hand and shaking it.

'Do we have a lecture tonight?' the officer exclaims, turning to the two sergeants questioningly, then dropping into a chair by the table.

But the pair of them just shrug their shoulders and animatedly swap knights.

The lecturer, ill at ease, draws on his pipe.

'Who brought him?'

'Ginger did,' says one of the men with a knowing little grin at his fellow, and the lecturer sees the mischievous twinkle in the officer's eye.

'Ginger? ... Where is she?'

'Went to see about the movie ... Probably looking for you.'

The officer seems flustered, picks up a short stick and begins to play with it.

'These past weeks,' he tells the lecturer as if in apology, 'we're simply being bombarded with lecturers, and they don't even bother to warn us ahead ...'

'We can drop it ... as far as I'm concerned ...'

'No, why? We'll fix something ... What do you talk about?'

And once again the lecturer, feeling a fool, starts carefully spreading his wares. Something about the situation of our universities, or maybe the Israeli's self-image, or, say, Zionism versus the New Left. He might get some argument going. Or let the men choose, let them ask questions ... anything ...

The two chess players bow their heads. The officer listens, reveals some surprise, ponders.

'Pity you can't talk on some other subject . . . Drugs, for instance . . . We had a lecturer here not long ago who did. Men were fascinated. What was he called?'

But neither of the two remembers his name, only that he'd really been great. He'd shown them samples of drugs, had burnt a bit of hash here, on this table, given them a sniff too.

'Yes . . . so I've been told . . .' says the lecturer at last, in a cold fury, controlling it, 'Sorry, but I'm no expert on drugs . . .'

A silence follows, and for a split second it again seems to the lecturer that night hasn't come yet, that the sky is still blue outside, a sweet clear summer sky.

'The color of these windows . . .' he says, 'So strange . . .'

But the officer sees nothing strange about it. Inspiration has come to him and he is taking charge:

'Had supper? No. Then go and grab something. Don't worry, I'll see you get yourself an audience that'll listen to anything you may say.'

And he sends the lecturer back into the night, and himself returns to chase the two chess players off his bed.

II

And descending the hill, on the way to mess, alone again, he takes stock of his surroundings, gazes at the missile pits, the radar scanners, the bunker entrances, the huge generators. And as he walks he meets a steady stream of soldiers coming towards him, and knows they will presently gather to hear him, and feels again the tiny thrill of anticipation. And the farther he goes the more people swarm about him – walking, standing about in groups. He looks out for the redhead, his lost pillar of fire, stops now and then at the sound of laughter. For a moment he imagines seeing her, a flash in the center of a merry crowd, but when he goes over to ask after the mess hall he discovers only a little ginger-headed soldier talking and gesturing, cracking jokes.

A bus is parked in front of the mess hall, and a newly-arrived batch of reserve soldiers wander about, in their sloppy fatigues, with their out-dated rifles, gather to arrange the watch, are already plotting ways to wangle a pass. And the mess is completely deserted, the tables bare, supper over. A graying, tired-faced cook serves him a meal of infantine food – a soft-boiled egg, cocoa, and porridge. As always, he devours his food rapidly, hungrily, the used dishes being cleared away as he eats, crumbs swept up around him.

He gets up still hungry, seeks to wash away the bitter taste in his mouth with something sweet, inquires after the canteen, goes and buys some chocolate wafers, a packet of razor blades which he puts in his pocket, starts peeling the first wafer out of its wrapper as he leaves, and drifts slowly back uphill munching. Three gray-haired reserve soldiers in cartridge belts and steel helmets stop him, wave check-lists in his face.

'You . . .' they demand, 'When's your watch?'

He smiles:

'I'm not one of you people.'

'What do you mean?'

'I mean you're wrong. I didn't come with you.'

But they refuse to let go.

'Aren't you here on reserves?'

'Not with you, though. I'm here to give a lecture.'

'A lecture? What about?'

But he remains silent.

'What do you lecture about?' they press him, disappointed, cheated out of a guard.

But he does not answer, studies the three crumpled, agitated figures in silence, does not answer.

And they wait, they still haven't grasped that he does not intend to answer them, but he is on his way already, up the slope between radar station and missile base, eating his wafers one by one, leaving a trail of tinfoil wrappings behind him in the dark, licking his chocolate-smeared fingers. Solitary – he has become a hermit of late, has fallen into the hermit's ways. He has started going to the cinema alone, has been caught talking to himself at traffic lights, to the amusement of people in nearby cars. Slowly he climbs on under the clear star-freckled sky, stops from time to time to peer at the missile pits, inspect them; the staleness of it, the hollowness, the tedium, the imminent divorce, the lone onanistic nights, the child being ground down between them. And suddenly making up his mind, casting a swift glance to ensure he is unobserved, he slips down into one of the pits to feel the missiles with his own hands. And there they are, pointed at the light horizon, stolid, their color a rosy pink. Cautiously he touches them, smoothes their flanks, is amazed to find them rather slippery, damp, as though covered in a fine film of oil or dew. He lifts a hand to the slender cone, takes hold of the fins. Such poised might. He squats and by the veiled starlight reads the numbers and letters inscribed on them, gently caresses the dark tangle of wires descending to the pad. And all at once a low buzz sounds and the entire platform with all of its five missiles stirs suddenly, veers left towards him as if to strike him. Hurriedly he flattens himself against the wall of the pit, ready to dig into it if needs be, but the platform lets go of him, swivels blindly to the right, then finally erects itself, aims upwards and stops. The buzzing lasts another few seconds and ceases. Someone is operating the missiles from afar, pointing them straight at the sky as if he meant to fire at the stars.

He picks up the fallen briefcase, climbs out pale and shaken, meets two soldiers coming down the road who look startled at the sight of a briefcase-carrying civilian emerging from a missile pit. They halt, wait for him to come up with them, grimy, his hands besmirched with missile oil.

'Who're you?' They bar his way, suddenly assuming authority, very serious.

'I'm here to give a lecture ...' he answers, putting on a frank air, a smiling face, suppressing his agitation.

'What were you looking for down there?'

'Nothing ... just wanted to see what they look like from nearby ...'

'They might have sent you sky-high, you know ...'

But that is just what I wish, he wants to tell them. His lips only turn up in a wry smile, however, and he resumes his casual walk, not to excite suspicion; saunters off to inspect other missile pits, lingers here and there, and the two soldiers stay where they are, following him with their eyes. Gradually he quickens his pace, falls straight into the hands of the officer and the girl who are waiting for him in the darkness.

'Had supper?' they ask anxiously, as if that were what he's come to Sinai for, 'Come on then, they're waiting for you ...'

And the lecturer gives himself up to them, follows the officer down steep narrow steps underground, tiny star-like lamps brushing his hair.

'Duck! . . .' he hears the officer's voice from the depth below him, and he bends his head a little and hits it hard against the ceiling.

A sharp pain stabs him. Gasping, he doubles up on the stairs, head in hands, his eyes filling with tears.

The officer turns, comes back to him, amusement in his voice.

'You too? Every damn lecturer has got to bang his head here. What's the matter with you fellows?'

But he is incapable of replying, chokes on the words, continues the descent at a stoop and enters the bunker bowing. The place is awash with a purplish light and there are instruments everywhere – a radar screen, control panels, small computer, sticks, levers, phones, wires, cables – all of it painted a greenish khaki. A low buzzing sounds from one corner.

'Here's your lecturer.'

There are only four men in the room – one at the wireless wearing a headphone, the same two chess players still at their game on a camp bed against the wall, and one other soldier, a dull, dumb face.

'Is this all?' the lecturer asks with a little laugh, he has never had such a small audience before.

'This is it.'

'Aren't you staying?'

'No . . . I've got to go . . .'

'And that girl . . .' – in despair.

'She'll come and fetch you after. You two there, break it up . . .'

One of the players freezes in mid-move.

'What's your subject?' asks the officer, but doesn't wait for a reply. 'You tell them . . .' – and is gone.

So the moment has arrived. To break the silence at long last, to start speaking. A dull ache throbs in his head. He has waited for this moment all day, has been brought from afar for its sake. Slowly he pulls the notes out of his briefcase, biding his time. Even though it's ridiculous to stand here in this dim mud-hole with four soldiers for audience and hold notes in his hand, as if he even needed them, as if he couldn't talk fluently, almost unconsciously, abandoning himself to the sweetness of his own voice, swayed by his own surreptitious, inescapable rhetoric, its slant of distortion growing as he proceeds.

The four of them watch calmly, wordlessly, no doubt used to have a lecturer dropped on them from time to time, here, between their beds, among the instruments.

Where to begin? Try something entirely new perhaps? Question them a bit about themselves. Personal questions: Who are they? What are they? How long have they to serve still? What are their plans after? Start perhaps precisely with that dumb one, who has a touch of violence about him, who needs a little sympathy perhaps, a kind word.

He takes the chair and places it in front of him, removes his watch, unbuttons his jacket, drops into the inevitable lecturer's mannerisms; rubs his hands, plans to open quietly, in a hush, now, the first phrases already welling up in him, not bearing on anything definite yet, only in due course edging towards one or another subject. What will it be this time? Perhaps the face of Israeli society in drawn-out struggle – a harsh political analysis which suddenly, towards the end, for no good reason, takes an optimistic turn. But then the lecturer catches sight of his own face on the radar screen, like a target in the grid of thin white numbered lines covering the area. Sunken eyes, a face drawn with fatigue, a mass of hair, and blood on his forehead. So there's blood. That's why the pain persists. He touches his forehead lightly, smiles at the dumb soldier. What time is it?

'Can I have some water? . . .'

The dumb one holds out a canteen.

He pours a little water over his head, then drinks some. The water soaks into the earth at his feet. He shivers a little. This silence of theirs. He approaches the instruments, smiling pleasantly. A large switch protruding from the board attracts his attention.

'What's this for?' he points at it as if it were the only one whose function he didn't know.

'To light this here up,' the dumb one answers patiently, the only one of the four to respond.

'Light it up?' the lecturer sounds puzzled, unbelieving. 'Can I?' and he pulls the switch all the way, secretly expecting a distant explosion, but all that happens is a row of little bulbs lighting up on the instrument panel. He turns them off. Emboldened by this apparent liberty to touch the instruments, his hand roves on, questing.

'Which . . . which one fires the missiles?'

'Why d'you want to know?'

'Nothing . . . just to see which button's pushed . . .'

'There's no such button . . . you don't exactly push anything either . . .'

He looks straight into the soldier's blank eyes. Is he being had? He moves back to his papers which have slipped to the floor. Here, in a bunker deep underground, in the middle of the desert, he stands opposite four soldiers and is supposed to speak to them, enliven the boredom of their long days, offer some information, possibly some ideology, best of all some faith. In short – inspire them; in return for which he is exempt from guard duty.

And now he decides to begin. There is no avoiding it any longer – he'll have to give this lecture come what may. The entire pointless, wasted day drops off him as an empty shell. Softly he embarks on the opening words. And at the same moment the signaler, too, starts speaking quietly into the mouthpiece attached round his neck; looking at the lecturer and talking to some distant person, who answers him now, who in a crisp voice reports the weather forecast, the wind force, visibility, his voice coming from a small loudspeaker fixed to the wall. And everybody strains to listen, while the signaler takes it all down in writing.

And with the return of silence the lecturer moves hesitantly back to the instruments, his embittered smile on his face.

'Can one get Tel Aviv on this too? . . .'

'Now?'

'If I may, just for a moment . . .'

The signaler rises, removes his headset, puts it over the lecturer's head, and instants later the phone is ringing at home, and the child picks it up again and his voice is clear and warm and close as if he were within arm's reach.

'Daddy's away, Mummy's asleep,' he says mechanically even before being asked.

'Yorami, this *is* Daddy . . .'

And now the child does hear him.

'Daddy?'

'Yes, this is Daddy here. Isn't Mummy up yet?'

'No.'

'Then wake her up. Go wake her up right away, you hear me?'

'Yes.'

But the child doesn't go, doesn't want to relinquish the

phone, his breaths verging on sobs.

'Yorami . . .' he whispers anxiously. The soldiers' faces are lifted up at him, following the conversation. He fondles the switches in front of him with both his free hands.

'What are you doing now?'

'Nothing.'

'Have you eaten?'

'No.'

'I'll be home soon.'

'Daddy? . . .'

'Yes.'

And all at once the child breaks down, cries from the depths of his abandonment, unable to stop, dry harsh wails, rising and swelling without interruption; and the men in the room with him smile a little, and only then he remembers they can hear it all over the loudspeaker, and he removes the weeping headset, casts about vainly, not knowing how to break the connection, till the signaler comes to his rescue and slowly the weeping recedes.

And all of a sudden he feels relieved. He abandons the idea of a lecture, collects his notes, replaces the watch on his wrist, makes to say something and changes his mind at once. Not a word will he utter. The chess players watch him briefly, quizzically, then start moving the few pieces still left on the board. The signaler picks up a screwdriver and starts taking the mouthpiece apart. Only the dumb soldier continues to stare at him, but the lecturer avoids his eyes, rummages through his briefcase, pulls out the volume of poetry received this morning, sits down, begins to read, barely taking in the shape of the letters, overcome by boredom. He is familiar enough with this clever-clever romanticism – sentimental stuff notwithstanding the ragged lines. He reads on all the same, turns the pages over wearily, his eyes almost shut. Ought to get the divorce, start a new life.

And still the dumb soldier's eyes haven't left his face. Is he still looking to him for a lecture, a revelation? He applies himself to the poems, skimming pages unhopefully; suddenly finds a wonderful poem, knows it to be so from the first line that is as a blow on the head. He reads quickly, once, then again. Three simple, lucid stanzas, each word in place, pearls on a dunghill. Maybe the fellow's pinched it from someone else? He reads it once more, then a fourth time, and it's as if it was meant for him personally. One more time he reads it, then looks up. The men in the bunker appear blurred, as if seen through a fog. And the radar screen in front of him fills with white scurrying dots, like a rash, like an air attack.

'There's something here . . .' he wishes to say to them, but no one is looking at him, each is intent on his own. Even the dumb soldier has despaired of him, has pulled a dime novel out of his pocket and sits reading it, his lips parted in excitement.

12

And at eight a shadow falls across him. The redhead stands in the doorway, has approached without making a sound and stands there tranquilly, a submachine gun over her shoulder, gazes at him seated there in the middle of the bunker, head bowed, the poetry volume on the floor at his feet.

'Finished?' she asks gently.

He makes no reply but gets up at once, stuffs the book into the briefcase, and without a word to the men in the room follows her up the steps, feeling his way, bent over, careful, but even so fully expecting to bump his head again, except that this time she waits for him beside the obstacle, lays a warm hand on the top of his head, presses it down low.

And then he is up the hill again, near the almost savage-sounding rumble of the generators, is signing a form which the skull-capped officer hands him, is looking stunned and bewildered, his clothes rumpled as though he had slept in them. Ah well, as long as he's *been* here. And a flickering light in one of the barracks reveals the audience they have deprived him of. Dozens of soldiers crowded into a smoke-filled room, absorbed in the movie he has brought. And he wants to lash out at these two here, but under his eyes she approaches the officer, kisses him, and the officer recoils slightly.

And then they are rolling down the slope, and the metal hissing under their wheels becomes earth again, the missiles and radar scanners are wiped out by the darkness as if they had never been. And the guard has changed at the gate too, and it is by elderly soldiers that they are stopped this time. The jeep escaping to freedom rouses their envy and they try to detain it, shine their flashlights into it, take down numbers, inspect papers; gray-haired, wrinkled, they fill in some form with stubborn zeal, gape at the redheaded girl behind the wheel, wink at him, and at last, reluctantly, raise the barrier.

And then they are on the arrow-straight road again, and he looks back and the missile hill is gone, only a red pinpoint floats high on a vanished aerial. And he is well content to have things dissolve like that, fade swiftly behind him. He looks at the silent girl by his side who strains over the wheel, intent on her driving, the submachine gun in her lap, her face illuminated by the glow of the headlights cast back from the road. A pale relic from another existence.

He reaches out and lightly touches her thigh.

'That hill ...' he waves a hand at the dark landscape, 'Have we passed it yet?'

'No ...' she smiles, and soon to his surprise the jeep leaves the road once more, and with the familiar sweep, without slowing down, starts the ascent.

13

And again he trails behind her, climbing rocks, wandering through small crevices, stumbling over rusty containers, tangles of canvas. By the feeble starlight he discerns the smashed munition crates, breathes the cool desert air, sees the land opening out to the coasts of Egypt, the distant Canal which even now, in the darkness, still glows with a faint incandescence.

How could he ever have forgotten this place? How come he hadn't recognized this rocky hill at once? This is where they had dropped him. He remembers it perfectly now. It had been on the fourth day of the Sinai Campaign, at night. The chief battles were virtually over, the war decided, and they had been spending all four days at a small airfield, sitting around beside an old World War II Dakota plane. On constant alert, cut off from events, disgusted at missing what seemed from afar like a grand adventure, they lounged on the asphalt at the edge of the landing strip, under the blades of the propeller, and once every few hours or so people would come and bring them yet one more machine gun, another munition crate, an intercom set, a stretcher. Their load grew bulkier and more cumbersome day by day till, towards dusk of the fourth evening, they were put on the plane which had suddenly come alive, and after a two-hour flight were dumped as a couple of live bundles of equipment in the no-man's-land between the two armies. A soft eastern breeze had carried them gently to this hill. At first they had tried to dig themselves in, then had just sat and waited tensely, shivering with cold, for the advancing troops. Towards dawn they had come under heavy fire from the very unit they were expecting. It took several minutes till contact was made and the shooting stopped. One of them was killed. Presently the riflemen arrived in person, gay and noisy, drunk with their swift advance through the vanquished desert. They took away the supplies and munitions, bundled him into a jeep with the dead body and sent him back to the rear. For a long time after he had still gone around feeling cheated.

'How did the lecture go?' She is standing a few paces away from him with her gun, watches his excited prowling among the rocks.

He stops, looks at her.

'The lecture?' he grins a little as if in recollection. 'There wasn't any after all . . . I kept silent . . .'

'You did, did you?'

'Yes, why not? I'm sure my predecessors said all there was to say. What more could I add?'

She laughs, appears relieved.

He approaches her.

'I mean, what's the point? Just talk for the sake of talking? Invent fake problems? Even though I could have . . .'

And suddenly he slumps on a rock at her feet, knocks his pipe out on a stone, sick at heart, stubborn.

'And I thought you'd fallen asleep,' she says.

He doesn't answer. It's as if a dam had burst in him. Hands thrown wide he touches a bush, bits of fabric, metal scraps; lies back among the shapeless debris around him, lowers his head carefully to the ground, looks at the rapid motion of the sky which is growing bleary behind a thin mist. Above him the ugly freckled face with the red crown of thorns. The sadness of it. He closes his eyes.

'This lecturer ought to be buried . . . mustn't leave him lying like that . . . there aren't going to be any more wars here . . .'

'Are you sure?' she says mockingly.

'I've seen the vast power ... touched the missiles ... Who could ever break through? ...'

'We ought to get moving ...' he hears her say.

But he doesn't want to move, he digs in, clings to the last of his liberty, is ready to stay the night in the desert, perhaps even deliver the missed lecture. And he – even his name she does not know.

But she doesn't care about his undelivered lecture, she wants to get rid of him, approaches the prostrate lecturer, touches him, tries to raise him, and he, as in a dream, bends and kisses her large foot, white sapphire no longer immaculate to his lips but filthy, filling his mouth with sand. And now she recoils, tries to shake him off, drags him along the ground a pace, pulls him up, and he feels the power in her, in her strong hands.

'You'll miss your plane ...'

14

The steps are all but dropped away under his feet, and he has no sooner got on the plane than it starts to roll as if his boarding had set it in motion. And once again he is the only civilian, and the soldiers, bare-headed and well-behaved, sit quietly rustling their papers, not even glancing at the late-comer. And he sinks at once on a vacant seat in the rear, fastens the seat-belt, watches the torches disappear on the runway one by one, and is already growing bored again, jumps up in his everlasting restlessness to find someone to sit by. And towards the front he discovers the gray head of the battery commander he talked to a few hours ago at the service base. He slips in beside him with a nod and a smile, but the colonel fails to recognize him, reads on, in the same manual still, with the same absorption. The lecturer waits awhile, then lays a tentative hand on the colonel's shoulder. The other starts.

'You don't remember me. I'm the lecturer.'

'What lecturer?'

'At the battery – 612.'

The man removes his glasses, stares at him as if he were seeing a ghost.

'You? ... You got back from there? ...'

'Yes. . .'

And they listened to you?'

'Certainly. In perfect silence. I had a hard time getting them to let me go.'

'You're lucky. They're pretty tough with lecturers as a rule.'

'Not with me, though. They were wonderful. Showed me the view, took me to the missile pits, spread out charts, showed me round the control rooms, the instruments, the radar, everything ... explained how things worked ... I nearly fired a missile myself . . .'

The colonel seems bothered, frowns. The lecturer's hands which are black with oil, the mud on his clothes, his flushed face and the blood on his forehead, and on top of that the shrill note that has crept into his voice—

'A wonderful experience to see that vast might . . . and the perfect camouflage . . . not a pinpoint of light . . .'

And beyond the window, between sky and dark desert, he suddenly discovers himself, sailing serenely through space, his features heavy, weary, the day-old stubble like a grayish vapor on his cheeks, stars entwined in his hair.

'There's just one thing I didn't quite get' – still clinging to the elderly officer – 'What depth do these missiles reach? . . .'

'What range, you mean.'

'Range. Of course: range.'

'Depends what exactly you're aiming at.'

'The maximum . . .' says the lecturer with sudden heat.

But the colonel waxes impatient:

'No. What it is you want to hit.'

'No, I mean – just at random . . . not to hit anything.'

'If it's not to hit you don't fire.'

The lecturer bows his head. No chance they'll ever understand him. And meanwhile the colonel is already engaged in getting rid of him, puts his glasses back on, returns to the manual and becomes engrossed in it again. And down below lights spring up from the emptiness, more and more lights. Signs of habitation, villages, lamplit roads, intersections, light upon light; and then there is the sea, and the shore, and Tel Aviv coming up at them.

And the doors open, everyone getting up, and the colonel swiftly escaping from him; and he is the last to step off the plane and finds it is raining outside. A spring rain is sweeping the town. And all at once he is reluctant to go home, wanders a little about the wet deserted airfield, turns to the emptying terminal and finds a telephone under a leaking booth-top, rain slanting in at him.

'It's me,' he tells his wife who picks up the receiver, 'You hear me—'

'Yes.'

And again, the chill—

'What happened? Where's the kid?'

'Asleep.'

'Managed to wake you up finally, did he? . . .'

'No . . . I found him asleep in front of the television set.'

The child wandering about by himself all afternoon. In the end they'll kill him between them.

'What happened? What happened to you?' he flares up, rain lashing at him, a headache starting.

'What do you want now . . .'

Her remoteness, her loathing.

'I've been in Sinai, at a missile base. I rang up several times. What happened to you? What made you sleep like that? Nearly all day . . .'

She remains silent.

'You hear me?' his voice softening all at once.

'Yes.'

'Look, is something the matter?'

'What's it to you.'

This endless privation, the unchanging hostility. Perhaps she even attempted suicide. So the war's still on. Whereas he would suddenly be willing to yield, to forgive. The headache mounts. The dead pipe in his hand drips wetly. He sways a little under the leaking roof. But he shall go home prepared to give battle.

Translated by Miriam Arad

Two Poems   *by* Moshe Dor

OCTOBER 1973

this morning in the circle of the sky strange
Birds pass. Don't hesitate: note seasons
And directions. The circle of the sky
Is ripped this morning by strange
Cries. Don't hesitate: note
Sounds and movements, Strange trees
Reach up this morning to the circle of the sky. Don't
Hesitate: note outline and colouring. Not for days
Will it be inscribed, neither on the sand nor on water, how
     war
Embraces the sky with the thin hands of pain, how
The morning, in clarity, increases despair and hope
In their simplicity. Don't hesitate,
You who compulsively count roots and light-years:
This morning in the circle of the sky strange
Birds pass.

REVOLUTIONS SPLIT MEN

Revolutions split men.
Stones stay whole, calm
In their cold completeness, between burnt orchids
With their identity.

From the top of Cabo Giraño, under the umbrella-pines, the
     sea
Attracts to a desirable end. Men are
Split, and can get broken. The endurance of stones
Is not theirs.

Recomeçar ... Let's start over from the beginning.

                              Madeira, Autumn 1974

                         Translated by Arthur C. Jacobs

Three Poems   *by* Amir Gilboa

I

I go on disappearing from myself and suddenly I see
myself walking ahead of me. If only I could cry.
No laughs no tears. Sad enough for tears. And I whisper to
myself oh my brother my brother. And my brother goes
        ahead
of me and bears
my face. His eyes in my eyes. And my being
in my non-being. And where shall we go. And we are over
a great abyss.

2

Those who know what's in heaven do not tell they
only dream visions and hear words
in the deep cellars they carry with them
and when they go out among people they are not noticed
only the blind ask them for help crossing the road
and the deaf long to read the right time from their lips
on the other hand the children don't want or ask anything
        from them
but look into and after them and dream visions
and hear words and the rest of their lives
recall a miracle they never tell

and always want to tell.

3

I knew in the dream the dream wouldn't fly like a dream.
I knew in the dream that in me myriads are dreaming the
        dream.
I woke. Midnight. Who turns the dark of night into the light
        of day?

And the sun stands still in the window in the dream as on
    that day in Gibeon I recall.
Look, here comes the night that is day and not night
and the endless day comes in the midst of night. And it will
    never darken.
And morning light glows. I wake. Look, here before me,
    Jerusalem.
And I see it. I see it with myriads of eyes.
Was there ever anything like this
a dream dreamed at the same time
by myriads while they dream.

From *To Write The Lips of Those Asleep*

Translated by Shirley Kaufman
with Shlomit Rimmon

Meir Wieseltier

A Dream of Death as an Angel

People wearing white linen robes
eating olives and sesame
reading scrolls
in walled cities
in forests
on pillows on stones,

dreamed the day of their passing

in the shape of an angel who comes
from the wall or tree
the knife
in his hand
makes explanations superfluous.

They go with him they don't complain
or they ask wait awhile
till I make provisions for my household
till I finish
my work
then you'll lay your hand on me.

And in special cases
found in the writings
it's possible to debate with him
to say you're early
go and return
in a couple of months, in a year,

for even an angel of destruction like him
retreats when he's faced with the facts
with a truth about life
nor dares
to presume
if there's substance in what a man says:

he goes as he came
returns some other time
from the wall or tree
the gleam from the knife
in his hand
shines like the shining of heaven.

Translated by Shirley Kaufman
with Shlomit Rimmon

Shlomo Nitzan

A Stolen Hour

(A chapter from a novel of modern Israel)

> *the hour*
> *that is not war*
> *and is not death*
> *that hour*
> *is a stolen hour*

*The setting is Tel Aviv and its outskirts, against a back-
ground of two or three generations of wars. Several boldly
contrasted characters emerge, each typical in a different way
of the people of Israel today, so that the reader is offered an
insight into the origins, the motivations and the way of life
of private persons behind wartime headlines.*

*The action revolves around Dita, a young war widow
whose husband's body has never been found, and Mike, his
enigmatical and contradictory twin brother. A strange love
develops betwen these two, for caught as they are between
the past and the present in a dilemma they can neither
escape nor endure, the conflict within themselves and with
one another cannot be resolved.*

FORBIDDEN thoughts. Hide, quickly. Hide from them but
hide, too, so as to be free to think. But where? Here? In this
exposed and tumultuous human wilderness? In the street?
In the bus? All those people ... The eyes, all those eyes.
Each of his movements, the lightest and the slightest,
trapped and caught in their network at once – I am totally
trapped in this place. Or perhaps not? Then where? Let me
get out of this, quickly. Out. Out! But where to? Where can
I find some nowhere of a place?

To be swallowed up into the bowels of the city at night.
Muddy, turbid bowels choked by teeming crowds lit up by
flashes here and flashes there, multitudes like holidaymakers
charging on to the pavements and into the coffee-houses,

lights in passing cars crossing with lights from the bright shop-windows all along the street with street-lamps glowing inside the green tree tops far beyond the traffic-lights red and green and yellow. Beyond them, beyond them, to hide and to be hidden. – Here at last, as if into the heart of this anonymous hiding-place: four walls and a closed door and a little window high up on the wall, open only for air.

Because the room was so very small its walls looked tall, taller than normal walls. Here was a bed and here was a table and this was all he wanted. To judge by the tiny window it must once have been a bathroom. To judge by its general appearance it was obviously the hide-out of a fugitive on the run. Who were Mike's pursuers? Perhaps his own thoughts that would not stay outside, that would insist on crossing the threshold with him and coming into his room. Far from giving him peace, the sound of his thoughts is louder than ever here, reverberating, even deafening in this tiny room cut off from the rest of the house, so utterly removed from the world, floating on its own beyond the city and beyond all boundaries and out towards unattainable places ardently longed for in vain.

Two cameras hung from hooks on the wall. A third, the one he had been using today, lay on the chair by the bed.

Here those forbidden thoughts of his were free to come out and display themselves. As in a secret hiding-place. Free of their prison at last, they could now openly display the ugly truth that they held, mean and trivial and shameless. For being what it was, it constantly avoided and evaded that other truth of the straight road used by the many. Like a secret scar it stayed hidden within him, and shame lest it be revealed made him feel cut off, hunted, banished. That he had become a solitary man, a foreigner in his own country and in the home town of his fathers, all this had surely come about because he had shrunk from standing up to his father, from setting up his own life against his father's life, his own truth against his father's truth. Not that he had any doubts about his own truth as against that of his father, but he certainly did feel ashamed of his own truth: ugly, petty, base as it seemed to be. The truth of a mere mole of a man, asking only to live, whatever the circumstances. The truth of a man who refuses to make his life a link in the chain of his nation-tribe's existence, who refuses to lay himself open to sudden death: who wants above all to live. Had they promised him –

had they been able to promise him – that bullets would not kill him nor any bombs destroy him, why then of course he would have been ready and willing to go to all the wars. But a soldier killed is a soldier dead. Even if his death does help to perpetuate his nation-tribe. If only he could have believed in an after-life ... But no, he didn't believe in such things. And this is what they wanted of him, and this is what they were demanding of him: to give up the one and only unique thing without which there can be nothing else. The strength and the consolation of a man who makes his life a link in a chain – that kind of strength is not his strength, such a consolation not for him. Well, what then? A dead soldier is first and foremost a dead soldier. Only after that is he a hero. After that they set him up as a model, so that others may follow in his footsteps and others in theirs and others in theirs and the thing has no end. They bring out a booklet to his memory and later on they place a memorial stone on his grave. If he has a grave. But whatever they built on his grave, the fellow hidden down there beneath it all wouldn't feel a thing. It's not for him that the memorial stone is intended but for those who are called upon to go the way he went, and for those who come after as well. This being so, what then? Where can he find a place where there are no tribes and no nations, just individual persons living their own lives and minding their own business? Ah, but that's the very thing he doesn't want. Now of all times he wants to be here. Why? Just to be contrary? Perhaps to provide a kind of perverted evidence. Evidence of what? It's of no consequence, so long as he can stay put. Even in this kind of existence, running for his life and hiding himself away and hatching out all these ideas about the survival of an ugly and lonely mole of a man.

Such things have always been from the beginning of time. Look, they've left us pyramids! A splendour of power and glory in a world that once was, a world that vanished long ago. But the pyramids survive. They say that hundreds of thousands of slaves met their death in raising them. And today? From all the ends of the earth people flock to the pyramids to wonder at their power and their strength. That's how it is today, and that's how it has been for countless generations. Well, what of it? Ask the opinion of a slave of the pyramids – any one of those hundreds of thousands who gave their lives for them – much consolation would all that glory be to him! Ask the opinion of any soldier in Napoleon's army who froze to death in the frosty fields facing blazing Moscow. Ask the opinion of any legionary in Caesar's conquering legions who was killed on the bank of the Sambre at the height of the Gallic wars. A slave who escaped from his master and who was killed in the battles launched by Spartacus. A French knight who fell for his religious faith, in the Crusades. People who have been shot in the most worthy and justified of demonstrations all over the world. Ask the opinion of all those myriads of people who have been killed for their beliefs and for their ideals, at all times and in all places. How many wars have erupted in this world since the time of the first war in this world? How many people have been killed in this world in all the wars since that first war? And isn't it true that every war had a purpose, and that there never was any war that didn't have a purpose? Wars of robbery, wars of conquest, holy wars, wars of liberation, wars of expansion, wars of self-defence, wars for survival, preventive wars and all the other kinds of wars.

Imagine an assembly of all the men who were killed in all the wars of this world since the time of the first war in this world. Every single one of them would voice his own motivations, his own ideas and his own ideals. Every slain soldier is a unique person in himself. Desires and ideas and ideals change and give rise to new ideas and ideals, and these in turn give rise to new wars.

But a man who fell in battle is a murdered human being, and nothing new can ever come from him. He is the sum total of a life that was lived and was then cut off, and there's no one else that could ever fill his place, neither in this world nor in the next.

For those who summon warriors and guide them to a special goal, their eyes are lifted to distant heights and their special goal is clear before their eyes. Those whom they guide follow after, trying to raise their heads so as to see that distant lofty goal, and by its power some of them might even feel slightly uplifted. And if there should be one who falls by the wayside, dying for his faith, his leader stops for a moment by the grave and sighs a deep deep sigh. However, he soon consoles himself and then he consoles the others too, and on they go in a great assembly, on towards their heart's desire, their special goal, their great ideal.

Perhaps the leader's eyes look sad – certainly they do look sad, but only too soon does he raise his eyes above the slain and beyond the slain and over to the far distance and what does he see? History. Meanwhile ... meanwhile history goes on swallowing up her children, and however much you try to satisfy her, and however many more you sacrifice, she will not say: enough. In the rest of the world wars begin and wars end and whoever remains alive goes home. Here, even if they come home they still remain in the war. Year after year after year after year. God! What a fate you've ordained for this people! Formerly it was years of persecution and slaughter all over the world, now they are being killed day in day out in wars for their own country in their own country. Wars that are fought and fought and never fought to a finish. And the efficiency. The terrifying efficiency. Gets more terrifying every day.

We are all like a great union marching head erect towards a goal. But the union itself has now become the goal. More and more efficiency. More and more decisive purpose. The army. Both secretly and openly the army here has become a model of highly organized and intensely purposeful living that will brook neither weakness nor failure. Out of the army into the army. There was a time when they used to call the army a melting pot; now it has become a primary school for the whole nation, a university of the future. But the one who fell, fell. The other one who refused to go, the one making his own paltry accounts, he turned aside. At one end the great and far-reaching vision and purpose of the union, at the other end one little mean purpose of a single solitary person. Stalemate. Perhaps quite a logical stalemate, but hardly valid, basically. Stalemate both for the living and for the dead. For those who make the big decisions and for those who lose their lives, for those who enlist and for those who volunteer. All stalemate.

This being so, for him – no. He will have none of it. If only everyone else could be like him – but they're not. Yes, that's how it is, so what? Is that a reason for him to copy all the others and agree to be a sacrifice? This being so, for him – no. With all that he's got he'll strive against this business of realizing any kind of ideal, whatever it might be. – Well, perhaps an ideal, all right. But sacrifice? Certainly not.

There is something else. Supposing he were to get caught up in circumstances that forced him to lay down his life in order to testify to his convictions – to justify this refusal of his, what then? – Of course this is a paradoxical speculation

– but even then, so far as he can tell now, when he can hardly even envisage such a possibility, definitely and clearly, still the same. No. – As much as he possibly can he will make it his business to avoid and evade any and every danger that could threaten him, whatever kind of danger it might be.

For in his opinion there is no faith in the world and no realization of any ideal that can be justified in assuming the right to demand a man's soul.

Well, even if this truth of his might look ugly and mean, to be hidden like a blemish, lower than grass and less than the dust – even so there's something in it. But nothing to be proud of: nothing noble and certainly no sacrifice. And therefore he won't show himself in public, he won't raise his voice – almost hiding himself from himself. This is the only way, keeping himself to himself. Total taboo. Like a thief in the night who has to steal his own life for himself every day anew, and who has to live in a hide-out. Yes, that's about it.

Had there been any room in this tiny room of his, he would certainly have got up at this stage to walk about for a bit. But what a room – can't even walk two steps in it. So all he could do was to stretch and yawn and perch on the edge of the bed for a bit. He passed his hands over his face once or twice, then leaned back and lay flat again, crossing his arms under his head as before.

Actually there is a laughable side to all this. To think that he is making all these efforts in order to preserve a life of . . . what? Wretched and full of weaknesses and shortcomings as it is – what is there that could make such a life worth protecting from any Moloch, worth guarding from any sacrifice? What is there in this life of his that it must be kept so holy? If only in order to be, simply to exist, then it is merely like the life of any animal or any bird in the sky. But then on the contrary it might well be that all their superiority, possibly even their discernment, their intuition – perhaps all this is theirs for the very reason that they are links in the chain of the great realization, and because they are always ready for sacrifice.

Well, that's as maybe. But as for him – no. What is it he wants, then? All that he wants according to the way he sees and feels, and all that he asks, in all humility, is to be allowed to live in peace, without wars and without getting himself killed even if it were to be for the sake of something greater, nobler, loftier and much more important than himself. Even though this life of his is nothing but a kind of grovelling alleluia, offered up by human frailties, each desperate in itself, with a way of life far from satisfactory, a dark and dreary existence staggering from day to night with no glory at all and of no importance whatsoever. – Even so.

To sum it all up, all he asks for himself is that he should be able to live just an ordinary life without any heroism. To be free to wallow in his own doubts and in his own defects, to live – without wars – the whole of this vanity of vanities that fills his life, even with all its faults and blemishes and little sins.

Translated by Shula Doniach

David Avidan

Antitear Gas

People we have never met, but who are not really strangers,
are people whose organic existence has been discontinued,
as the physical integrity of what has been termed 'this
                    country'
has been violated and violated again, just to escape more
                    violation.
before after and while people we've never met, but who
                    aren't really strangers,
were having their last, indeed first, respects paid to them.
People we've never met aren't necessarily strangers,
for they belong to this place, and that's what always counts
                    here, and as a result
they just go on assuming most key responsibilities (with or
                    without party-key priorities):
they are still to be found and will be, for many more years,
among moviegoers enjoying lousy war-films, at any
first second third fourth chessboard, section

A-B-C, and equally so
in good or bad or mediocre poems
that might have been written and published – altering
the 'Forties, the 'Fifties and the 'Sixties.
Man, they keep manning anything mannable in this country,
                    going
for every government tender, opportunity, initiative,
                    enterprise, competing for the best girls, the best
                    jobs, making it
in swinging discotheques, flying abroad
by El Al Airlines, evereluding,
with an elegant rustle, hospitals, cemeteries and, in fact,
for the sake of nonhistorical record, draftboards
and junior colleges and university campuses and memorial
        meetings.
What more can be said – this country is just packed with
                    them, and they have
every right to stick around, observing us with sheer curiosity,
                    shielding
their eyes with lowflying woolly clouds rather than
with their Japanese sunglasses, lost in a bright June Sinai
                    battle.
For after all an experiment is an experiment,
even though it has been going on, in a rather improvised
                    laboratory,
for twenty years or so.
Now it may already be said:
Second World War Jewry
has no more monopoly on death—
the local industry has been making marked progress.
This is how we manage with them, authority within
                    authority, the living among the dead among the
                    living among the dead,
with a double constitution double passports double mobility,
in between constantly contorted borders of a swelling-
                    shrinking, shrinking-swelling geomutation,
quite like spacetime as believed to have been conceived by
                    the departed Albert Einstein,
left behind by mutants still alive and mutants yet unborn,
and those in times to come who'll never have to die.

Translated by the poet

When God Said for the First Time

When God said, for the first time: Let there be light—
His intention was to rid Himself of the Dark.
He wasn't thinking at that moment of the sky,
but already the waters began filling the trees
and the birds took shape, and the air, to fly.
Then the first Wind blew into the eyes of Our Lord
and he saw it with the Eyes of the Cloud of His Glory,
and thought: It is good. He didn't think then
that the children of Adam would
ever become a multitude.
But they already began to think of themselves without fig
    leaves,
and in their hearts already they were thinking of a way
to cause what pain they could.
When Our Lord at first thought of the Night
He did not think of Sleep.
It was just: I'll be happy this way – that's what the good
Lord thought. But already they were
a multitude.

Translated by Sholom J. Kahn

OCCASIONALLY

Occasionally I leave the room to ring my own bell.
 When I look outside I astonish myself.
Who would have guessed I'd been out there so long?

But the one I'm waiting for never comes, I write
a letter, winter ends grimly, spring
begins in the flowerpots on the roof. I promise
when his honour comes to prepare a great feast.

Meanwhile the wind is cold and the only warm town
screens me from the noise of the sea. Bundles of
starlings screech, and drop into sleep.
The trees are black hulls. I am very cold.

But I want to tell His Honour something I have not
yet found. I grope on the table. there are the
    matches again.
This all goes on turning, doesn't it? Round and round.

Translated by Elaine Feinstein

AGAINST PARTING

My tailor is against parting.
That's why, he
said, he's not going away;
he doesn't want to part
from his one daughter. He's definitely
against parting.

Once, he parted from his wife, and
she he
saw no more of (Auschwitz).
Parted
from his three sisters and
these he never
saw (Buchenwald).
He once parted from his mother (his father
died of a fine and ripe age). Now
he's against parting.

In Berlin he
was my father's kith and kin. They passed
a good time in
that Berlin. The time's passed. Now
he'll never leave. He's
most definitely
(my father's died)
against parting.

Translated by Jon Silkin

Aharon Megged

From Abiathar Levitin's London Notebook

The following is the final chapter of a novel, The Richter File, *consisting of four notebooks by Abiathar Levitin, a proof reader in a Tel Aviv publishing house. Discovered after their author's untimely death in an accident, the 'notebooks' centre around the character of Joseph Richter, a writer, the focus of Levitin's life from the 1930's into the 1960's. The first notebook, 'Memoirs', comprises biographical notes on Richter, and was intended for publication, while the second, 'Confession', not intended for publication, is Levitin's personal diary, containing many details left out of the first notebook. 'The Watchman' and 'Our Turbulent Age', of the third notebook, is a commentary on one of Richter's short stories, which Levitin uses to express disagreement with the ideas of a certain established literary critic. The fourth notebook describes Levitin's humiliating meeting with his 'hero' in London.*
The Richter File, *published originally in Hebrew under the title,* Mahbarot Evyatar, *won for its author the Bialik Prize for Literature in 1974.*

IT's evening, and I'm sitting in my room in Mrs. Hilman's boarding-house in West Hampstead, near the Jewish section on Finchley Road. It's already springtime – at least on the calendar – but outside it's raining, and inside it's cold. I'm not lighting the gas stove, since I have to drop a shilling into it every time I turn it on. It's a narrow room, with a bed and worn-out bedspread, a chest-of-drawers and a mirror, a table at which I'm writing and a chair in which I'm sitting. Why am I writing? No one will see these lines anyway. 'I shall speak, that I may find relief.' Perhaps things will be easier for me afterwards. Perhaps.

Last night at eleven o'clock, I returned from a meeting of the World Association for Hebrew Language and Culture, held at the house of Mordecai Engel. A meeting in honor of Joseph Richter, guest-writer from Israel. I came back with a feeling of unfading humiliation. Unfading, for no vengeance can make me recover from this insult; no desperate act can restore me. The feelings that had come over me so often in Israel, that had brought me to the edge of destruction, that were the cause, to tell the whole truth, of my fleeing here, to England.

Never, in my worst dreams, did I ever imagine they would follow me here.

I returned at eleven o'clock, like a beaten dog slipping back into its kennel. I plopped into the chair, still in my wet overcoat, venomous. I reached into my pocket, took out my pen and tried to write. I hoped that putting things into writing would make the venom drain out of my body into the paper. But I was paralyzed. I wrote not even a word.

A night and a day have passed. It was a night that let me fall asleep only as dawn approached, and then I slept like a rock for two or three hours. It was a day on which I walked mile after mile, from here to Regent's Park, from Regent's Park across the entire length of Hampstead to Hampstead Heath, from there to Highgate and around and around until returning here—

Now that I have calmed down a bit, I can write. The cold wind, the budding gardens, the walk up and down the many streets, the old houses, inns, churches – all these things have helped me somewhat to forget. They have quieted the storm.

Ten days ago, on March 13th, Richter arrived in London. I went to the airport to meet him—

But I must start at the beginning.

Seven months ago – in September – I landed in England. I had prepared myself several years for this trip. I hadn't left Israel since my arrival there in 1921, and the thought of leaving – even for just a year – was dreadful. But the need to leave, to free myself from the strangle-hold I was in, kept pressing upon me. It became a compulsion. The final impetus for my decision came after my break with Richter. It was a break that occurred not all at once, but in stages, ever since his fiftieth birthday celebration about ten years before.

I was the initiating force behind this celebration. I organized the planning committee and conceived the idea of *Golden Sheaves*, the literary collection published in his honor. And I was the one who was rejected, most humiliatingly, from participation in the festivity. And the one who rejected me was the honoree himself.

I submitted an article for inclusion in the collection, an analysis of one of Richter's works, an article deserving of the editor's praise. But despite the editor's promises to include this article, it did not appear. I soon learned that Richter himself had a hand in this.

To this day I find this hard to explain to myself. Did he fear the wrath of the critic Ernst Landauer, with whom I had dared to engage in controversy? Did it disparage his own honor, that my name, unimportant as it was, should be included along with the names of the major figures adorning its pages? Was my interpretation of the story, 'The Watchman' – an interpretation which exposed some secrets behind his literary personality – unacceptable to him? Did he find it unpleasing? Did he hold a grudge against me, for some cause unbeknown to me, and find the opportunity to get even? I looked for one justification after another for him, but not a one of them was enough to expiate this blow.

I ceased meeting with him. I didn't see him for months. This wasn't easy for me, after some twenty years of friendship and collaboration.

But one day in December of 1954, Richter appeared at my office at the publishing house. He said a bright hello, sat down by me and acted as if – as if nothing had come between us. As if we had seen each other just the day before! He reached into an envelope and took out a large bundle of manuscript pages, handed them to me and said: 'I've finished a novel. I've brought it for you to read.'

Just like in the old days: I would read, make my annotations, and be the sponsor of his literary produce before the publishing house ... And I knew how indebted he was to me ... 'And you know how indebted I am to you', he would say ...

I had no choice but to accept my fate. After all, it was within the realm of my obligations, and twenty years could not be blotted out as if they had never existed.

I did my work, as I always had done. I read faithfully and made some annotations, corrections and suggestions. Again we were meeting almost every week.

Except that our relations had cooled. *I* was responsible for this. I was no longer receptive of his interests outside the bounds of work, and I didn't engage in much conversation. Such was the case afterwards as well, when he brought me a new collection of stories and another novel ...

I immersed myself in what I had been doing those many years: in exploring the books of the Kabbalah. Every day I'd go to the library, and in the evening I'd examine the books at home and write articles.

Thus evolved my decision to travel. I had to leave, due both to my research work and to the increasingly burdensome weight of our relationship. There was just one way to get away from him: to go far away, to a place where I wouldn't have to see him again, where I wouldn't have the chance of seeing him.

I'm a solitary man, with few needs, and during the years I had saved up my money. I resigned my position at the publisher's two years before my retirement date, in order to add some of my early retirement funds to my savings. A sum that would allow me to travel and pay my living expenses for a year.

On September 13th, 1962, I landed in England. I went to Oxford, to be close to the Bodleian Library.

I had previously been corresponding with the librarian of the Hebrew collection, Dr. May. What brought me to Oxford was this:

During the course of my study of Kabbalistic literature, I came across the volume entitled *The Garden of the Palace.* Reading it made me have grave doubts concerning both its source and the identity of its author. The commonly held opinion was that it had been written by Rabbi Meir ben Todros Abulafia. The only documentary evidence I found for this was in the book *The Lips of Sleepers.* By reading two exegetical works on *The Garden of the Palace (G.P.),* one by Rabbi Isaac ben Todros of Barcelona, another by Rabbi Shem Tov ibn Gaon, my suspicions were roused that *G.P.* was a forgery, a pseudo-epigraphical work. First of all. I found a similarity between this book and Rabbi Meir ben Eliezer's *The Tradition of the Covenant and The Epistle of the Unity.* Second, I found that many chapters in *G.P.* were copied from *The Order of God* and from the commentary of Rabbi Judah Hayat. Third, *G.P.,* an apocalyptic book, fixes the year of the final revelation of the Messiah to be 1598, and could not possibly have been written before 1500, the year that Hayat wrote his commentary, according to all the textural evidence existing in his work. These doubts encouraged me to work on until I should either discover the true identity of the author of *G.P.* or learn that it was only a combination of passages from other works.

I learned that a complete manuscript of *G.P.* existed at the Bodleian Library (Oxford MS. 1577), and that an incomplete one was in London at the British Museum (Gaster MS.

1398–1701). I wrote to the Bodleian librarian with regard to this matter. He assured me of the existence of the manuscript and promised to assist me in my work and help me find a place to live.

I spent four months in Oxford, and those were the happiest months of my life since youth. One thing led to another, and when I completed my study of *G.P.*, I began examining other old manuscripts, both from the Cairo Genizah and ones written later: *The Book of Magical Secrets, The Book of Raziel, The Book of the Vestment* (which lay in disarray with *The Book of Righteousness*), and many more. Each day I would spend hours in the library, and except for the librarian and for Professor Remington, a great expert in Semitic languages and Midrashic literature, I hardly saw a soul. In the afternoons, when the weather was not too cold, I'd stroll through the gardens alongside the river and walk among the ancient college buildings. In the evenings I'd read English books on philosophy and Judaica, borrowed from some Jewish lecturers with whom I had become acquainted.

I was exalted the whole day long. When a man like myself enters the Bodleian Library, he feels as if he were Ali Baba in the treasure-cave, not knowing what to take first. The long, high rows of bookshelves contained bundle after bundle of parchment scrolls and manuscripts, hundreds of some of the rarest books in the world, collections of old periodicals no longer found anywhere else! Hidden treasures! Tears came to my eyes as I reverently turned page after page of earliest editions of nineteenth-century Hebrew journals, such as *First Fruits of the Times, Daybreak, The Declarer, Dawn,* or as my fingers ran over the brittle pages of R. A. Braudes's novels *Whence and Whither?* and *The Two Extremes*. What a feeling it is for a man such as myself, to turn, with his own hand, the parchment pages of the divan of Isaac ibn Khalfun, the earliest example of a Hebrew divan, transcribed in the eleventh century! Or when his eyes meet the lines 'Then were the chiefs of Edom dismayed,' written in the original hand of the poet Joseph ibn Abithur himself! What a thrill goes through you when you hold in your hand a first edition copy of Isaac ibn Ṣahula's long poem, *The Ancient Proverb*, printed at the Soncino press in the fifteenth century! Or the Talmudic tractate *Interweavings* printed in Wad-al-Hajara – Guadalajara! Or *The Four Rows* by Jacob ben Asher, printed in Constantinople in 1494! There were also many volumes printed by the Bomberg press in Venice or by the houses at Frankfort, Wilhemsdorf, and Amsterdam, in the seventeenth century; books printed in Vienna, Lvôv, and Cracow in the eighteenth and nineteenth centuries! Once, while I was browsing in the Hassidic collection, I chanced upon a certain tractate which at first glance I could not recognise because of its worn cover. Then my flesh tingled: it turned out to be *The Tent of Isaac*, by my own grandfather, may he rest in peace, Rabbi Isaac Leib Levitin; it was commentary on the writings of Rabbi Shneur Zalman of Lyady, printed in Lvôv.

Glorious days. To tell the truth, there were many days that I neglected my work and did not engage in research per se. I was drawn instead to some old volumes from the nineteenth-century Hebrew Enlightenment and to some sacred texts from earlier periods. It was a temptation I could not resist! The smell of the pages, the sight of the Hebrew letters, the flavor of antiquity, even the touch of the old leather covers, were enough to make my head spin! I plunged into the books and forgot all else; I indulged myself in this paradise of letters and verses, sacred lore and poetry.

I was exalted the whole day long. This Oxford – so quiet, so serious, with its ancient, stone buildings, its pathways, upon which scholars walked about like priests in divine service, its wide, grassy meadows, its awe-inspiring mansions and churches, with their dimly lit, vaulted corridors. And even the city streets and alleyways, full of ancient taverns, coats-of-arms, clock-towers, so many stately, historical houses! I loved to walk about these streets and alleyways, to wander into a shop here and a shop there, into Rosenthal's bookstore on Broad Street, with its large collection of rare Hebrew books, or into the Ashmolean Museum, where I found some Jewish marriage contracts, or into the magnificent Sheldonian Theatre ... And as for the two or three Hebrew scholars I met, even though I got together with them only once in a blue moon, I loved their company, their conversation, whether in the college resturant at lunchtime or in their homes, in the evenings. Unlike the pointless banter and drivel that go on at the writers' cafés in Israel, our conversations were always aimed at delving into the depths of the issue; they were characterized by attentiveness, broad-mindedness, good manners and mutual respect. For the first time in years I could join in and contribute to a discussion without the constant interruptions that had taken place back in Israel, interruptions which either tied my tongue completely or made it say things that I didn't intend to say.

I was sorry to leave Oxford and the Bodleian Library which had become almost home for me, Dr. May, who had treated me so warmly, the gracious Professor Remington, the moss-covered stones, the green meadows, the castles and the turrets – in order to come to London. But I had to do this in order to complete my research on *The Garden of the Palace*; a second textual version lay in the British Museum, and I needed to go over it. I therefore packed up my books and my few belongings and came here, to Mrs. Hilman's boarding-house in West Hampstead.

In Oxford I had no Jews, but I did have Judaism. And I swelled in the midst of it. London had many Jews – but a Judaism of ignoramuses. As soon as I got here, I turned to Mr Abraham Sheldon, a member of the World Association for Hebrew Language and Culture, whom I had met in Israel during a trip of his some years before. I asked him if he could help me find an inexpensive place to stay. The London hotel where I first stayed was beyond my means; nor could I work there in peace and quiet. He found me Mrs. Hilman's house, located in a Jewish neighborhood. He then invited me to a meeting of the Hebraists, which was scheduled to be held a fortnight later; it was to be an evening dedicated to Saul Tchernichovsky on the anniversary of the poet's death. I went to this meeting, which took place at the home of Mordecai Engel, a well-to-do, observant Jew who spoke Hebrew with Ashkenazic accent. I met about twenty or thirty men and women, most of whom were also observant, whose knowledge of Hebrew language and literature came partly from childhood education a generation earlier and partly from what they read in the handful of newspapers, journals and books that found their way to England long after publication. There were also two Israelis there, one of them an emigrant teacher who taught Hebrew and Bible in a Jewish high school, the other a student at the University of London. Mr. Sheldon, chairing the meeting, opened and solemnly welcomed 'our distinguished guest from Israel.' He attached to my name every sort of embarrassingly flattering adjective: 'a superb scholar', 'a student of Kabbalah and Jewish philosophy', 'a loyal friend of the Hebrew book', and, last but not least – 'who has written a number of important essays in the field of Jewish studies.' (!) I was forced to rise and take a bow before the applauding audience ... And the lecture! Someone spoke 'On Tchernichovsky and His Works'! Those worn-out, hackneyed phrases about 'Judaism and Hellenism,' about 'singing the praises of Nature against the background of exilic suffering', and other similar phrases lifted out of Klausner and Lachower! There was not a single ray of originality to freshen up all those stodgy clichés! Finally, when the lecture was over and the readings finished, it came time for tea at the other end of the drawing room. Some of the guests politely gathered around me, inquired about my work and asked my opinion on such-and-such book by Agnon, on Shamir's *King of Flesh and Blood* on Yizhar's *The Captive* ... That is how I became acquainted with a few of them; they also invited me to their homes and to dreary meetings of the Association.

Twice again I attended those boresome meetings, in order to relieve some of my loneliness. I also visited a few times with Dr. Manzer, a Talmudist and great scholar of Kabbalistic literature. Most of my mornings were spent in the library of the British Museum, and most of my evenings were spent in my room, as I completed my research.

This is no Oxford. In the library here, you take the book you want, sit down at a table underneath a deathly gray light, among people you don't know. You have no contact with the librarian or with the other readers or with any books other than your own. The room is filled with a kind of cold emptiness. But all the same, I was content here as well, content with my work and with London itself; there was so much to see and so much to learn. I was even content with my solitude.

Then, all of a sudden, Richter's ghost caught up with me.

Two and a half weeks ago, on a Friday morning, when I opened the pages of the *Jewish Chronicle*, as I did every week, I was startled to read that Joseph Richter was about to arrive in London.

I read it and reread it. My eyes did not deceive me: Joseph Richter, 'one of the most eminent Israeli writers', etc., etc., author of such-an-such books, is about to arrive in London on such-and-such date to receive an honorary doctorate from the School of Jewish Studies at the University of London.

I cannot describe what came over me during those moments! It was as if every ounce of humiliation and resentment stored up inside me suddenly jumped out of their lair and overwhelmed me. A mixture of various feelings, all gloomy and bitter. On one hand: why hadn't he notified me of his coming? He surely knew that I was in London! On the other: why was he pursuing me to the ends of the earth? Why couldn't he leave me alone? But could there possibly be another meeting between us, a new start? And again, on the other hand: why was he getting an honorary doctorate? Why in London, of all places . . .?

It was quite clear that from that moment on I couldn't get anything else done. I couldn't go to the library, I couldn't read, I couldn't write. That peace of mind that I had enjoyed for more than half a year, had been shaken, stolen away. For almost an hour I sat at this desk, incensed, enraged; I couldn't find strength to get up. I picked up the paper and put it down, picked it up again and pushed it aside. Then I walked downstairs to the foyer and telephoned Mr. Sheldon at his store. I asked him if he had heard about the impending arrival of Joseph Richter . . . Yes! he said joyfully, of course he knew about this! They had even written him about this from Israel! Not only that, but the writer was going to appear at a meeting of the Association; a time, date and place had already been set, and I was invited to come, naturally . . . I told him that I knew Joseph Richter personally. I asked him if he knew the exact time of arrival, since I wanted to meet him. Of course! he said. Of course! He himself would go out to the airport to meet him and would be happy if I were there too . . . He gave me the time, date, flight number, and so forth.

This conversation left me even more upset. I was especially surprised that Ethel had not written me about his coming.

But Ethel never mentioned Richter in her letters.

All day Saturday, and every day after that, I didn't do anything but roam the streets and parks, occasionally going into a museum and hurrying out, spending lots of time on the underground, absent-mindedly reading the newspapers. When I got home in the evening, I was weary; I tried to sleep but I couldn't.

On Thursday afternoon I went out to Heathrow. Upon my arrival I went to the customs station exit. There I came upon a dozen or so people, including someone from the Israeli Embassy, two or three men from the Culture Department of the Jewish Agency, Mr. Sheldon, along with another man whom he introduced as Professor Ohrbach from the University of London, and some public figures I had met at the Association. We stood and waited a long time and talked about one thing and another.

I don't know how it happened. As soon as Richter came through the gate – neatly dressed in a new, gray overcoat, all pale and confused (I was astonished what a handsome and tall figure he cut, as if I were seeing him for the first time) – the welcoming party swooped down upon him, each and every one of them hurrying to shake his hand and greet him, one man taking one suitcase, another man taking another ... And I, who didn't consider myself a part of the official entourage, stood over to the side, trying to catch his glance, waiting my turn as last in line to greet him. But as I waited, the entourage, he included, passed by me, moving through the exit. As I toddled behind trying to catch up, they all got into three cars waiting for them along the curb, closed the door and drove off. I was left all alone.

Could he not have seen me? Did he see me and purposely feign unawareness?

I returned to the city by bus. I said to myself: It is quite possible that he didn't see me; I stood there, off to the side, among other people waiting for other passengers. He might not have noticed me during that reception business, with all that confusion a person goes through when he gets off a plane in a strange city.

That evening I called up Mr. Sheldon at his home. 'Where were you?' he exclaimed when he heard my voice. 'We were surprised that you disappeared from sight! Mr. Richter said, as a matter of fact, that he knows you. He too asked where you were ...' I asked him where Richter was staying, and he gave me the name of the hotel, the room number and the phone number.

I didn't want to disturb him the first evening after his arrival, since he was surely tired and in need of rest. I waited until the next morning. I also felt a little bit better when I heard that he had asked about me.

The next morning I called the hotel.

For three hours, from ten until one, I sat by the telephone in the foyer of my boarding house.

At first his phone was busy; the hotel receptionist asked me to wait. I waited with the receiver to my ear, and in a few minutes I heard her voice: 'It's still busy.' Since another boarder and Mrs. Hilman herself needed to use the phone, I had to put down the receiver and call again later. I called him five times, and each time the phone in his room was busy. The receptionist had already taken pity on me and suggested that I leave her my name and number, so that she could have him call me. I did as she suggested and waited by the phone. I sat and waited more than half an hour. I was amazed at how many people were either calling him or being called by him. Did he have that many acquaintances here in London? The phone here rang a couple or three times; each call was for Mrs. Hilman, who jumped up and came out of her room to answer people inquiring about lodgings. When my call didn't come, I thought that the receptionist might have forgotten to give him the message, or that he might have called and gotten a busy signal. I called the hotel again. The receptionist, who knew my voice by now, said: 'Yes, Mr. Levitin, I gave him the message, and now it seems that you are in luck, because the line is free.' Yes, it was free. The voice of a mature woman answered in Hebrew. When I told her who was calling, she asked me to wait a moment. After a few seconds, she came back and said: 'Perhaps you could call back in a quarter of an hour? Mr. Richter is in the bath right now.' It all seemed very strange to me. If she had told him who was speaking, couldn't he have asked her to say hello for him? Anyway, I waited twenty minutes and called again. I heard his phone ringing. After a few minutes the receptionist told me: 'Sorry, Mr. Levitin, but there's no answer. It seems he's gone out.'

I gave him the benefit of the doubt. I said: He must have waited fifteen minutes, and when my call didn't come, he went out. He must have hurried on his way.

In the evening I called him again. There was no answer. The hotel information clerk said that he had gone out. The next morning at ten (I was afraid to call earlier than this, lest I waken him), there again was no answer. When I asked Mr. Sheldon where Richter was, I was told that he had taken an escorted trip to Oxford and Cambridge and wouldn't be back till Sunday. On Monday afternoon at five the doctoral presentation would take place in Goldsmith's College at the University of London. During that time

Richter would deliver a lecture on 'Ancient and Modern Legends in Hebrew Literature.' If I were to go there I would be able to see him.

Again I was flooded with waves of resentment and humiliation. Surely he already had my telephone number; surely he knew that I had been in Oxford several months. Couldn't he have informed me that he was going there? I would have been pleased to accompany him, to escort him through the city, it's colleges and its libraries.

Or was he being held captive by his hosts?

On Monday afternoon I went to the University of London. Although I arrived early, it took me a long time to find Goldsmith's College. The University is spread out over a good number of city blocks. Several times I was mislead and ended up at the wrong building; the distance between buildings is great, and inside each building one encounters long corridors, labyrinths, and numberless rooms and halls. When I finally found Goldsmith's College, it was already twenty minutes past five.

I arrived in the middle of the lecture. The hall was filled to the brim with three or four hundred people, most of them wearing skull-caps. It seemed that all the Hebrew-speaking students from the various colleges had gathered there. I slipped in and for a few very bewildering moments, I remained standing, standing alone at the back of the hall, which was built like a theater, the floor slanting downwards toward the stage. Then one of the people in the audience touched me and pointed out a free seat on one of the front rows. I leaned forward and tiptoed down toward my seat. The lecturer was the same Professor Uhrbach I had met at the airport. He was reading his lecture, and I didn't listen. All my thoughts were given to Joseph Richter, who was sitting upon the stage between four other persons, two on the left and two on the right. I couldn't take my eyes off him. It was strange to see him in tuxedo and black bow-tie. Although he had always been pale, he seemed younger than he did the last time I had seen him, more than seven months before. Despite the fact that he was over sixty, he had not turned gray. His hair had faded somewhat, but not grayed. His eyes – the color of the sea – still contained that same haughty indifference. From time to time, I thought that he saw me and that we were looking at each other eye-to-eye. A great distance separated my seat in the audience from his on the stage, and I could look at him through my glasses without flinching.

Then he got up, the audience applauding, and approached the podium. He had a stack of papers in his hand and lay it down in front of him. When he began reading, a chill went through me.

I listened to what he had to say, and as I listened, a change began to take place inside me, the same change – I don't know whether it's praiseworthy or reproachable – that had always occurred when I went over his stories; all my resentment, all my bitterness concerning his humiliating behavior toward me, gradually melted away, dissolving through the mystifying power of his words, then disappearing entirely.

No, his lecture did not show any special depth of thought or erudition. It didn't kindle any new lights for me. As a matter of fact, all the things he said about other people he really meant about himself. But when he spoke about the legend of the River Sambation, about the ninth-century traveler Eldad Haddani, about the sixteenth-century Italian Kabbalist Joseph della Reina, about the dreams of the Safed Kabbalist Hayyim Vital, about the Messiah bound, about the seventeenth-century pseudo- Messiah Shabbetai Zevi, and about the tales of the great Hassidic sage Rabbi Nahman of Bratslav, carrying the chain from them to the modern writers Frishman and Berdyczewski and Bialik and Jacob Steinberg (the only post-Bialik writer mentioned in his lecture), the ideas were expressed with such inspiration, with such lucidity and depth, with such dignity and aggadic melodiousness, in the same style in which his stories were written – clear, full of distant echoes – that their essence was not in their content but in their melody. Their enchantment hovered over the auditorium, inspiring the listeners and captivating them completely.

It is no wonder that when he had finished his speech, the whole audience rose and gave him a tumultuous standing ovation.

At the end of the meeting, as the audience was leaving the hall, I waited beside the door. I was hoping that as he left with his escorts and passed my way, I would have a moment to congratulate him.

But he and his escorts left the stage through another door. When I left the building, I saw the entourage walking across the wide, grassy square across the street. There was no sense in chasing after them.

It was already evening, and I turned to walk on home. As I walked, I thought to myself: I have no sense of humility. Who am I, what am I, that he would pay any attention to me? What right have I to demand this from him? He is a great man, deserving of all the praise and honor they have bestowed upon him. He has acquired it through his productivity and talent. What does he owe me? Reimbursement for the labor I've invested in preparing his stories for publication? I've already received my reward! How base, how contemptible are all my insubordinate musings – as opposed to his greatness! The former will disappear in the dust, but the latter will last forever.

Last night I returned to Mordecai Engel's house for an Association party given in Richter's honor.

I sat in the last row. The party was supposed to have started at eight-thirty; the guests waited and waited, and at nine-fifteen he finally arrived, escorted by Mr. Sheldon. They both turned directly toward the lecture table. Mr. Sheldon opened the meeting by apologizing for the delay: so many admirers had come to his hotel room that it was hard to get him away . . .

The same man who had lectured on 'The Works of Saul Tchernichovsky', again delivered an insipid talk, this time on 'The Works of Joseph Richter'. It was obvious that he had read only one or two of his stories.

I tried to catch his glance through the people sitting in front of me. The drawing-room was not large, and we were separated by only eight or ten rows of chairs. For a moment it seemed that he had noticed me; he might have seen me, but then he turned his gaze away to another side, toward the lecturer, and down toward his hands. He seemed extremely tired. Even his clothes were slovenly.

When he rose to address his admirers, the same thing happened that had happened ten years before at the Ohel Shem Auditorium during his birthday celebration: here, like there, he spoke only five sentences. Five sentences spoken in fulfillment of an obligation, five sentences devoid of content or grace.

Only I, among all the congregants, knew that he was doing this not out of humility but out of contempt.

When the guests got up and moved to the other side of the

drawing room for tea, I said: The moment for our meeting has come.

I waited. I stood by the wall and waited. People thronged around him and held him under siege. I saw him throw his arms around one of them, give him a hug and a kiss and exclaim: 'Ornstin! So you're here! So you're alive!' And to those around him he said: 'I've not seen him for over thirty years! Since Berlin!' For long moments they stood there and exchanged graces with each other. Finally, Sheldon took him by the arm and brought him toward the serving table; the whole crowd trailed along with them. I left the place I was standing and approached him. He called out my name.

'*Evyosor!*' He smiled as he held out his hand. 'So you're in London. As a matter of fact, they told me that you had called . . .'

But at that moment an elegantly preened lady brought him a cup of tea; he drew his hand away from mine, took the cup and immediately turned to her. He thanked her, asked where she was from, where she learned her Hebrew, as if I didn't exist.

Evyosor! As he called me always, when he was drunk and his true self came through. My name, Abiathar, in Ashkenazic pronunciation of the ghetto.

I couldn't bear it any longer. I fled the place.

The entire way home, more than two miles, it rained.

I got back here wet from head to toe. I plopped into the chair. My blood was boiling. I couldn't forgive myself for this humiliation, which I alone had brought on. My trip to the airport, my chasing after him, my pitiable waiting for him to leave the University auditorium, my sitting by the telephone hour after hour, waiting for any crumb of kindness that he might throw to me . . . And this insult, thrown right into my face: 'Evyosor . . .!'

There is no deliverance from this humiliation. Neither in deed nor in word. I write, and the words seem repulsive; they themselves are pitiable. It would seem that since my suffering is unadulterated, the words would be pure, redeeming. But no. There is no redemption in them.

If only I could find some justification for him, I would be left in peace. I could bear my yoke if I knew his reasons, if I could find some justification for his reasons. The foundations of the universe are not crumbling. But—

And perhaps, I suppose, perhaps all this is just his revenge for my having left him without permission, for having left him alone with his manuscripts, with his tales. Paying me back for my one and only sin against him.

Translated by Samuel R. Whitehill

Avner Treinin

The Day Is Coming

The age of the first crocus will never
return. Always move on.
Level by level, the crossing, then
bridge over bridge, curving and climbing
to be stopped at the wall. The edge
of the carport. This is the time
to switch off the motor, begin to go down.

Bricks block a window, that is,
someone has changed his mind, does not want
to see what he wanted so much at the start
and already he tries
to wipe out the error, a flower pot
still there, but simply undone
like a heavy bird suddenly gone.

A dog at our window. Dog tells dog.
But what's he to me, my neighbor removed on a stretcher
even his name I don't know, when the balconies
were removed, the mint plants, a street facing
comfortable chairs. When man spoke to man,
someone could get there, could tell us
while his body was still warm.

The day is coming when heavy waters
from the sea will no longer spread
over a bright beach, a boy building temples
of sand, shell castles on tunnels
with rivers streaming. The day is coming,
already logs from forests of dark
nations, sticky pitch and oil spreading.

Jerusalem below is a field of olives
under house joined to house, a crocus
that can't break out of the asphalt,
tangle of roots, bones that no horn
can arouse. Jerusalem above
is smoke falling from concrete chimneys.
A shriek of sirens wakes us in the morning.

On the Mount of Quietude he will lead me among the
        nations.
A beating of drums, covered with deerskin.
The old world down to its bedrock. And what is the secret
of a bright morning in this alien city where I was born?
Three blacks and a cinnamon, kings of the earth.
Golden dome, crescent on cross, David
shields Israel in a morning of grapes.

At noon the town square is empty,
a swarm of robes cut through, makes me remember
what happened in Hebron. Locked in
green glass, bubbles we never will breathe.
Still I believe. As in a crystal ball
that tells fortunes, the heart of the grape
still shows through the clusters of Hebron.

Many omens and Muftis, their Holy War,
swear death on these infidels who multiply
cells to the tissue, the tents, the arab
at his wheel, the potter from Hebron – Elhalil
is Abraham, Ibrahim, is
the beloved, the leader, come near,
coming near, the blood will stand up and cheer.

As if the sign were given
every alley swarms. They shall enter in
at the windows, they shall run
upon the wall, storm in the streets—
I, me, why have I forsaken me
to walk in the valley of Hinnom
for I fear evil.

Hour after hour they cried,
all at once stopped. I think
of the frozen lake, that someone
did walk on the water.
Something
has got to move.

                              Translated by Shirley Kaufman

From *Maariv*, 14-4-76

Yitzhak Orpaz

Little Woman

I

THE destruction of the world will almost certainly begin like its creation – with the movement of a tiny grain from its place.

At first everything was simple. I asked her and she agreed. Before I even put out the light she was in my arms. There was a soft sadness in her silent face. I looked at my watch: not an hour had passed.

I saw her small, fragile, engraved in the black of her dress. Her face was narrow, transparent, the expression like a nun's. She stood in the corner of the bar, leaning on the wall, and didn't want to speak. I said to her: 'Let's go get some air.' She nodded and smiled. I said: 'Let's go to my place for a cup of coffee.' She nodded and smiled. She wasn't wearing a thing under the black dress, and she took me in voicelessly. And afterwards with an indistinct sound, a kind of hum.

Suddenly I asked her if she was a widow. Perhaps because of her white skin, the flush which had started flooding the whites of her eyes. There was something painful in her slow and thrifty movements.

She smiled:

'My name's Anath,' she said.

How hadn't I even thought she had a name, I thought.

When I came back from the shower she was sitting on the edge of the bed, whiter than the sheets and smelling of resin. Not the liquid resin, with its sharp smell, but solid resin, its smell dense.

She didn't ask for a thing, just sat there and

I closed my eyes and saw Anath in a white headdress, walking on the stones of Talpioth, bowing her head and crossing herself before every bell tower.

'My name's Gomer,' I said.

That wasn't my real name. A refugee from the city, from

troubles, from myself, what could I say to her in this far-off place on the edge of the desert. In July, at the height of the hot days, it had seemed that everything was working out, taking shape, and there was even the hope of some peace, to sit down to my life's work: 'On the Beautiful as a Monster'. The scores of pages, notes, outlines, tables, files, looked down like a bad conscience from the shelf, from all the shelves. Types and archetypes, infant giants, Medusa and the wife of Lapidoth, Huldah and Cassandra, the great mother and the sacrifice of the seven sons, the big woman and the sacrifice of the seven husbands, gods, and moles and the beetles of the sun. And then, in the middle of August, in the space of two days: the publisher went bankrupt, the order from overseas was cancelled, the wife demanded increased maintenance payments, and the children – how they stared sidelong at me from the kitchen door, frightened, ready to flee into their mother's arms, from me, their father. They covered their faces with their tender hands when I tried to kiss them goodbye. I packed a small suitcase, took the remnants of my savings, and fled to here.

A city on the edge of the desert. Everything dries quickly here – a shirt on the washing line, a bad idea, memories. The bare hills, the white glare, the cold, sharp, nights, the whirlwinds of dust at three or four o'clock – wandering cones, heads rising, wandering and falling. A drifting garment hung upon them is sure to dry. It seemed that I'd started to forget. And then – Anath.

She sat curled up on the edge of the bed, so small.

'You're so big' – she laughed.

True. I could have leaned my chin on her little head, if I'd wanted. And she had two small dimples. She played over them with her hair. Her teeth were healthy, their fierce gleam bluish.

Suddenly I was afraid.

'I'd like a child from you,' she said simply, with no connection to anything, laughing.

We both laughed. She playfully shook my right ear with her fingers, and almost stuck her strong teeth into it when I rose upon her.

Again I heard a kind of hum, like the sea. I asked her if she'd said something.

'Nothing,' she said, and smiled.

On the fourth or fifth morning she stood before me in the

doorway, and her eyes were moist behind the smile. When I asked her to come in, she shook her head in shamed refusal, as if pleading for her life.

'Can I stay?' she whispered.

Two tears rolled down from her eyes into the dimples in her cheeks. She was so little. The light seemed to fall on her from above; from her eyes down she was enveloped in shade. She stood ready for anything, even to leave.

I'd come to a place on the edge of the desert. This small apartment which I'd decided to make into my solitary cave. But Anath takes up so little space. And she doesn't talk. She doesn't even ask for anything.

Already on the second day she disappeared for several hours and returned, small and smiling, a strange glow in her eyes.

Towards evening we stood at the window and looked. Darkness started descending. The darkness, like the light, descends here unobstructed. Opposite us, two or three forms stood shuffling in the doorway of a kiosk, making strange, silent movements, as if conspiring in some plot. Beside them was a garden of stones. Low trees and bushes, bent to the ground, and, rising above them, structures of stones. The stones are hard, their hue from gleaming black to purple brown like clotting blood. A garden of naked forms, and two or three houses as far as the eye could see. Nothing moved, the customers next to the kiosk were frozen.

'You're sad,' she whispered into my armpit, where her head used to show up sometimes, during the first days. I picked her up in the air and kissed her face.

'Imagine the voice of a child,' she said in the softest of whispers, and wrapped herself around me.

Horrors! I didn't imagine that. I imagined a lot of thin voices while she hummed upon me. A stone, give me a stone. There's something noble in a world that's barren, stone-like.

'Look,' I said.

Anath looked and smiled inwards. A whirlwind of dust. Suddenly it started swelling, lifting a head. If not for the strong afternoon light which distorts things, I would have said that I saw Anath rising, growing, higher and higher.

'Like a queen. She crosses the mountain accumulating dust. Into her belly, gathering, gathering. See, she's got a head, hasn't she?'

'You talk like a poet,' she made her voice hoarse as if

trying to disguise an old contempt.

'No. I worked at it. I tried. No matter.'

I went out of the house for long hours. I went walking on the mountains, among the stones. My pockets filled with stones, in my hands – stones. When I got home we'd have a quick roll – I soon discovered, to my amazement and perhaps even to my comfort, that Anath cut all the preparatory acts as short as possible – on the bed, beside the bed, on the step, the doorway, anywhere. Afterwards Anath would bring me sandwiches and coffee, and wake me. Sometimes salt-herring, a slice of sausage, almost always olives. Soup very rarely, with kinds of vegetables, white roots which Anath brought from somewhere. She didn't ask, but apparently she understood that my means, now our means, were limited. And she didn't complain.

One day she drew my hand to her belly. 'Can you feel?'

I didn't feel anything, of course. Better that my hand should turn to stone. Hadn't she always calmed me: no need to worry.

'Sweet,' I said. I meant her belly, the pulsing in it always on the ready.

But, true, Anath had grown a little. In more than one direction, I'd say. Otherwise it's hard to explain why recently I'd been finding myself pushed increasingly to the edge of the bed. And even off it. After all, it wasn't the smallest of beds.

The little joke cost her dear. I went through her like a threshing tank. If there was something alive in there, it must have burst, turned into air, into acids. And now it's your turn, Anath! I'll tear you apart, Tilhamath! A new heaven and a new earth I'll make of your body!

Anath wanted more. She parted her lips; they were moist. Her teeth were in my flesh.

That day I saw on the western ridge a kind of open structure on six columns. Then the structure divided into two and I saw two camels. I sat on a rock and saw the round sun hiding, very yellow among the stones. The hydra had twelve heads. When one was cut off, two grew in its place. How much time was needed to fill the world with them? And she also had an eternal head which some ancient hero had hidden among stones.

Some five weeks after our meeting Anath informed me that there was no longer any doubt. Her eyes were good, promising. For some time now I'd been ready, not without dread, to hear anything from my little love. Hadn't I seen her swelling? And maybe there was more than one in there. In my mind's eye I saw a huge queen bee, its belly swarming. Nightmare! That thought alone was enough to make a man shrink. I played the shrinking man in front of the mirror in the wardrobe, during the hours when Anath went out bare-foot to the mountains. Or maybe it wasn't play, the light made me smaller, the closed shutters, Anath loved a sad coolness.

I am a sullen man by nature. The smile I borrowed from Anath. She looks at me with a demanding smile, until I respond to her. Sometimes she's away all night and comes back before morning, dew in her tangled hair and the soles of her feet black with the dust of black rock, gleaming. She smiles, and without a word descends upon me, a mountain of sweetness and grace.

And later, 'Move. You're hurting them.'

There was no point in my pretending I didn't know whom she meant. Once I saw, in a movie, a queen termite, her tiny ones bustling under her belly, rolling her about, getting squashed, but not ceasing. And all that time she kept pour-ing out new termites, tiny cubs for the morrow, for the future, termites for all intents, to get squashed by her belly and to keep rolling on.

After all, I had offspring of my own, somewhere, deserted. I fled to the barren stones, the first and last of a world that was solid, dead.

The circles widened. I encompassed the mountains, up to the highest peak, where the Dead Sea plain comes into view. And a vapour rose from there as from a furnace – sometimes that is how the radiance looks – silent, crystalline. On the other side were the dismal hills of Moab, and beneath them – the surface of the sea, polished like a mirror. There, on the hills of Moab, human sacrifices had been made. That was where I looked, leaning on a rock, the sun of noon in the circle of my eyes, silent like a thing among things.

Anath didn't ask questions, her eyes didn't search. She was certain I'd be back.

Once I asked her – what'll happen when the money runs out. She shook her head quietly as if to say: we'll find a way.

The big mirror in the wardrobe no longer contained us both. At the start of our relationship we'd both be embraced, and more than that, and the big mirror didn't hide a thing. Now I had to rise up behind Anath to steal a glance at my dusty unkempt eye above her shoulder. Unless she stood behind me, big and wonderful. Lilith spreading butterfly wings.

I could no longer avoid her. She was everywhere in the apartment. I fled and I came back. I sought her face, in my own way.

Her houserobes amazed me. They filled the wardrobe. She didn't need any other clothes, almost. Her black dress, in which I'd met her in the bar, two or three panties and bras heaped in a little pile in the corner of the wardrobe, and all the rest, apart from my few clothes – houserobes, house-robes. One in particular especially amazed me – a huge houserobe which didn't fit into the width of the wardrobe and was rolled twice around the hanger. It was painted with innocent little flowers with few leaves, clusters of yellow and purple. And more trees, shade, streams of water. The smell of moss came to my nose. I asked her where she'd got such a huge thing, like a giant's garment.

'I brought it with me,' she answered innocently.

I wanted to ask: From where? I didn't ask. I was afraid she'd say that *she'd already worn it in the past*. When? Where? How many offspring had she already given to death? I burst out of the house.

'Bring something. We're hungry,' she whispered after me.

Anath's appetite, which from the outset hadn't been small, had increased greatly. We didn't eat delicacies. Olives, salt-fish, peas, sometimes tomatoes and potatoes. Even now she didn't ask for other foods. She cooked soups from strange roots, white, like worms, but hard. She would squeeze them out, finally, and give them to the cats. The cats fled from her, the lizards didn't. Gleaming back, they stood over the roots until they'd finished them. The problem was quantity. It started with paper bags; now even two baskets a day barely sufficed. I had only the smallest part in it, which grew smaller and smaller. Of late I'd go through a day with one tomato and some olives, which I kept in my pockets.

Full of wonder I gaze at Anath. She eats slowly, with an economy of movements, but, it must be said, chewing to the end, deriving the last juice out of everything. Peels and all. Anath doesn't spit, she likes cleanliness. She passes the tips of her fingers with a kind of regal grace over the olive, the tomato, the fish, the potato, before eating them. And then over her mouth. No belch of nauseating satiety, as is the custom of the vulgar. And already she's set to start all over from the beginning.

Fascinated, I watch how she finishes off two baskets of food a day, now more. I've read about species of insects which in one day consume a quantity of food greater by ten times and more than their weight. For Anath that doesn't hold. Because she's big, too.

And still she grows. It's easy to see that the centre of growth is in the pelvic area, and from there outwards – to the head and limbs. When I look at her, I forget things, and that's good. Unfortunately, I also forget to eat and when I remember, there's only scraps left. And a hum rising, soft and spreading, encompassing you like a sea. I don't have the strength to stand her.

I drown. Anath wakes me with slaps on the back, like a baby, pulls me out, trembling, licks me, stands me up on my feet. She even gives me a thin slice of bread and a few olives, which she's kept aside for me.

2

In October the *khamsin* winds of autumn came early, and a kind of seasonal disquiet, somehow heavy, expectant, rising on desert sand, started to seep in among the few houses, sprawled on the stone paths, and covered people's faces with a secret silence. Anath barely went out, or moved, perhaps to gather strength for the main effort – growth. She willingly received whatever I brought her. My savings were running out quicker than I'd imagined. And the day came when I brought her two full baskets with the last of my money. I didn't say a word, but Anath knew. She ate slowly in a kind of quiet rite, as if giving thanks, and only when she'd finished everything did she raise her eyes to me, big and pleading. I knew I couldn't abandon her. I went to work.

This strength that's in stones. Black, glowing, lying on the mountain, deaf to time, accumulating sun. We come, pull them up, throw them into the box of the truck, roll them on the road, build traffic islands. And the good burning in the hands. The blisters and scratches too. And the strength rising in the hips.

And what clarity.

They respect my silences, the others. I don't take part in their breaks, I don't smoke cigarettes. I don't like in-between bites, when my mouth is dry, and the sun hangs over us and over the dead plain, unobstructed.

Perhaps they don't notice me. They don't even notice a rock until they cut their hands on it. I've become small, I don't take up much space any more, but I pave it, black stone beside brown stone, paving and cutting, working quickly, eagerly, paving myself into a continuous path. Especially during those hours when alone – the others sprawled out munching their lunch in the shade of the tin white plaster of a new house – I catch a broken ray of sun, an arrow of light which breaks on a stone and pierces my temple.

All of me, then, turns into a crystal of clarity. My eye closes and I see a mighty wave of little creatures, quivering, hungering for life, sliding down the mountain, and on top of the naked mountain, looking down on the plain, Anath, huge and majestic, her teeth gleaming.

It was no hallucination, I knew that it comes. My mind was clear.

The lazy, big-shouldered, chattering workers – it was they who brought me back from the edges: I lost measure, slipped away from the straight islands, continued the paving to a garden of ornamental cultured plants, fenced in. My stones covered up the bushes one by one. They were small, miserable, making no protest as they were stiffed. The men tried to fix them, to revive them. I promised a stone monument in place of each plant, stinted leaves moving, moving towards some urgent tomorrow. They laughed at a joke. Nothing matters to them. They move like dinosaurs. And at the end of the day, while they go home, I go to the grocery to load three full baskets on my diminishing shoulders, for Anath. And Anath is happy.

It's good to see Anath happy. The quiet radiance in her eyes. She sits there broad, sheltering, her soft eyes on the hard mountain opposite, from where they come and to where they vanish, the agamas. A whole school, some of them are always next to the house, burrowing around it or freezing in the sun like small copper tombstones. Suddenly they move, lick the sharp air with darts of the tongue, and freeze again, waiting, as if they know it'll come in the end, the great prey.

The house is very clean. Dust is nothing to Anath, who walks in it clean and broad as a queen. She chews slowly but all the time, almost. In between she falls upon me, a sweet mountain, thawing, engulfing me all around like a river of delights. The agamas don't disturb us. It's reasonable to assume that it's they who are our cleaning-workers, cleaning our room, finishing off every scrap. At any rate they won't do this during our comings-together. They come afterwards, collect, go out, gnaw their scraps among the stones, with a politeness that is all patience. When I go I see them come, when I come back they are no longer there, and Anath – her arms are always stretched out towards me. Tired and longing, I fall into them, plunge into the delightful velvet which goes on and on until waking.

At night, in dream, rocks bend their heads over me, bull heads, gleaming, grey, crumbling. I thank Anath who raises me at every corner, encompasses me with pulses, pulls me out half alive and brings me back to life, to the stones.

Once Anath woke me to look at the sunrise. Never had I seen her so aroused – a quivering mass of love and pity, spreading out her arms to the world, to the sun, which had just risen on the horizon. A small, hard, circle, very clear, turned on her forehead, sailed between her arms. And I too. We both lost ourselves there, and when I got up to go I said to myself: see, this great big wonderful thing, all this grace, to me it is given, and I support it. Recovered, I went out to my day's work.

If only my day's work were enough for Anath. But it wasn't enough any more. I took on credit. To fill four baskets is no little thing, nor is it easy to carry them on two ropes over my shoulders after a wearying workday. But, I must admit, it also clears the mind. Sharp as flint, my brain now raced over the islands of stone spreading out on all sides and even climbing up the fronts of the few houses, engorging them into the cold landscape. All the avenues of stone run up to the ridge and climb up it – and there the plain opens. Like a polished stone, the sea between mountain and mountain. Anath between the pillows, a huge garden, trees with curling roots, secret paths and moss. Her eyes pulse before me and my mind clears up, tracking and counting the creases of Anath's desire.

Sometimes everything looks like a single desire. More food. The house has grown very cramped. When Anath passes through it I push myself into the recess in the wall meant for cleaning utensils, and wait. And when she calls me I know.

Now she called me. Softly she passed her hand over my head and asked me to listen to her belly. I listened. I no longer had to bend over – when I stood erect now my head touched her belly. I heard many lives. Whole days, the stonecutters chisel in my hand, I pursued them, or perhaps they pursued me, wanting to separate, to recognize, to burst out. I became tired, I fell in a heap at the end of the row. The workers woke me with splashes of water. Was I at the end of my strength?

I knew where her eyes were looking. To the cold store. One entrance and only one man guarding it. An erect structure, grey, hostile, peeling plaster, no stone had been added to it. It looks like a blend of three towers placed side by side, supporting each other on the edge of the desert. Fruits and vegetables from places of soil and moss were brought here in big sealed containers. Every day ten containers or more. One a day would supply Anath's needs. At least for a while.

Perhaps I was slow with my response. Could I have had any doubts? Her hair covered her eyes, and from in there came her voice, stifled with sorrow:

'You know we need it. For our children. For tomorrow.'

I trembled. It was the longest speech I'd heard her make. It was accompanied by a host of little voices, from where I stood at her feet I could hear them clearly – a growing exultant chorus, rising from some place inside her huge houserobe.

As soon as night came I was at the place. There was no fear that the guard might identify me. An old man, half blind, smiling at everyone who came and went, he seemed unseeing, listening. At night, listening – during the day, sitting in the sun, rubbing the cataract in his eyes.

'Take, Mr. Gomer, take whatever you want,' he whispered between empty gums.

So the old man had recognized me. He sat small and helpless on a straw stool in the doorway. A small blow with a stonecutter's hammer would silence him for ever.

I went back, my hands empty.

Anath didn't reprove me. She embraced me in her big warm arms. She loves me in her way, this big, wonderful woman. She forgave me for everything, and in the abundance of her grace, amid convulsions of her great body –

convulsions of hunger – now seething with so many lives, so many hungry lives, she didn't leave a crease or crevice of her body which didn't envelop me.

That's Anath. She didn't reprove me, and didn't complain. Not even on our last night. Listening inwards, her eyes dreaming, she wouldn't say: we're hungry. She'd say: we're young, full of strength. A young world. She wouldn't speak. Her giant body would speak, now wrapped inside the biggest houserobe of all, the one I'd seen in the wardrobe rolled around the hanger twice, perhaps three times.

I was afraid and fascinated. A sweet mountain. I was lost among its ranges. I clung to her, tooth and nail, as if seeking, in her, protection from her. I knew this characteristic of Anath's – when they're hungry she wraps herself over me with ever-growing desire. All this vast beauty, now so active, not a single part of it will give up its avidity to caress, to bite, to suck. A hunger full of power, intoxicating.

But my mind was very clear. I tried to count them, all the little heads which pressed from every place in her body. They were beyond measure. They looked as if they were all pressing at every place at one and the same time. The hum, too, could be heard from every place.

Anath's white teeth, charmingly spaced but strong, smiled at me as the sun cast its first light upon us. Perhaps I had wanted to go outside, to the bald mountains, the barren stones. I'm not sure, I didn't want much any more. Anath didn't prevent me from pulling my head out of her and looking. My eyes climbed with the islands of stones to the top of the ridge, where they fell into the salt break. There was no point in resisting. A giant camp of hungering, quivering creatures slid down from the mountain, ran about from stone to stone, their colour a transparent green. How green Anath became. All of her, except for her white teeth, which gleamed like blades.

I knew she'd start from the extremities, at any rate from the lower parts. Her fingers fluttered over my face, delicate, and only her tongue and her teeth, from time to time, with the first taste, were avid, but not hasty. So I will finally be able to follow systematically the last stages of the process of shrinking. I will try to keep my mind lucid until the end. How much solace there is in the thought that after me it will be the others' turn.

Translated by Richard Flantz

238

Hanoch Levin

Pshishpash's Plight

1. PSHISHPASH AND THE CHAMPION WRESTLER

IT had always pained Pshishpash the thief that he was working while the people he was robbing slept. On the face of it, it was the nature of his work that it be done at night, on the sly, in the rooms of sleeping victims unable to notice his activities; on the face of it he should have thought it a blessing. Sleep, if you look at it objectively, is a terrible state, a man is so helpless when asleep. He sinks into unconsciousness, leaving himself at the mercy of the unknown, his heart full of cold misgivings. Who knows what may happen while he sleeps; any child whose attack we could, when awake, repeal with the slightest kick can, while we sleep, bash our head in with a kitchen utensil or a heavy toy. And the world is so full of children, dogs, women and diseases and you never know who you can trust and who you can't. A great fear, accompanied by a procession of small ones march over us as if we were a mat. And so this situation, in which the robbed are asleep and the thief awake, gives the robber an advantage – but Pshishpash refused to take this point of view. His constant enviousness made him see it as his fate to be spending his strength in hard night labor and in fear of discovery and capture among people resting in their beds and breathing in serene oblivion. (By the way, it is true that as soon as someone falls asleep he ceases to fear it and so behaves calmly as if his situation were excellent and free of danger and as if he were not alarmingly helpless. That is the paradox of sleep. If only we could find a way to sleep and yet continue to fear sleep at the same time, we will have solved a basic human problem.)

Lately Pshishpash's resentment had grown to such a degree that he would intentionally create a noise in the room of the robbery in order to desecrate the sleep of the occupants, with their open mouths and cosy movements. He didn't even mind that the price was the success of the robbery itself. The first to wake would jump up and call out 'Who's there?' and Pshishpash would run away or get caught by a brave person who had actually left his bed and launched his warm body into the dark. The second to awake would then also rise up and ask 'Who's there?' and on hearing the first cry 'Thief! thief!' would switch on the light. Mostly in these cases, if caught, Pshishpash would get not too badly beaten because people recently awakened are not at their strongest. He would beg them, using cunning and flattery, to leave him alone and not call the police. His flattery would usually create a more cheerful atmosphere in the room, and the newly awakened assembly would start laughing, the laughter emanating from relief. And why not? The robbery had been averted, no harm had been done. The first to raise the alarm would laugh the hardest, because in addition to his relief there was the pride of possessing the keenest senses. He would be content and merciful and suggest the release of Pshishpash. Everybody would go back to bed and sleep the better for it as none of their property had been lost and they had gained an exciting criminal experience in which they were firmly on the right side of the law. It is good to uphold the law and pleasant to sit in the lap of righteousness.

Old women, stubborn and cruel would not forego calling the police when they caught Pshishpash, and in time he learnt not to wake them and would complete his mission successfully; indeed they were his bread and butter. O stupid women, you are evil because you are poor and you are poor because you are evil; too bad about you. But there were meagre takings in such houses and Pshishpash, who continued to awaken his other victims, was definitely going downhill professionally speaking. He couldn't get over his petty enviousness which arose in him whenever he saw his victims restful and snug in their nightclothes.

One night Pshishpash was climbing up a drainpipe as usual, thinking about the water going down the drain as he was going up – a simple-minded analogy, which, because of his tendency to belittle himself, he could not put out of his mind. In the top storey a little window was open and Pshishpash climbed on to the sill and looked in. A minute or two later his eyes began to see a small room, untidily furnished, a bachelor's room in which women come and go, each one leaving behind little trinkets that clash with one another. Newspapers were strewn over the floor and photographs cut out of them were hanging on the walls. On the bed lay a young man, heavy and well built, wearing only white under- pants and with no blanket over him. He was deep in slumber of the kind that makes sleepers resemble profound philo- sophers with important ideas to express. It is a well known fact that people wear profound expressions while sleeping or eating because they are deeply involved in these activities. Men sitting on the toilet get the dreamy aspect of poets, eyes wandering in space and lips half open, and women with artistic inclinations seeing them in this position often fall in love with them.

Pshishpash hopped into the room soundlessly. His eyes searched for the place where the man might be hiding his money. He looked at a pair of trousers on the floor and tried to get nearer and grab them before his usual resentment against sleepers interrupted his work, but even as he was bending over the trousers he knew that his resentment had taken control of him. Head down he stood over the trousers, captive to resentment and anger which were taking over limb after limb: here am I, on a stifling summer night, wear- ing sweaty clothes, with a burglar's cap on my head and a burglar's mask on my eyes, climbing up pipes, straining my eyes in the dark to look for the money and possessions of others, always others, humble servant to a powerful need to meddle in other people's things, standing in front of this well built young man, whose chest rises and falls with his breath- ing as though breathing were the most natural thing in the world and not an act of perpetuating the burden, whose face is completely calm and who permits me to run around and air his trousers while he dreams of success, of honour, of beautiful women! Pshishpash could stand it no longer, he came nearer the bed and as he did so the figure of the man upon it grew larger and Pshishpash suddenly realized that here was an unusually large and solid man, his calves and thighs and arms firmly muscular. His anger mounted at the thought of the extra strength this man was accumulating as he slept.

The familiar moment arrived: the desire to waken the man took complete possession of him and became a necessity – but the thief's advantage over his sleeping victim is a basic rule of burglary and Pshishpash would have sinned against his profession if he had openly given up this advantage. Therefore he pretended to have arrived at the professional conclusion that a man like this would probably sleep on his money and so he would have to slip a finger underneath him and poke around. In this way he could waken the man as though unintentionally. He started pushing his finger under the sleeping man's back, slightly above his waist. The man turned his head round and a sweet groan escaped his lips, but Pshishpash didn't stop poking.

'Mmm?' the man said, hovering on the narrow border between sleep and wakefulness – and opened his eyes. He saw before him a dark shadow and impulsively put his hand out to grasp. His hand rose and touched Pshishpash's face and, failing to find anything to grab hold of, it slipped down and stopped, firmly grabbing his shirt collar. With his other hand the man pressed the switch on the night light at his head and the room was lit. Pshishpash, bent over the man with his finger still stuck under his back, felt some satisfaction for having damaged the man's sleep, but on the other hand began feeling fear as well. Softly he said:

'Have I disturbed you?'

And after a little while:

'I guess I did.'

After another short silence he said:

'O.K., so I got caught.'

And after another:

'Sorry.'

Gently he extracted his finger from under the man's back and said:

'Thanks.'

The polite words were meant to spare him a beating. The man didn't let go of Pshishpash's collar, but neither did he pull him towards himself or look as though he might be about to hit him. Apparently he was still too sleepy and was waiting to regain his wits before he decided how to react correctly. Pshishpash, however, was already impatiently waiting for the blow both because he knew it was inevitable and the sooner it came the better and because he was already regretting having wakened the man, hating himself and longing to be punished. Anticipation of a beating is terrible torture because we don't know how bad it will be and how injurious as well as insulting. Waiting on the edge of patience, fondly hoping that our body remains unscathed and that we shall feel not the slightest pain. O how we yearn for there to be no unpleasantness. In order to cut the waiting short Pshishpash said:

'Thief.'

and in order to avoid any misunderstanding he added:

'I mean me.'

With a sneaking glance he observed that the cuttings hanging on the walls were photographs of the man stretched on the bed underneath him. In the pictures he could be seen leaping in the air naked but for shorts, in a boxing ring, waving his leather gloved hands. In all the pictures his rival would be flat out on the floor, or leaning weakly against the ropes, or holding on to his aching head. Well, thought Pshishpash, this time I got caught by a professional fighter. This time I'll really get shaken, this time I shall be punished like never before. My limbs will get rattled either side of my spine, my heart, stomach, liver and kidneys will all drop down to gather at the bottom of my belly, broken loose from their arteries. How many vulnerable parts there are in a body. Yes, this time the hand of justice will not strike lightly. And I shall suffer, I will suffer and writhe round the strong hand. How good it is to writhe and curl up in pain round a real, strong hand. Pshishpash was already visualizing himself circumventing the hand as the pious circumvent the altar, screaming and shouting in the pains of hell and in the desire give the hand thanks and praise to the high heavens. This is the hand whose blow I have been seeking all my life.

The wrestler pulled Pshishpash's shirt collar slightly and drew him nearer effortlessly. The ease with which he was pulling the burglar towards himself drew his attention to his strength and to the total ease with which he coped with life in general. He drew his torso backwards, propped a pillow against the wall and leaned on it in a nearly seated position. Life often brought him situations in which he felt sure of himself, strong and potent, immediately able to break, bend and twist everything about him. But this occasion surpassed them all for easy confidence. The wrestler could not recollect a previous occasion in which it had ever been simpler to smash somebody's face. He was fully awake now and could observe, at an angle, his golden-brown shoulder; he followed the glance down his arm, wrist and hand until his eyes rested upon Pshishpash. The difference between his shoulder and Pshishpash's face was enormous and not at all favourable to the owner of that face. It was not merely the rich brown colour, full of sun-given health, against the spotty paleness with the occasional red patches which filled the burglar's face, but mainly the astounding and wonderful smoothness of the shoulder compared with the clutter of features – nose, lips, eyes, forehead, chin, etc. – on such a limited space, a jumble of shapes and substances which nature had unloaded upon this smelly head. The wrestler felt so good confronting the thief that it made him feel quite weak and the hand holding Pshishpash's collar fell on to the bed. As often happens with people overcome with joy, who are virtually paralysed by it, so the recognition of his own strength made the wrestler suddenly limp. Weakly he said: 'Get me a glass of milk from the fridge.'

Pshishpash did not hesitate. His body grateful for not having been beaten, he went to the little kitchen rather elated. He returned immediately with the glass of milk in his hand. The wrestler raised the glass to his lips with a trembling hand, looked at it briefly and pushed it away.

'I can't drink,' he said, 'you make me feel weak.'

A little milk had spilt from the shaking glass on to the bed. Pshishpash pulled a handkerchief from his pocket and hurriedly began rubbing at the stain. He rubbed vigorously, knowing that for once he was doing something useful. 'Stop that this minute. You're making me weak,' the wrestler said. 'A glass of cold milk served in bed at night, cleaning and polishing – it's all so pleasant that I can't bear it any more.'

A soft and pleasant sensation was filling his brain, spreading through his entire body and paralysing it. Anxiously he gazed at the glass of milk and handed it to Pshishpash, who put it on the night table next the bed, and dropped his hand to his side as if after some exertion.

'Bastard, you've made a fly out of me,' he muttered heavily – even his tongue was getting weak – as Pshishpash leant over him worriedly, 'and the championship fight is the day after tomorrow.'

Pshishpash, the joy of having been spared a terrible beating now evaporated only to be replaced by the fear that he may not be beaten at all, couldn't bear the wrestler's words. How could he, himself, make people weak? If he could make people weak, that would make him a somebody, the possessor of a degree of strength and responsibility. And that would be impossible, the results far too complicated. Pshishpash was ready to carry many heavy burdens, but not that of himself. So he must do something to give this wonderful man, the fruit of wise nature's own will, his strength back. This man has to fight for the championship the day after tomorrow and there is the risk he might lose because of Pshishpash. A flood of self-destruction swept over him and he was near to doing something irreversible – only he knew there was no one to save him. For deep down he wanted to live after all. But if not destruction at least he must do something to correct the damage, to give the wrestler his strength back. Pshishpash lifted a finger, brought it near the fighter's eyes and moved it along, very close to the lashes, whistling through his teeth at the same time:

'zzzz . . . zzzz . . .'

He paused, bent over, looked at the wrestler closely and continued

'zzzz . . . zzzz . . .'

After two or three minutes of this childish irritation, the wrestler began to feel annoyed. His anger started to well up. Pshishpash would pause every once in a while to see how the anger was coming along, and the man's strength with it. At first he tried to drive the moving finger away by batting his eyelashes, but Pshishpash carried on in the unshakable faith of a man convinced that his action is for the fighter's own good. The man's anger increased, wonderful power poured into his arms and – by jove! – he put out a swift hand, grabbed Pshishpash's moving finger and bent it. An unpleasant crunching noise was heard, and Pshishpash yelped shrilly. The wrestler's hand dropped to his side and his head fell on to the pillow. 'It's so easy to break fingers,' he whispered, powers ebbing, 'So easy that I shall never be able to move again from weakness. I am lost.'

Pshishpash, who had just paid a heavy price for his avid dedication to saving the fighter, sat on the floor, his entire body focused upon his bent, broken finger, and groaned with pain. There's gratitude for you, he thought, he'd break all my bones before I make him well again. I'm getting out. As far as I'm concerned he can lose the championship. Let him become the ring cleaner. Pshishpash was quick to forget his self-hatred with the slightest pain. Like everybody else, he too wanted to be safe and well whatever the cost. He would leave the soul-searching until after his recovery.

He jumped on to the window-sill, held on to the drainpipe with his legs and one arm. His first thought was to slide down without saying a word and without looking back at the wrestler, so great was his concentration in his pain. On the other hand, he wanted the satisfaction of seeing the man lost and helpless on his bed. He turned his head towards the lying man through the window square, against the night background, only to see the fighter's face slowly turning towards him, his lips silently mouthing:

'So easy . . . so easy . . . I shall never get up again . . .'

For a brief moment Pshishpash still attempted to derive satisfaction from the sight, but to no avail. He slid down the drain with one finger sticking out, crookedly, in the air.

2. PSHISHPASH AND THE MIDGET USHER

Pshishpash loved to hate many things about himself. He hated the shape of his head, the build of his body, his nose, manner of speech and walk. It was a natural hate of long standing which, in time, faded and was almost forgotten. Above and beyond this routine, trivial hate was his hatred for his lips, because these pretended, more than any other part of his body, to show simultaneously a strong passion for life and an ironic view of it and Pshishpash who was far from having the pretense of such an attitude to life and who spent most of his time despising himself, was ashamed that his lips expressed things he could not live up to. And beyond the two hates, at the summit of his baseness ruled his deep hate for his own ambition to improve his life. This was a real hate, a substantial hate, a fever, the revolt of a man like him against the very thought that his life might have a chance, against his inability to let go of life, against the impertinence of trying again and again.

The heavy burden of the three hates brought to Pshishpash the image of a man urinating into his own mouth. But we are hard-bodied people, our bones are solid, we are clumsy. We cannot urinate into our own mouths. We can urinate on our feet, yes, anybody can do that, but we want to do it into our mouths, our mouths, our mouths! But our mouths open wide, we shovel food into them and swallow air sorrowfully and ask ourselves when will we have the strength and agility to punish ourselves in more unusual, more imaginative ways? Acrobats must be happy people because they can urinate into their mouths. I shall go to the circus, Pshishpash thought, and ask one of the acrobats to demonstrate how its done and train me so that I may reach the same achievement. There was no circus in town at that time. For six months Pshishpash waited impatiently. At the end of that time a circus came to town. The children were happy and so was Pshishpash, but differently. His was a heavy hearted, apprehensive happiness, the joy of the anticipated burning insult. The children, as usual, experienced that noisy, mindless happiness which we are inclined to find charming only for the sake of their soft, smooth flesh. We forgive a child like we forgive a bottom.

In the evening Pshishpash went along to the circus, made his way among the gay crowds who were queueing to get in. As a thief he did not buy a ticket but crawled in through the back fence, near the animal cages. Suddenly he felt something tugging at his trouser leg. Looking down he saw a midget dressed in usher's uniform holding on to his thigh and looking up at him.

'Thief! where's your ticket?!' the midget usher shouted. Pshishpash immediately made the most of the other's size to hurt him:

'And what can a midget do to me?'

From childhood the midget was trained to recognize the insults and react in angry desperation. He held on to Pshishpash's leg like a drowning man: 'If I were taller I'd have grabbed you by the collar! Unfortunately I'm not tall!' 'Not tall!' giggled Pshishpash. It wasn't a true giggle because he was not a jolly, carefree giggler. It had been many years since he had laughed or smiled wholeheartedly and the bad feeling of doing the wrong thing was always behind his smiles. But giggles are one thing and the desire to free his leg from the midget's grip are another. He said:

'Get off my leg at once!'

The midget was furious with the sneak's impertinence. He knew full well that if only he were a normal sized usher, the man would have been fearful. It wasn't fair that his height should make criminals feel unruffled.

'You'll be sorry you were born!' he screamed. When furious he had the tendency to exaggerate. Pshishpash was afraid he might start giggling again, and nearly wagged the midget's cap to show his contempt, but the pain in his leg made him more practical.

'Take me to one of the acrobats,' he said.

'Take you to one of the acrobats?! have I become your

guide? Phooey! And since when have we had acrobats in this circus? This is a circus of old animals and deformed people. Phooey!' With each spit the midget tried to release some of the anger bubbling inside him.

'If so let me get out and let go of my leg,' said Pshishpash.

'Without punishment? Are you mad?'

'Look, I've been caught and I haven't seen the show,' Pshishpash tried to reason. He was very worried he might be drawn into making fun of the little man again.

'Oh if only I were a little taller I'd get you by the collar and drag you along! I'd stand at the gate and get you all by the collar, one by one, you with your collars, I'd crumple them in my hand and press on the napes of your necks!'

'Let go,' Pshishpash said again.

'You're not going without being punished!' the midget usher shouted in a thin, reedy voice, probably because of all the talk about collars, which had always been his favourite target and made him increasingly excited. 'I may not be able to reach your collar, but there are parts which I can reach, by God, yes I can, easily!'

And he wasted no time abandoning Pshishpash's leg, jumped back, bent over Pshishpash's shoe and with a quick movement unlaced it and was about to run off with the lace. Pshishpash caught him by the collar and was unable to control the malice:

'You can't reach collars – but I can.'

The midget usher, with a shoelace in one hand, swung his other hand upwards in an attempt to leap in the air and slap Pshishpash's face, but Pshishpash did not loosen his grip on the collar, pushed the dwarf down and pressed him to the ground. The midget gave up trying to do what he had known all along he couldn't. In quiet frustration he remarked:

'Because you're taller than I am.'

Pshishpash shook him and replied:

'Yes, I'm tall, I'm tall.'

'Beside me you're tall!' The midget whined loudly. 'You can thank God for making midgets for you to compare yourself to! Go and get a photographer to take a picture of the two of us as a souvenir of your great height!'

It didn't take long for Pshishpash to lose his patience with the suffering midget and his endless discordant whining about his size. After all, we save up what little patience we

248

have for our own troubles, not others'. He shook the midget again and pushed him away. The dwarf fell and rose again quickly due to the short distance between his head and the ground. He waved the shoelace in his hand and said:

'And this goes straight to the lion.'

He turned and started running. Apparently the midget often used the lion threat and saw himself a part of it. Pshishpash quickly caught up with him and grabbed his collar again.

'Again! Just because I'm a midget!' the dwarf screamed. He had a perpetual need to explain and excuse his weaknesses. 'You could beat me at anything because of my height!' He was about to explode from the pressure of his urgent demand for justice.

'What do I care,' said Pshishpash, 'I want my shoelace.'

'Take it. Who needs your shoelace? Who needs a shoelace anyway? Or do you want me to kneel and lace your shoe for you?'

And he quickly bent down and grabbed Pshishpash's shoe. Pshishpash freed his leg with a powerful jerk and shouted:

'Let's have that shoelace now!'

'Take it, take it!' The midget said disgustedly. He got up on his feet, threw the shoelace on the ground and added:

'Phooey!'

He spat at the shoelace. Pshishpash realized that he had just lost his shoelace, as he would never touch anything with somebody else's spittle on it. He leapt on the dwarf and was about to grab, for the third time, his crushed and crumpled collar. But this time the midget was expecting this and, knowing he could not escape, fell backwards on the ground, lay there prostrate and said:

'Please carry on.'

Pshishpash bent over him.

'There's no need to hit me,' the midget said, 'You can stamp on me with your foot. Phooey! I'm fed up with fighting about my size. A dwarf must pay the price. Please. Stamp away!'

Pshishpash got down on his knees and breathed in the little man's face.

'Why the hesitation?' the midget usher asked. 'Why do you hesitate, all of you? I demand a final decision about myself! A final decision!'

'I have no interest in beating you up,' Pshishpash said.

'Why not? I'm a healthy man, I can still take some good strong beatings.'

'I'm looking for an acrobat who can piss into his mouth,' Pshishpash said, his face all red from bending down.

'Piss into his mouth? What for? Are you miserable? Yes, I guess you must be miserable.' The midget usher chuckled, his mood elated by the discovery of this new misery. 'You look O.K., on the outside, but you're probably a cripple inside. Midget inside? Hunchback inside? Worm inside?'

'Where can I find the acrobat?' Pshishpash asked.

'We haven't got any acrobats. I already told you.'

'And in what circus can I find them?'

'I don't know. You think that just because I'm with a circus I know all about them. I know nothing about circuses and circus affairs, and I don't care either. The only thing I care about is the fact that I'm a midget and nothing else. My dwarfhood, my dwarfhood and my dwarfhood again! MY DWARFHOOD!!!'

And he quickly added:

'For a small sum my friend, who is also a midget, and I would be willing to piss into one another's mouths. It won't cost you much.'

And he began drumming his heel nervously, like some tense businessman.

'No,' said Pshishpash, 'I'm looking for someone who can do it to himself.'

'You're crazy. You're mad. What acrobat would do a thing like that? What for? Is he miserable? Does he suffer? He wouldn't have any of your afflictions. He'd beat you up for even suggesting such a thing. My friend and I, on the other hand, would put our souls into it. What do you say? Don't be stubborn. You don't know acrobats, I do. An acrobat is a strong, agile man. His body is perfectly built and he moves as if he's dancing. More often than not he's handsome too, because he must cultivate his appearance if he is to captivate an audience every night. An acrobat performs difficult and complicated exercises, he works with his body. His work produces power guided by knowledge, it's beautiful, liberating work, like life itself. He has no time for and no interest in soul-searching. He is always outward looking, his eyes see what goes on outside, not inside, he laughs in company not in maddening solitude. He has no reasons for morbid introspection. His love life? when he decides to get married he has no difficulty in finding a woman. He gets to know many women in his travels. He can easily have rich women, beautiful women, even Swiss women, women outside the circus, and then he abandons his profession and goes into business using his wife's money. Money, money, money, he can enjoy life. And the money is, naturally, safe in a Swiss bank. And even if he marries a woman from inside the circus, a trapeze artist, singer or horse trainer, then she is a marvellous thing, blonde, who wears short white skirts, her thighs beautifully tanned and her teeth white and even. True, they lead nomadic lives in the circus and live in caravans, – by the way, very comfortable caravans – but they rule! They rule! He rules his body, the trapeze bars, the air he flies through. She rules over the midget, the orchestra or the horse who are partners in her act. And both rule over the audience. And don't worry, in time they'll save up money and start their own business. The fact that they haven't much money just now makes no difference to their outlook on life. They have no inclination towards self-destruction – quite the contrary, they, like most other people aspire to wealth, food, pleasure and comfort, and to reach a stage from which they can mock the have nots. They have not the faintest doubt as to whether they deserve anything. They are sure they do, and they are right, and that's why they're already halfway there, they'll get what they want, have a good time, eat, burn and leave a filthy world behind them; with a smile on their lips they will leave a lot of filth in the world. And who is this filth? You know who. You and me for instance. We've always felt filthy, haven't we. So, everything should be just fine, it should be ideal: they want to leave filth and they do; we know we're filth and we stay in it. So why do we complain? Why aren't we satisfied? Why aren't you content, filth? The fact is you're not. You get no satisfaction. Because you'd like those who are leaving you behind not to travel so quickly, not to leave you so hastily. You'd like them to stay beside you for a while, to look and smile down at you, you want to feel their laughter gushing over you like a terrible blow, you want a sharper, more bitter pain, at last the terrible pain of looking up at their happiness has become the only pleasure you're made for. But it is not to be yours. They, of course, have no intention of staying near their stench, no interest in fulfilling your pleasures – they have their own. Unfortunately for you they are quite innocent in their behaviour, they lack that true malice you so fondly imagined they held for you, they don't want to dance on your head, they want to dance on marble. Great disappointment, eh? You cry out for bigger punishment, deeper humiliation, you yearn for pain unto death – and what do you get instead? some punishment, a little humiliation, a touch of pain, not enough of anything. In short – neglect. Yes, our plea for punishment goes unanswered, we're bastards on both sides, we're in a vacuum. Our nights are full of visions of dreamy, endless degeneration. A mirage! We wake up in the morning, banished from true punishment, our hands held out to the castigators as they pass us by. I've said all this by way of explanation why I must tell you that it would be foolish of you to expect them to be your salvation. You musn't have any illusions, I can see you too have that tendency – why, you were going to approach an acrobat – and I want to warn you. I'm a veteran midget and experienced in bitterness. I've sobered up. I know that we must help ourselves, get organized, first of all get organized, because without organization we won't advance a single step. When we're organized and our steps are well planned and thought out, then we can fulfil all our aspirations by ourselves. We can attack ourselves, commit the most terrible atrocities, punish ourselves in ways a happy person could never imagine, because only we understand one another, only we know exactly what we want to do to ourselves. I can see us now, a solid cluster turning on its axis, turning fast, faster and faster, taking off like a propellor, the speed increases and we turn and turn, the outer edges burning with the acceleration, the cluster shrinking in size, we disappear, up, up, the whole organization is shrinking, we burn, we are consumed, nothing left but a tiny dot, and then that's gone too. We are gone! Hurrah! We no longer exist! That's the way I imagine it. You no doubt have your own ideas. Anyway the motto must be organization.'

Pshishpash's face was getting redder and redder all the time from bending over and was now nearly purple. The dwarf lying underneath him had become silent and was now gazing past Pshishpash's shoulder with the satisfaction of a clever director who had finished giving his instructions and was now expecting the others to get on with it while he could take a rest, Pshishpash straightened himself slowly and turned to go, his heart full of ill will towards the midget

usher. The latter remained flat on his back, but when Pshishpash had put a few steps between them he suddenly yelled
after him: 'You see? instead of getting organized we run
away from each other! We're ashamed, what? Ashamed!
We'll never succeed! Phooey!'

Pshishpash didn't turn his head round but went through
the now empty circus gate and walked on, with one unlaced
shoe and his three old hates joined by a new hatred for himself, for being too much of a coward to recognize his true
friends, and get organized.

Translated by Mira Bar-Hillel

Abba Kovner

I Don't Know If Mount Zion

I

I don't know if Mount Zion would recognize itself
at midnight in the fluorescent light
when there's nothing left of Jerusalem
but its beauty wakeful
in the milky light that glides over its limbs still wings
lift it from the sunken desert
slowly slowly higher than the stars
this strange shell that floats out of the night
transparent giant
so much sky

253

washes over it
I don't know if Mount Zion looks
into my heart holding its breath now in pain and pleasure
behind a barred window and who it is meant for
at midnight.

2

These olive trees that never knelt
their knowledge hidden their
wrinkles carved this whole blue fan
on the road of the Hinnom Valley
I don't know if Mount Zion sees the things
that have changed our image
out of all recognition. Hands that touched it every day like a
    mother's
touching the forehead of her son sank
dropping into the sleep
of the Dead Sea—
does it hear the cry
from the market of the gates or the rush of my prayer from
    the shadow—
what's the use of friends who watch from the galleries
while our hearts struggle in the arena
and what's the sense of poets if we don't
know how to say
—Mount Zion does it really exist or
is it like our love that glows from another light
rising night
after night

Translated by Shirley Kaufman
with Judith Levy

From *Maariv*, 19–9–74